EDUCATION
AND THE
GOOD LIFE

EDUCATION AND THE GOOD LIFE

Beyond the National Curriculum

John White

LONDON EDUCATION STUDIES
KOGAN PAGE
Published in association with
The Institute of Education, University of London

For Pat

First published in 1990 by Kogan Page Ltd.,
120 Pentonville Road, London N1 9JN

Typeset at Selectmove, London
Printed and bound in Great Britain by Biddles Ltd, Guildford

British Library Cataloguing in Publication Data

A CIP catalogue record for this book is available from the British Library

ISBN 0–7494–0096–X

Contents

Introduction

The National Curriculum introduced into English and Welsh schools by the Education Reform Act of 1988 combines extraordinary richness of detail at the level of specific objectives with extraordinary poverty of ideas as regards fundamental aims. Since its arrival teachers have begun to grapple with the complexities of the massive assessment system that goes with it, aware that the central controls to which the details of their work are now subject will become even more extensive when the rest of the scheme is phased in over the next few years. As they get further entrenched in these new ways of working there is a danger of their losing sight of what the National Curriculum is basically about: it is often only too easy to forget larger aims when coping with more immediate objectives. Yet if they do turn to statements of these larger aims in the Education Reform Act and other official documents, they will find no more than two or three lines of the utmost platitudinousness. I cannot believe that everything will suddenly click into place and their day-to-day work be seen in its true significance when they read that the school curriculum must 'promote the spiritual, moral, cultural, mental and physical development of pupils at the school and of society', or that it must 'prepare such pupils for the opportunities, responsibilities and experiences of adult life'.

Whatever powers the National Curriculum, it is not a carefully worked out set of publicly stated aims. It consists of ten foundation subjects, dozens of attainment targets, hundreds of more detailed statements of attainment, yet the educational aims behind this proliferating structure are non-existent. Although few critics of the National Curriculum have commented on it, this aims-vacuum seems to me a defect which a democratic society should not tolerate. In planning *anything*, from the production of computers to a family holiday, one has to know – given a minimal rationality – what one is basically trying to do. One starts with one's overall aims and works from there towards the details. Planning a national curriculum is no different. The fact that official documentation on the 1988 National Curriculum patently does *not* do this may well lead one to wonder if it begins instead from *covert* aims which it might be politically inexpedient to reveal: the only alternative would seem to be that it is not a rational enterprise at all, and this may be hard to credit. Whatever truth there may be in this, in a democratic society we take it that citizens have a right to know what purposes so powerful an influence on the life of every pupil is intended to serve.

The 1988 National Curriculum goes against the spirit of our democratic constitution.[1] As I shall explain later, although opposed to *this* national curriculum, I am firmly in favour of the principle of a national curriculum in general. This has led me to ask in this book what a more democratically acceptable national curriculum might look like. In line with what was said above, this has meant being as clear as possible about fundamental aims from the start.

This is not an easy job at all. For one thing, there is no long-standing tradition of thought about such matters. When setting out to write a previous book on the aims of education (White, 1982), I was amazed to find that, although there had been plenty of short essays on specific aims, no one had until that time written a full-length book giving a synoptic view of aims in general.[2] The historical explanation of this fact would be interesting to investigate. I suggest that one factor might be the lack until recently of a philosophical treatment of ethics concrete enough to throw light on substantive values and how they interrelate. Now that ethics has begun to tackle this, a more systematic approach to educational aims has become possible.[3]

The root problem in providing this synoptic view lies in charting conceptual connections between a few fundamental categories. A first is the notion of personal well-being or personal flourishing. Although the National Curriculum does not say anything explicitly about this, it would be widely, and almost truistically, accepted that school education, like education in general, should help pupils to flourish. No teacher is likely to deny this. At the same time, few teachers, I suggest, are likely to be very sure just what flourishing consists in. This is not at all surprising since the topic is a philosophical one of no little complexity. Despite this, until recently general philosophers had little to say about it. In the last few years, however, a number of excellent works have appeared on the topic,[4] so it is now easier for educationists to be clearer about what the aim of promoting the pupil's well-being might involve.

A second near-truism is that education should not aim *just* at furthering the pupil's well-being, but should also have in mind the flourishing of people other than the pupil. Sometimes this is expressed in terms of the 'moral aims' of education. This brings us to our second major category: morality. This, too, needs elucidation. Every teacher will agree that children should be brought up to be morally good people. Yet here, too, uncertainties abound about what morality is and what form moral education should take. Recent ethical philosophy can help on this issue also. Some of it even questions whether we do well to use the category of 'morality' at all. I shall come back to this.

A third category is personal autonomy. Although one will look in vain for any reference in the National Curriculum to pupils' being empowered to lead self-directed lives, some such ideal has long been popular among teachers. Once again, there are difficulties just below the surface about what personal autonomy encompasses; the remarkable attention that this concept has recently received in general philosophy, especially ethics and political philosophy, can be put to good use in tackling them.

Elucidating these three concepts one by one would itself be a major contribution to providing a well-founded set of aims for a new national curriculum. However, the work would still be piecemeal: we would still not have reached anything like a synoptic view. To get further we would need to look at how these three categories – personal well-being, morality and personal autonomy – might be interrelated.

These possible interconnections are the central philosophical topic of this book. One might interpret my project here as a response to a challenge. The problem is that, viewed one way, the three concepts each stand on their own, resolutely refusing a closer union with the others. Personal well-being, for instance, stands apart from morality in the sense that even the most anti-social or immoral of individuals may in certain circumstances be said to lead a flourishing life. Similarly, personal well-being does not seem to necessitate personal autonomy: individuals can in certain circumstances flourish even though they are not directing their own lives but rather are responding to the demands of custom or authority. Personal autonomy, finally, can exclude morality: think of a completely self-centred person determined to lead his or her own life as he or she sees fit and with minimum external constraint.

The challenge comes in trying to bind together these categories despite their reluctance to be more closely interconnected. My response to the challenge is to argue that *from the contemporary educator's point of view*, but not necessarily from any other, it makes good sense to think of the child's well-being both as embracing a concern for others' flourishing and as premissed on a self-determined life. In stating things this way, I have not used the concept of morality but that of altruistic concern. This may not seem to make much difference, as for many people the terms will seem interchangeable. I explain later why I have made this change.

If the central argument of the book succeeds, we can think of education as having a single overarching aim: the promotion of the pupil's well-being. Although it is a unitary aim, it is internally complex. A large part of the detailed argument of the ensuing chapters is intended to reveal something of this complexity.

All this is not, however, an abstract exercise in philosophizing. The book has in mind throughout its length the task of working out defensible aims of education, including the school education that might replace our multiply defective National Curriculum. The immersion in philosophy is unavoidable. Once one accepts that any adequate discussion of aims must get to grips with notions like the three categories I have mentioned, one has to go beneath the surface and explore some of the deeper issues – *not* as an intrinsically absorbing activity, although it is this too, but as an essential first step in improving what goes on in schools.

The later chapters of the book relate the aims worked out in preceding chapters to the more specific content of education and to the 1988 National Curriculum and what might replace it. A new category now takes the stage: knowledge. In some treatments of education, and quite markedly so in the case of the National Curriculum, knowledge-aims have pride of place. I shall argue that, important as they are, they must be seen as subordinate to wider ethical aims concerning personal well-being, altruism and autonomy.

The last two chapters of the book bring us back to current politics. Chapter 8 is a critique of the National Curriculum from the point of view of the complex of aims spelt out earlier. Not surprisingly, given what I said above about the poverty of argumentation about aims in official documents, it quite fails to meet them. In this chapter, too, I explore the possible covert aims of this curriculum.

The final chapter seeks a more soundly based alternative to the National Curriculum. It tries to do this by taking as read a commitment to liberal democracy and asking what democratic constraints there should be on any national curriculum. As we shall see, this ranges beyond the content of the timetabled school curriculum into a wider discussion of the role of the school in general. Part of the argument touches on another major category – art – and its place both in the curriculum and in human flourishing.

Those readers unfamiliar with philosophical argument may find it most profitable to begin with these last two chapters and from there to work their way back into the main body of the text, beginning with the first chapter. I do not think they will find this particularly hard going. I have avoided technicalities and have kept the main lines of thought fairly simple. Some philosophers, I know, would think it all too simple and would want to introduce all sorts of qualifications and subtleties. In a

longer, more exclusively philosophical, work I would too, but I follow
the advice of a fellow philosopher of education of my acquaintance,
very active in the earlier efflorescence of the discipline in the 1960s,
who insisted then that what needed wielding was 'the hacksaw, not the
scalpel'. In many ways this is as true of the 1990s as it was 25 years ago:
once again we are embarking on a new movement in defence of liberal
values in education, and once again we have to get the main headings
in order before we can proceed to details.

The philosophy of education can expect to play a major part in this
new movement. This is because a liberal alternative to the National
Curriculum and the wider educational policy in which it fits must
be based on a coherent and defensible set of values, and working
these out is a largely philosophical task. The 1980s, preoccupied with
educational policies based on utilitarian goals whose value has been
assumed without question, have seen the discipline, for two decades
a major contributor to educational thought, reduced to a dangerously
low ebb. This has come about largely through government funding
policies on teacher education, which have reduced the numbers of
teachers studying the subject almost to zero. Philosophy of education
has not been the only victim. Every educational discipline which
helps teachers to think critically about what they are doing has felt
the pinch.

As critical educational thought in Britain has thus come increasingly
to be curtailed by central government, Eastern Europe has begun
to witness an intellectual liberation. While British philosophers of
education have been effectively debarred by financial manipulation from
teaching their subject, their Eastern counterparts, formerly forbidden to
teach by government order, are now occupying key roles in universities
and turning their attention to the democratic values which must replace
those of communism. If British philosophers of education have now no
approved role in their own country, their services are currently much in
demand in Eastern Europe. If the discipline survives its present crisis,
this may well be due in no small part to the support which the USSR
and its ex-satellites are giving it. If the country of John Stuart Mill has
temporarily no time for it, the land of the KGB can still come to its
rescue.

One last comment. My last book on educational goals *The Aims of
Education Restated* (White, 1982), already mentioned, also dealt with
interrelationships between the central concepts of this book – personal
well-being, morality, autonomy and knowledge. It is because of later
dissatisfactions with the account I gave there that I began the work
afresh and now feel I can relate them in a less problematic way. At
several points in the text and in the notes I indicate where I have diverged
from the arguments I relied on then.

I am grateful to those critics of my earlier book who set me on the path towards this one, as well as to fellow-students in philosophy of education with whom I have discussed various of the ideas below, including Anne Astwood, Ann Bird, Jeff Davis, Graham Haydon, Roger Marples and especially Terry McLaughlin and Patricia White. My thanks, too, to the members of, and readers appointed by, the Publications Committee of the Institute of Education, who helped me considerably in the final shaping of the text. Denis Baylis, the Institute's Publications Officer, has been to me, as to all authors who have had the pleasure of working with him, an unflagging source of encouragement and support.

Chapter 1

The Aims of Education in the Liberal Democratic State

The aims of the 1988 National Curriculum

It's amazing how wrong one can be. It is nearly 20 years since I first began to argue for a national curriculum. In all that time, I have been assuming that once the need for such a curriculum had been established and people began to think about its more determinate shape, they would be embarking on a pretty complex task. They would have to work out a coherent and defensible set of overall aims; examine what sub-aims, or intermediate aims, these might generate on logical, psychological and other grounds; bear in mind the wide variety of ways by which aims might be realized; and try to work out criteria delimiting the role of central government from that of local government, governing bodies and schools . . . all of which would be a long and massive undertaking, requiring the collaboration of professionals, civil servants, politicians and others in some kind of semi-independent but politically accountable national educational council.

When the British Government published its National Curriculum proposals in 1987, I felt a complete idiot. They showed that devising a national curriculum is simplicity itself. You pick ten foundation subjects to fill most of the school timetable, highlight three as of particular importance and arrange for tests at different ages. I could have worked out the national curriculum years ago. Anyone could.

But perhaps things are more complicated than this. There must be some reason, surely, why the Secretaries of State picked out their ten foundation subjects and their three core subjects as particularly important. There must be some underlying ends to which they see these as means. What could they be?

Statements of rationale are sparse. The Act itself says merely that the school curriculum must be a 'balanced and broadly-based' one which:

[a] promotes the spiritual, moral, cultural, mental and physical development of pupils at the school and of society; [b] prepares such pupils for the opportunities, responsibilities and experiences of adult life.

Apart from these few words, there is no indication of what sorts of people pupils are expected to become or of what kind of society they are expected to live in. The words themselves, moreover, are so general as to give no clue about these matters. What is meant by 'spiritual development', for instance? How does it differ from 'moral development'? What are 'cultural' and 'mental' development? And what sorts of 'opportunities, responsibilities and experiences of adult life' are meant?

These bland phrases might mean virtually anything – or nothing. There is no obvious reason, for instance, why a tyrant like Hitler or Stalin should object to [a] and [b] as statements of *their* educational aims. And speaking of Stalin, it is instructive to see what kind of national curriculum *he* had. Leaving out tiny inputs on the USSR Constitution, astronomy and psychology, it consisted of: language and literature, mathematics, history, geography, the sciences of biology, physics and chemistry, a foreign language, physical education, drawing, singing, and practical work in agriculture or industry. The list is almost identical to Mr Baker's ten foundation subjects. Not only that, three of Stalin's items were classified as 'important subjects' – language, mathematics and science. Today we call these 'core subjects'. Detailed syllabuses for every subject mentioned, covering the ten years of compulsory education, were laid down rigidly from the centre.

None of this implies that our government's policy is Stalinist or that there is an affinity between Russia's Man of Steel and our own Iron Lady. But it does prompt the question: in the light of the surprising similarities between the two curricula, what differentiates them?

We come back to the importance of providing a rationale for National Curriculum proposals – and a rationale, moreover, of some determinateness. In examining such a rationale we should take care to distinguish publicly avowed from covert intentions. In Stalin's case the task is pretty easy. Behind the Marxist-Leninist rhetoric about the making of the New Soviet Man lay Stalin's desire to harness the school system to the demands of his police-state autocracy. What about Mr Baker?

As we have seen, the Education Reform Act itself is not helpful. Will we do better to look at some of the earlier documentation? The 1987 Consultation Document on the National Curriculum contains just three pages of rationale. Most of it Stalin could have accepted. To equip pupils 'for the responsibilities of citizenship and for the challenges of employment in tomorrow's world'. No problem. To ensure that all pupils 'study a broad and balanced range of subjects throughout their compulsory education'. Ditto. To ensure that 'all pupils, regardless of sex, ethnic origin and geographical location, have access to the same good and relevant curriculum'. Da! To 'check on progress towards those objectives at different stages'; to 'enable schools to be more accountable..' Da again!

The only hint of distinctiveness comes not in the document itself but in its approving reference to the White Paper *Better Schools* (1985). This gave us a very brief list of aims, including such things as helping pupils to develop lively, enquiring minds and the ability to question and argue rationally; to acquire knowledge relevant to adult life and employment; to use language and number effectively; to develop personal moral values and acquire respect for religious values and tolerance of other races and ways of life; to understand the world in which they live; to appreciate human achievements.

Apart from the references to personal moral values, religion, tolerance of other ways of life and the ability to question, there is again nothing here to which Stalin need have objected. Agreed, though, these do give us something.

But how much? Three lines of text scarcely provide a fully worked out underpinning for a non-Stalinist National Curriculum. They are capable of innumerable interpretations. Not only this: we are not told how they are supposed to map on to the curriculum subjects. The most puzzling thing about this National Curriculum is that it includes no obvious vehicle whereby to develop personal values, including tolerance of other races and ways of life. True, some of the foundation subjects, especially English, history and geography, can play a part – not that the Baker curriculum says they should. But there is in any case only a limited amount the *academic subjects* can do to promote these aims – as compared, say, with whole-school policies on respect and tolerance within the classroom, the pastoral curriculum and non-authoritarian forms of school organization.

Mr Baker failed to explain why he said nothing about other means of realizing aims than traditional subjects. But this is only one instance of his more general reluctance to give us more than the glimmerings of a rationale. We simply don't know, on the information given so far, how un-Stalinesque the National Curriculum will turn out to be. Part of the problem is that the Act gives ministers very wide powers to determine the details of curricular programmes, all these being as yet unspecified. Since public statements about underlying aims are so meagre, the way is left open for Mr Baker and his successors to gear the syllabuses in different subject areas to virtually whatever purposes they think fit.

What is odd about the Baker proposals is that they *begin* by laying down the timetabled curriculum. They are not only vague about the wider aims which this subserves, but they also fail to explain why *this* way of realizing aims is singled out in preference to others. But the gaps in explanation do not end there. Even if one begins only with the formal curriculum, there are still various possible ways of proceeding. The most logical would seem to be to start with broad curriculum objectives and only then attend to the vehicles by which these might be attained, whether these be traditional school subjects, interdisciplinary courses, projects, or whatever. The Baker curriculum goes straight for subjects, as I have said, but does not say why. There is only one point in the Consultation Document at which its thinking goes momentarily beyond a subject framework. In paragraph 18 it acknowledges 'subjects or themes such as health education and the use of information technology'. However, it quickly makes it plain that 'such subjects or themes should be taught through the foundation subjects'. The wayward horse is soon reined in.

A final lacuna. As well as the question 'Why *subjects*?' one should also ask 'Why *these* subjects?' Why, for instance, are Latin and sociology excluded? (I am not necessarily advocating these.) No reason is given for choosing the ten foundation subjects. Unless, that is, one sees one in the statement in paragraph 16 of the Consultation Document that 'the foundation subjects commonly take up 80 per cent of the curriculum in schools where there is good practice. The Secretaries of State will take that as their starting point . . .' But this does not get one very far. If good practice can be identified, of course it is a good idea to use it as a starting point. But how do you identify good practice? And what criteria, more particularly, are the Secretaries of State using to pick this out? We are not told.

One should not confuse favouring the principle of a national curriculum with favouring *this* National Curriculum. The main argument for shifting from professional to political control of the broad framework of the curriculum is that questions about the aims and content of education are intimately connected with views about the kind of society we wish to live in. They are as much political questions as issues of taxation policy or defence. Every citizen in a democracy – as we, but not Stalinists, understand these terms – should have an equal right to participate in the control or exercise of political power in these and other areas. The problem with leaving curricula in the hands of the teaching profession is that it is, after all, only one section of the citizenry and there is no reason why its opinions should be privileged over other people's.

This argument does not show that there should be *central* control of educational content, only that there should be political control. It is compatible with wholly local control. But there is nevertheless a good reason for *some* central control. If British people saw themselves only as citizens of Lincolnshire or Gwent, wholly local control might be in order. But we do not. The 'kind of society we wish to live in' is for us in large part our national community, and our educational planning needs to be premised on this. This is not at all to exclude some element of both local control and of supra-national, eg European Community, control.

The case for political determination of aims and content does not rule out some element of professional control. Teachers may have no privileged status in setting the wider, political goals, but they do have a special expertise when it comes to applying general prescriptions to the complexities of actual schools and actual classrooms. Where the line should be drawn between political and professional responsibility is a further question.

The only defensible form of national curriculum is one that is genuinely committed to democratic principles, not least equality of political power. A minimum test of its commitment is whether it includes among its goals preparing all young people to become equal citizens of a democracy. There is nothing in the Baker curriculum about this – nothing about the prerequisite understanding of the socio-economic structure or the principles of democracy, about fostering the virtues necessary in democratic citizens, about equipping people for critical reflection on the status quo, or about building the imperfect democratic structures we have now into something more adequate, through extending democracy into the workplace, for instance.

All of which raises again the question: in what way does Mr Baker's National Curriculum diverge from Stalin's? If it does nothing to celebrate and nurture our democratic values, wherein lies the difference?

The state and the good life

The general argument for a national curriculum rests on the notion of democracy. This has been taken to be a form of government in which every citizen has an equal right to participate in the exercise and control of political power. Suppose now a democratically elected government decided to shape its educational and other institutions so as to promote a certain view of what human well-being consisted in and to discourage rival views. Suppose, for instance, it sought to set up some kind of theocracy in which the good life for the individual was premised on the love of God and obedience to His will. We can have in mind, perhaps, the religious communities of seventeenth-century New England for a partial parallel.

All of us, I would imagine, would reject such a polity. If we did so, we would be appealing, I suggest, to something like the principle that, in a *liberal* democracy, the state should not steer people towards determinate ideals of human well-being. In so far as we accepted some such principle, we would be implicitly accepting that it is not enough for a government to be democratically elected to be justified in imposing a national curriculum. That curriculum must also conform to this basic liberal principle: the government would be exceeding its powers if it steered pupils towards determinate pictures of the good life. These need not, of course, be religious.

It is important, I think, to look further into how we should formulate this basic liberal principle, of which we all have, I suggest, a rough intuitive idea.

A common way of expressing it among philosophers of liberalism is in terms of *neutrality*.[1] They hold that the state ought to be neutral with regard to different conceptions of the good life. Dworkin (1978, p 127), for instance, starts off from the claim that:

> Each person follows a more-or-less articulate conception of what gives value to life. The scholar who values a life of contemplation has such a conception; so also does the television-watching, beer-drinking citizen who is fond of saying 'This is the life', though he has thought less about the issue and is less able to describe or defend his conception.

Dworkin argues that if the state is to treat its citizens equally it has not to prefer one conception of the good life to another. Rawls (1971) and Nozick (1974), who differ radically in other ways about the proper sphere of state action, nevertheless agree with Dworkin that conceptions of the good are not for the state to promote.

If one accepts this, then how is the state's proper sphere to be delimited? One argument might be that it should have a hand in trying to ensure that the necessary conditions are provided for everyone to lead his or her preferred way of life. These necessary conditions may take different forms.

There is first of all what we might call the 'moral framework' of the society.[2] This is a set of rules which protects or promotes the actions of individuals in pursuit of their own well-being. Examples might be prohibitions against murder, physical injury, stealing, breach of contract, lying, infringements of liberty, as well, perhaps, as positive injunctions like that of helping those in distress.

The state may also have a role in helping to provide other necessary conditions of the good life which we may label 'welfare'. Whatever one's particular view of the good life, one will need, among other things, food, clothing, shelter, good health, a secure and predictable environment, an income. (The list is not intended to be complete.)[3] The state can play a part in providing these goods, although people will differ about how far its powers should extend.

Educational implications

While it may be true, then, that educational aims carry with them some picture of the good society, it does not follow that the state must have a hand in determining them. On the neutralist liberal theory of politics just outlined, it would be debarred from laying down any aims which encapsulated a view of the good life.

On the other hand, it might be possible to distinguish among aims between those which carry with them a picture of the good life and those which have to do with necessary conditions for leading the good life, however that be conceived. If the state can legitimately be concerned with helping to supply those necessary conditions, then it could legitimately help to determine aims falling in this category.

Following the distinction made above, it could be involved in aims concerning the moral framework or aims to do with welfare.

This still leaves the state a broad territory. As to the moral framework, it might lay down aims to do with law, or aims regarding that part of morality not enshrined in law. It could, for instance, insist that everyone is brought up with some knowledge of what law is in general and its function in promoting individual well-being. To that aim it might add an acquaintance with major particular laws currently in force. Again, it might also think it important to build up dispositions in children not to want to break these laws and, more widely, dispositions to conform to moral rules that lie outside the legal framework. Some people would want state prescription under this heading to go still further – beyond law and order and conventional morality. Part of the moral framework within which we live is our democratic constitution. One can argue on neutralist grounds that the state should develop in future citizens the understandings and attitudes necessary to making democracy work. One might also want to argue that the state should not only promote conformity with moral rules but also a reflective attitude towards them.

Welfare aims might also be various. The state could lay down, for instance, that children should be acquainted with the different forms of welfare and their contribution to individual well-being: this might cover work on subjects such as peace, the police, health, the social services, and the economy. Preparation for roles within the economy might also fall under this heading: this might range from equipping pupils with useful general skills, dispositions and knowledge, in the areas of science and technology, for instance, to more specific training for particular types of job.

It is not difficult to find examples of state determination of moral and welfare aims in the recent history of education in Britain. Before the shift away from professional and towards political control of aims and curricula that has recently taken place, the only compulsory curriculum subject in state schools was religious education. One of the reasons why this was included in the 1944 Education Act was that it was felt that it would help to shore up moral values in the post-war period. There may be philosophical difficulties about basing moral values on religion, but, these aside, this looks like a particularly clear illustration of the neutralist liberal theory of state control in action.

More recently, since the 'Great Debate' of 1975–6, and more particularly since the Thatcher Government of 1979 to date, we have seen a marked emphasis on economically orientated aims. The balance of curriculum subjects in various national curriculum proposals has been tilted increasingly towards mathematics, computer studies, science and technology; and government initiatives like TVEI and proposed City Technology Colleges have been targeted at improving the economy.[4]

To return to more general considerations, suppose the state restricted itself to moral framework and/or welfare aims, who would be responsible for aims to do with the good life? Could these be justifiably left to schools and/or parents? A difficulty is that if those educators steered pupils towards some ways of life rather than others, they would be in the same position as a non-neutralist state and neutralist objections to the latter would also seem to apply to them. One alternative would be to exclude life-ideals from educational aims altogether, but this would seem to leave children without any guidance, except what they might pick up incidentally, about what goals in life they should follow – and this is especially hard to defend.

But is it clear, in any case, that a neutralist state must restrict itself to aims concerned with the moral framework and welfare? There is one further way in which it can help to provide the necessary conditions of the good life without favouring a particular version of it. It can aim at acquainting pupils impartially with a whole range of different ideals of the good life, without steering them towards any in particular. I had this principle very much in mind in writing *Towards a Compulsory Curriculum* (White, 1973).

Critique of neutralism

There is one major problem with this line of thought. Is it true, in fact, that being acquainted with different ideals of life is a necessary condition of personal well-being? A positive answer here presumably takes for granted that this knowledge is indispensable for *choice* of a way of life. But this itself embodies a particular view of the good life – namely one in which the individual chooses his or her way of life, rather than having this determined by others. Because this conception is so much a part of our cultural background, it is often difficult for us to see it for what it is. But it should be clear enough on reflection that the autonomous life, as just described, is not without its competitors. In more traditional societies than our own there are many other versions of the good life which do not embrace personal autonomy: societies, for instance, in which life-goals are determined by caste, gender, fortune-telling or magic, parental profession, religious doctrine, or various combinations of these. In supporting autonomy, a state would be abandoning neutralism since it would be favouring one particular version of the good life.[5]

This means that a neutralist state cannot consistently lay down aims to do with acquainting pupils with different life-ideals. It also brings us back to the problem of what guidance any pupil can expect, on neutralist principles, about what kind of life he or she should lead. Nothing now seems to be available.

But this in its turn provokes further questions about the role of a neutralist state in laying down aims regarding the moral framework and/or welfare. The reason for doing this is to help to provide the necessary conditions for people to lead a life of well-being, yet if no guidance can be given on what such a life might consist in, one wonders what the point is of building a substructure where there is no superstructure to support.

The truth is, however, that there *is* a superstructure, after all. In the kind of society in which we live, that is a liberal democracy built around an advanced industrial economy, welfare provision and a moral framework only make sense if seen as necessary conditions for an autonomous way of life.

It is true that some version of a moral framework and some version of welfare will be necessary for *any* type of society, including those resting on non-autonomous forms of life. Every society will need prohibitions on murder, bodily injury, stealing, lying and promise-breaking; and in every society people will need food, clothing and shelter. But in a society such as ours, more is included in the above two areas than these very basic requirements. In particular, we see it as a vital function of the state to protect various individual liberties: there are, for instance, legal or moral prohibitions on interference with freedom of expression, freedom of movement, freedom from indoctrination or manipulation, and freedom from intrusion into one's private affairs.

Why do we consider personal liberty important? One could take the view that this is an ultimate value which cannot be supported by reference to anything more basic [6], but such a position would be hard to maintain. If it were true, then *any* form of liberty would be seen as valuable. It is noteworthy that the liberties we see as requiring protection, like those mentioned above, are of a particular kind.

Charles Taylor (1985, Vol 2, p 219) has recently pointed out that although there are far fewer traffic lights per kilometre in the streets of the capital of Albania, Tirana, than in, say, London, we would not call the Albanians freer than the British because they are less constrained in this way. A liberal's attachment to negative liberty – that is, freedom from interference in doing what one wants – has to do with forms of interference which most seriously impede the kind of life one chooses to lead. Impediments to the realization of one's most important desires are of more moment than others. It is because people's desires to practise their religion, express their ideas, control their own lives, and determine where they will live and what kind of work they will do, are seen as more important to them than the desire to drive unimpeded through city streets, that political liberty has to do with the former rather than the latter. If this is right, then negative liberty is desirable not in itself, but as a requirement of positive liberty – that is, of one's leading a life which one has autonomously chosen to lead.

All this means that neutralism is an untenable position: in refusing preference to some ideals of life over others, it overlooks the fact that it is tacitly presupposing the value of personal autonomy. This comes out not only in its commitment to negative liberty, but also in the underlying reasons for advocating neutralism in the first place. Why, after all, should it be thought desirable to avoid entanglement in different conceptions of the good? Why should one try to ensure that one conception is not favoured over another? The root anxiety here seems to be that non-neutrality brings with it the danger of *imposing* one way of life rather than another. But this is only an anxiety for someone who is already wedded to the view that individuals should freely determine their own way of life, ie for someone who already places a high value on autonomy.

The state, education and personal autonomy

All this has important implications for the conduct of government in a liberal democracy like our own. Political battlelines tend to be drawn between those on the right, who advocate freedom from state control in sphere after sphere, and leftwingers, who call for an extension of state welfare provision. In so far as negative freedom derives its value from positive freedom, or autonomy, and in so far as welfare provision likewise subserves autonomy, then left and right could well be united in a common goal: the promotion of general autonomy.

I shall take it henceforth that a *justifiable* government policy is one which seeks to promote the autonomy of all its citizens and does not favour some at the expense of others.

How does education fit into this picture? We have seen that the autonomous life has many prerequisites, covering both what we have called the 'moral framework' and 'welfare'. The state has a role in both areas. Some of its work has to do with trying to ensure that its citizens' autonomy can be *exercised*. To this end it maintains a framework of protective laws, provides health and other social services and endeavours to keep internal and external peace. But one cannot talk about individuals' exercising their autonomy unless they have become autonomous in the first place. The state can help in this task, too. Of course, many of the institutions needed in order to protect the exercise of autonomy are also necessary for its formation: if children were brought up without health care, or in a society in which law and order had broken down completely, then their chances of growing into self-determining adults would be severely reduced. But other policies and institutions are needed, too. In order to become autonomous, there has to exist a range of options from which one can choose preferred alternatives. How extensive this range should be is a further question, but, whatever its extent, the state can and should have some hand in ensuring that it exists.

It is not enough, however, that a wide range of options *exists*; those who are to choose them must also *know* that they exist. This is where education begins to enter the picture. More generally, in order to become autonomous one needs to have acquired various capacities, dispositions, and types of understanding. If a government is committed to the promotion of autonomy for everyone, its aim must be that everyone should be educated to enable them to exercise it. A fuller account both of what autonomy is and what is educationally necessary for it will be given in later chapters, but for the moment it will be enough to bring out the following points. To become self-determined one needs, as we have seen, an understanding of the various options that are open. Some of the available choices are more important to one as an autonomous person than others. Knowing the differences between the types of socks, or baked beans, or television sets from which one can choose is normally less important than understanding what differentiates the life of a religious believer from that of a sceptic, or being a trade union official from being a manager, or voting for the policies of one political party over another. Behind such more specific knowledge will be knowledge of a more general sort – about religion, for instance, about the structure of one's society, or about the physical sciences. But autonomous persons need more than knowledge or understanding. They also have to have certain dispositions of character. If they are to withstand possible manipulation or coercion by others they need independence of mind, resoluteness and courage. If they are to be free from obstacles arising from their own psyches, they need to be clear on where their major priorities lie and firmly committed to those priorities over values of lesser importance. Much more will be added later about the virtues necessary for autonomy. In particular, nothing has yet been said about attitudes towards other people. But even this brief introduction should be enough to underline the point that a state committed to autonomy must see to it that certain educational aims are met which go beyond those to do with welfare and with the moral framework that we earlier described. To these – which are concerned with knowledge and dispositions pertaining to the necessary conditions of personal well-being – are now added aims to do with the nature of that well-being itself. How all these various aims are to be related each to the other is again something that must occupy us at a later stage. The main conclusion at this point is the extensive responsibility that liberal democratic states should have for laying down educational aims which prepare their citizens for autonomy.

The value of personal autonomy

All this, however, is to presuppose the value of autonomy itself. This has seemed legitimate enough, working as we have been within the framework of liberal democracy. We have shown how neutralism collapses into a hidden perfectionism in favour of autonomy; and we have shown how the value which is central to liberalism, liberty itself, also rests on a prior attachment to autonomy. But we have still done nothing to show that autonomy itself is to be desired. Even if convincing grounds have been given by the above arguments as to why a liberal–democratic state should lay down autonomy-supporting educational aims, it could be said that these grounds don't go deep enough: further reasons have to be put forward as to why autonomy is a good thing.

We will be looking at what these reasons might be in Chapter 6: until then, the value of personal autonomy will be taken as read. It might be useful, even so, to point to a particularly powerful obstacle which any justification of autonomy will have to face. As we shall see, this is not purely theoretical, but intimately touches our living together within a multi-cultural society.

We have already referred to the point that conceptions of personal well-being do not all incorporate a high regard for autonomy. In traditional societies one's main goals in life are laid down for one by custom; and for many religious people the ideal of self-determination is anathema, since one's task in life is to subjugate oneself to the will of God. This raises a problem within the theory of liberal democracy itself, since societies like our own contain certain ethnic or religious minorities for whom autonomy is not a value. This means that one cannot make the straightforward claim that liberal democracy is committed to autonomy. If certain strands in it lead us in that direction, others, notably the freedom accorded to religious and ethnic minority groups to disvalue autonomy, are at odds with it. From an educational point of view the conclusion at the end of the last section, that the liberal democratic state ought to lay down autonomy-supporting aims for all its citizens, is now open to challenge. If certain minority groups disassociate themselves from this value, is there any good reason why young people being brought up within those communities should be educated in accordance with it?

If it could be shown that all other conceptions of personal well-being were in some way *mistaken* and that the autonomy ideal were not, one would have the makings of a strong argument in its favour. Can this be shown? On the face of it this would be a hard task, since however many alternatives one managed to exclude, there might always be others, as yet unexamined, which passed the test. One could, it is true, restrict oneself to examining the credentials of those alternatives which are found in our own society. One could look at what is presupposed in the values held by those Islamic or Christian believers, for instance, who reject autonomy. Incoherences, or unsupported assumptions, might be found in the metaphysical doctrines which they embrace. On the other hand, it is notoriously difficult to produce cast-iron refutations of religious positions, since all kinds of countermoves have been assembled over the centuries in their defence.

In any case, there do seem to be *positive* grounds in favour of some non-autonomous conceptions of well-being. Suppose we take a traditional society from another time and place, say a North American Indian community or an African tribal community before the coming of the Europeans. Personal well-being, let us accept for the moment – although we shall need to investigate this further later – consists in the overall satisfaction of one's most important informed desires or goals, taking one's life as a whole.[7] A person who has had most of his or her major desires fulfilled can be said to have had a life of greater well-being than someone whose major desires have been checked and thwarted at every point. Given this, then if a member of a traditional society lives a broadly fulfilled life in this sense, then he or she has achieved a high measure of well-being. Would that well-being have been increased still further, or indeed shown to be illusory, if that person had been an autonomous agent? There are difficulties about conceiving what it would be like for him (or her) to be autonomous. For one thing, there would have to be a range of options among which he could choose, but this would be by definition unavailable in the traditional society. For another, he would have to have been educated in the ways of autonomy and this, too, is ruled out. But if we try to ignore these problems and imagine someone who had somehow acquired some of the cognitive requirements of autonomy – independence of thought, some arrangement of preferences in a hierarchy of importance, or whatever – even though he were still unable to make the choices which he envisaged owing to the tradition-bound nature of his community, there are good reasons, perhaps, for thinking that this frustrated autonome would lead a life of less overall satisfaction than the unimpeded heteronome.

The autonomous way of life is not the best way of life in *every* set of circumstances. Nearly all human beings who have ever lived have belonged to traditional societies. *Their* well-being has consisted in living, as far as good fortune has permitted them, a broadly fulfilled life according to the mores and expectations of those societies. How, then, can the autonomous version of the good life be justified? And how far does the fact that non-autonomous versions exist bear on the question of whether a liberal-democratic government can legitimately lay down the educational aim of promoting autonomy for all, in view of the fact that some ethnic and religious minority communities do not value this? As promised, these questions will be taken up again in Chapter 6. Meanwhile, I shall be taking it for granted that autonomy is desirable. This causes no problem if one assumes, as I have been doing in this chapter that we are operating within the framework of a liberal-democratic state, since the notions of autonomy and liberal democracy are so closely interwoven. Even so, the deeper problem remains.

Chapter 2

Personal Well-being

Personal autonomy and personal well-being

Chapter 1 revealed the commitment which a liberal democratic society has to promoting the personal autonomy of all its citizens. What this implies about educational aims must now be spelt out more fully.

We saw that all kinds of other agencies besides education can help people to become, and/or remain, autonomous. Prerequisites of autonomy include such things as food, shelter, clothing, income, health, and a framework of law and morality including various liberties. The specific contribution which education can make lies in equipping people with the various capacities, dispositions and kinds of knowledge and understanding needed both to become and remain autonomous. It is these that we now need to examine more closely.

So far not much has been said about the characteristics of autonomous persons. We know that they are self-determining, that they make their own choices about how they are to live and do not let others make them for them. But this is to say very little. Vastly different character types can seem to come together under this umbrella – the Mafia boss, for instance, as much as the Oxfam field worker. We need now to see what further shape can be given to the autonomy ideal, which characteristics are to be ruled in or out. This is obviously an important task for anyone looking at the explicitly educational prerequisites of autonomy: unless one knows in broad outline which virtues and capacities are to be promoted, one can say very little about educational aims. Those concerned with many other agencies than education have no such professional reason to concern themselves with personal characteristics, however much as citizens or in other roles they may have views on this. Providers of food, shelter, and clothing do not need to know whether their beneficiaries are courageous or cowardly, altruistic or self-centred, knowledgeable about their culture or ignorant. But these matters may be of primary importance to the educator.

A familiar problem that arises from making the promotion of personal autonomy the *only* aim of the educator is that this seems to leave morality out of account. Parents and teachers do not see themselves as bringing children up to become Mafia bosses, however autonomous, but to become morally good people. Are there not, then, moral aims of education, perhaps to do with the 'moral framework' discussed in the last chapter, which somehow circumscribe autonomy aims? Or will the further shaping of the notion of autonomy, just promised, enable us to include moral aims within the autonomy aim?

Over the next few chapters I will try to answer these questions in the course of a fuller delineation of education for autonomy. I shall build up to this gradually, as the issues it raises are complex and need careful disentangling. The first task will be to examine more closely the notion of personal well-being which we encountered in Chapter 1. We saw there that circumstances can exist where personal well-being and personal autonomy come apart: members of traditional societies may live a life of great well-being, but in a heteronomous way. For us, however, living in non-traditional societies, the two things go together. Educationally speaking, an upbringing which has the good of the child in mind intends him or her to become an autonomous person; and to understand what the latter involves, we have to be clearer about the former. As we shall see, too, it is through investigating well-being that we shall be able to throw light on the relation between education for autonomy and education for moral goodness: for the underlying issue here is whether well-being includes or excludes moral goodness.

Education and the structure of desire

Is a life of well-being to be identified with a life in which one's desires are satisfied? There are several problems with this, some of which, to do with the structure of desires, will be mentioned later. An immediate difficulty, however, is this. Suppose one has a desire (eg to go to America) and the desire is realized; but when it is, the person is disappointed: it is not what he or she wanted, after all. To meet this point, one has to relate well-being not merely to desire-satisfaction, but to the satisfaction of *informed* desires. If the person who wanted to go to America had known what America was like, he or she would not have wanted, after all, to go there. Informed desires are desires which are based on sound empirical information about their object and avoid logical confusion.[1]

Defining personal well-being as, *inter alia*, the satisfaction of informed desires is different from defining it, as I have done elsewhere, as 'post-reflective desire-satisfaction'. The latter applies only to autonomous people, to those who *choose* their way of life from among various possible options. Their well-being, from this point of view, is the satisfaction of those desires which they come to have after reflection on which of these options they prefer. These desires may still not be informed, even if they are post-reflective.[2] We saw in Chapter 1 that non-autonomous people living in traditional societies can be said to lead lives of greater or lesser well-being. Personal well-being, for them, is still a function of the satisfaction of informed desires, even though reflective choice is not a possibility for them. A boy is brought up to be a carpenter like his father. This is what he wants to be. He has a good idea of what the life of a carpenter involves. His desire is thus an informed one; and if he lives out this life, that counts towards his well-being.

Is well-being quantifiable in some way as a function of the number and/or strength of the satisfied informed desires one has? Suppose one person has twice as many informed desires satisfied in his life as someone else. Would he or she necessarily have had a life of more well-being? This cannot be right. Some of the desires we have are desires we would rather be without. I may want to run away when I am in any danger, for instance, and yet feel that very often I should stand my ground. Or I may like heavy drinking or smoking and be only too glad if I could find some way of cutting down. If someone's life is full of satisfied desires which he or she would rather not have had, it is difficult to see how this could count as a good life for that person.

The same is true of strength, as of number, of desires. The satisfaction of any intense desire that one does not want to have – to smoke, drink, be cruel, injure someone or whatever – does not count towards one's well-being but rather detracts from it.

This reinforces the point already made, that personal well-being involves the satisfaction of *informed desires*, not of desires *per se*. I may have a desire to smoke, but satisfying this does not benefit me because it is not among my informed desires: knowing what I know about smoking, I would rather be without the desire.

Among one's desires, therefore, can be desires to have or not to have certain desires. As well as having a first-order desire to smoke, for instance, one can have a second-order desire not to have this desire. Our desires are not all of a piece. We come to impose a structure upon them, regulating lower-level desires by higher-level ones.[3] The acquisition of virtues is an example. Temperance is the regulation of the bodily appetites for such things as food, drink and sex. One is born with innate desires for these things and they cannot be regulated, as with lower animals, by instinctual mechanisms; we can eat and drink too much, for instance, or eat and drink the wrong things. In the course of growing up we have to learn to control such desires. This is a matter of acquiring appropriate second-order desires (Dent, 1984, ch 5). These will not be desires not to have the desire to eat or drink at all, but desires not to have the desire to eat or drink to excess, for instance, or to lose the desire to eat sweet things or drink alcohol.

But not all second-order desires spring from virtues. Roman banqueters used to visit the vomitarium in order to make themselves sick and revivify their appetites. In our present terms, they desired to reactivate in themselves their desire to eat and drink.

Neither are second-order desires confined to desires to regulate bodily appetites. In wanting to become courageous I want to withstand my desire always to flee when faced by danger. In wanting to devote myself to teaching I may have a picture of myself as having certain desires and not others – the desire to encourage people, for instance, to explain things or to be fair.

We have spoken so far of second-order desires; but there is no reason in principle why there should not also be desires of higher orders. Thus a third-order desire would be a desire to have a desire to have a desire (and so on).

The upshot of all this for personal well-being is that it has to take into account the hierarchical structuring of desire. The satisfaction of higher-order desires, since they regulate other desires, counts more towards well-being. Talk of hierarchical structuring does not imply an elegant system, with one or two master desires at the top and everything else subordinate to them. For our major desires may themselves conflict and there may be no superordinate desires to regulate them. We may both want to stay at home with our family and to follow our career as an international reporter, to devote ourselves to politics on the one hand and live as a creative artist on the other. At a more metaphysical level, we may want both to fulfil our social roles and to reunite ourselves with nature or the cosmos. In some way we have each to find some resolution to these kinds of conflicts, but the ways we do so may be unsystematic, idiosyncratic and incapable of being contained by general rules.

Personal well-being, then, consists in the satisfaction of one's most important desires, taking one's life as a whole. Desires are not all on the same level. This poses a difficulty for a utilitarian account of well-being, which looks instead to quantity of satisfaction. Educationally this is important, because prominent among notions of well-being which affect in an often unrecognized way how children are brought up and schooled is some such utilitarian idea: it may, indeed, be embedded in the thinking behind the English National Curriculum (see Chapter 8). At the level of national economics we have become used these days to equate an increase in people's well-being with an increase in their ability to consume goods and services. But this is far too simplistic. There is no reason to assume a priori that the good life consists in just one kind of fulfilment. This goes against what we know about human nature. In making rational decisions about our lives we are none of us simple 'economic men', doing no more than weighing up the consequences of doing this or that in terms of the overall quantity of satisfaction. We make choices not only between types of car, or between buying a computer and having a holiday in America; we can also choose to *be* a certain sort of person rather than another: to be self-controlled, generous, committed to scholarship or family life, confident. Thought about education, including thought about the proper basis for a national curriculum, should begin with the articulated, complex picture of personal well-being outlined in this chapter, and not with the flattened-out, uni-dimensional account of the utilitarians and economists.

Well-being, finally, is not all or nothing: there are degrees of it. A life, or period of a life, is higher in well-being the more one's more important desires are fulfilled.

Education alone cannot bring about well-being. As we have seen, and will explore further, all sorts of other necessary conditions have to be met. But education is itself a condition of well-being and can thus help to promote it. We saw in Chapter 1 that education is necessary for autonomy; here we are dealing with the more inclusive claim that education is necessary for well-being, whether it is autonomous or heteronomous. If one's more important desires are to be fulfilled, one must *have* those desires in the first place. Although there is a biological basis to desiring, in that wanting to eat, drink, sleep and avoid danger is implanted in us innately, the desires we come to have are shaped by our culture. The first task of upbringing is to equip us with desires we previously did not have, at least in that form: we come to want to eat with cutlery or chopsticks, watch television, play games. The second task is to help us to organize our burgeoning desires, to impose a hierarchical structure on them and resolve conflicts between them. This, too, is a matter of creating, or shaping, desires within us, only the desires are now of a higher order. Implicit in these tasks is a further role for education. We are talking not just of desires, but of informed desires. Children have to be brought up to have some understanding of what the objects of their desires involve.

Desire and value

The account that has been given of personal well-being has been intentionally a formal one. All kinds of substantive examples may fit under it. It covers both autonomous and non-autonomous ways of life, the difference between these being that in the former one chooses one's major ends oneself, while in the latter they are determined for one. It also covers – so far, and unless our later discussion changes the picture – both the life of a person who is responsive to the moral demands on him or her and that of someone who is not, ie an amoralist. And it covers both the life of someone whose major ends raise no eyebrows and that of someone like Rawls' notorious imaginary person whose chief interest is in counting the blades of grass in city squares (Rawls, 1971, pp 432–3).

Is the account *too* formal? If it lets in as much as this, perhaps it needs to be narrowed. Is it the case that there are some desires which people ought to have, from the point of view of their own well-being, whether they in fact have them or not – desires for autonomy, for instance, or living morally, or devoting oneself to non-trivial pursuits?

Reasons have already been given in Chapter 1 to support the claim that well-being does not necessarily go with autonomy; and there will be further discussion of the relations between well-being and morality in Chapter 4. But there is also a more general point to be dealt with. We have so far followed the suggestion that personal well-being be understood via the notion of desire-satisfaction. But could it be, after all, that what constitutes our well-being is independent of our desires? Could some things – autonomy, morality, intellectual pursuits, art or whatever – be essential constituents of the good life regardless of whether any individual actually wants them?

If there is anything in this, our account so far seems to have got the relationship between desires and values the wrong way round. Instead of what is valuable for people depending on their desires, it looks as if we begin with what is valuable and see to it, if we can, that people's desires conform to this. How is this issue to be resolved?

The account given so far roots our well-being in empirical features of our make-up, namely our desires and their satisfaction. It sees human beings as animals of a certain sort, endowed with certain innate desires, and their well-being as constituted by the fulfilment of desires ultimately based on these. (It is possible to talk of the well-being of animals other than human beings. A cat's well-being is increased by its being able to hunt, sleep, feed etc when it will, and it is diminished by being beaten, kept in confinement and deprived of food.)

This view of human well-being has in its favour that it is wholly intelligible in terms of the world with which we are familiar. But the opposing view, that what is valuable for us is independent of our desires, lacks this advantage. It faces the problem of having to give some account of the values which it claims exist. What kind of thing can a desire-independent value be? Where does it exist? How does one know that it exists? If x is said to be valuable for any individual, but someone does not desire x at all and would be deeply distressed if he had x, then how could it be shown that x was really good for him or her?

The onus is on the defender of desire-independent values to answer these questions. One source of the desire-independent view lies in a different picture of human nature from that implied in the account just given. Whereas the latter sees a human being as a sort of animal, other views locate our essence elsewhere. Platonic, Christian or Kantian views of man, for instance, hold that our embodied selves – which bring with them desires and the satisfaction of desire – are not our real or essential selves. What we fundamentally are are members of the world of Platonic forms, or immortal souls, or Kantian things-in-themselves. The well-being of entities like this cannot consist in desire-satisfaction, but must be defined in other-worldly terms – as having to do with the contemplation of other-worldly reality, for instance, or communion with God, or membership of a community of noumenal rational beings.

Metaphysical theories may thus lie behind desire-independent views; in which case the latters' acceptability rests on the acceptability of the metaphysics. There may also be other sources of claims about desire-independence. One such derives from overlooking the difference between giving an account of personal well-being in general and giving an account of what type of personal well-being one finds important for some reason. It is easy to write one's own values into one's definition of the concept, without realizing that this is happening. We saw in the last chapter how naturally one can take it for granted in an autonomy-supporting society that personal well-being must take an autonomous form. In seeing autonomy as a universal value which exists even for those who lack any desires in that direction, it may come to seem to one that the value exists independently of *any* desires, in some external realm of its own. But what is taken to be external may, after all, be something which is deeply internal (cf Williams, 1985, p 191), in this case *one's own* attachment to autonomy which one has unknowingly taken to be a universal value.

In so far as one does hold that values are independent of desires, one has to show not only what their metaphysical status is, ie what kind of existence they can be credited with, but also how they can have any bearing on our lives. Suppose someone does not want to be autonomous at all, but autonomy is claimed to be valuable for her (or him). (Any other value could be substituted here for autonomy.) What might this mean? Suppose she now has a rather inadequate understanding of autonomy and is provided with a better one. She comes thereby to see much more clearly what autonomy involves. Could it still be that this clearer perception fails to instil in her a desire to become autonomous? If so, then what bearing do values have on our lives? How can they help us to live if they can be perceived in this wholly intellectual way, as something as much outside us, and unconnected with us, as anything perceived physically, like a tree or a table? But suppose her acquaintance with the value did move her in its favour, how could it do so unless she already had a desire of some sort which caused her to be moved in this way? If so, would this not lend support to the desire-dependence thesis? It seems that its rival claim is caught in a dilemma: if we can be acquainted with values in a purely cognitive way, then it is hard to see how they can affect our lives; but if the perception of them does affect us, this must be because of some desire we already have. One way out would be to suggest that our perception of the value creates in us a desire which we have not had before and which is unconnected with any desire we already have (Bond, 1983, pp58ff). But this move has the appearance of a last-ditch attempt to save a theory for which no grounds have in any case been produced: it would need to be supplemented with an account not only of the metaphysical status of values which exist independently of our desiring them, but also of the causal mechanisms whereby our perception of them can generate desires in us.

Conclusion

We have looked at several difficulties facing the desire-independence thesis. Leaving aside further complications, I conclude that we have seen no good reason to reject the original suggestion that personal well-being is to be understood as the satisfaction of one's major informed desires, taking one's life, or a portion of it, as a whole.

Finally, I should reiterate that the account of personal well-being that has been given is a formal one only and various substantive fillings can be provided for the concept. There may be good reasons, depending on circumstances or on one's point of view, for pressing for some such more substantive account. We saw in Chapter 1 how a notion of personal well-being which includes a commitment to autonomy can come to be appropriate in some societies, even though it fails to be so in others. It is as yet an open question whether there are good grounds for adding other substantive features to the formal concept. Are there circumstances in which it is appropriate to write in, for instance, an attachment to the pursuit of knowledge, or to art, or to morality? Educators, including educational planners, have an obvious interest in the answer to this question. In so far as they are aiming at promoting the pupil's well-being, they will need to know whether there are good reasons, in their particular circumstances, for giving this ideal some more determinate shape. While it is useful and necessary for them to see the limits of the formal concept, they also have reasons for pressing beyond this.

In this connection a possible pitfall for the educator, or, more likely, for the philosopher of education interested in clarifying educational aims, is to take the formal concept of well-being as that which should determine aims. This connects back to the discussion of neutralism in Chapter 1. One motive for espousing neutralism, as we saw, is to avoid the danger of illicitly imposing on others one's own values. Since one common though covert and often unconscious way of privileging one's own values is by writing them in as logically necessary features of the concept of well-being, it may be thought that the best way of avoiding this is by rigidly excluding any such personal admixtures from the concept; and this in turn may be thought to be the same as aiming at a wholly formal account of it. But the latter identification is questionable. No reason has yet been given why the educators should base their thinking about aims just on the formal account. It is sensible that they should try not to base it on accounts of well-being which simply reflect their own or others' preferences; but there may be other determinate accounts which are more solidly based and which there are good reasons to follow.[4]

Chapter 3

Beyond Moral Education?

What do we mean by 'moral education'?

Education aims at promoting pupils' personal well-being. In a liberal-democratic society, we have suggested, this will include personal autonomy. What about aims concerned with morality? Do they, too, fit under the well-being umbrella? Is it, as many philosophers have urged, in the individual's interests to behave morally? Or do moral aims lie outside well-being aims, on the grounds, perhaps, that morality is a constraint on, or in conflict with, the pursuit of one's own good, rather than a part of it?

What are these moral aims? One of the great difficulties of writing about the moral side of education lies in knowing how this is to be understood. Superficially, there may seem to be no problem. We all want children to grow up with some concern for others' well-being. We all want them, for instance, to keep their word, to tell the truth, to refrain from physical and mental maleficence, to be helpful to people in distress or need, and to be tolerant and fair. We would all agree that learning these things is different from acquiring knowledge or skills. It has to do with the acquisition of *dispositions* to behave in these ways. Children must learn not only *that* they should tell the truth (it is hard to accommodate skills in this connection); they must also learn *to be truthful*.

So much is commonplace. However, scratch a little deeper and the impression of solidity disappears. I have given examples of what would be generally taken to be moral behaviour. But what makes them *moral*? Is it that, as I half suggested, they all involve a concern for others' well-being? Is acting morally promoting the good of others? If so, are parents who look after the interests of their own children necessarily behaving morally – even where this means giving their children benefits and privileges denied to others? Or does morality require impartiality?

A second problem. How are we to react to claims that one should do what is morally right even when this does *not* serve others' interests – that one should always keep one's word, for instance, even though doing so may on occasion cause others harm? Again, if one takes the injunction to help those in distress or need, how are we to apply this? Is it to be restricted to cases of immediate succour, like lending a hand when someone is drowning in one's vicinity; or does it include helping the starving in the Third World? If the latter, how demanding is it on our time and resources?

These are only some of the issues that now come to the fore: a dozen others are waiting just out of sight. The nature of morality – and with it moral education – is deeply problematical.

Disputes about particular issues mirror larger differences about how human life is to be lived. This makes it difficult to locate the subject matter of morality. Teachers developing policies for, or devising programmes in, moral education confront an unmanageable task. It is not just that there is controversy at the margins while the central features of the subject are clear. The subject has no centre. The only statement likely to be generally accepted about morality and its education is that they are important. As soon as we begin to ask in what ways they are important, all kinds of divisions appear. But the fact that morality is so widely seen as a centrally important aspect of our lives is a clue to its nature.

Education and the moral framework

Why is morality important? We have already encountered one answer in Chapter 1. A framework of basic moral rules, with or without legal backing, is necessary in a society for its members to achieve personal well-being. If we lived every day in danger of being killed, injured, robbed, deceived and coerced, things would be worse for us than if there were widely accepted prohibitions against them (Warnock, 1971, ch2).

What kind of moral education might this view bring with it? It would seem difficult to embrace it wholly under education for the pupil's well-being. Even though my conforming to moral injunctions against maleficence, lying and intolerance is in other people's interests, it seems it may not necessarily always be in mine: I might do better not to conform on occasions that suited me not to do so. (See Chapter 4 for further discussion of this issue.) One task for moral education might then be to tie such conformity to personal well-being by making pupils aware of, and wary of, the penalties for transgression. Some of these will be legal penalties, since part of the moral framework will be enshrined in laws. Others – shame, social disapproval, the pains of conscience –

will not. If one relied wholly on this approach, moral education would be thoroughly instrumental: children would learn to behave morally so as to avoid the pains of immorality. One difficulty with it is that there might be some occasions when the potential benefits of transgression outweighed the likely pains: some people might still find it worth their while to steal things, break their promises or torture people. To try to prevent this, children would have to be brought up, therefore, to behave morally at all times and not only when it was convenient for them to do so. They should learn that they must do what is right because it is right, that virtue is its own reward.

One problem for this view of moral education is: *how* can children be taught that virtue is its own reward? Another has to do with disagreements about the extent of the moral framework. Much of it is prohibitory: one learns *not* to do various things – kill, steal, injure and lie. But the positive injunction to help others in distress is also generally recognized. Everyone will accept that this includes cases of immediacy, of sudden disaster in the here-and-now, such as when someone falls into a canal or is knocked over by a car. More distant sudden disasters are more controversial. What should one's reaction be to catastrophic flooding in another part of one's country? Or to famine in another continent? Does the injunction to *individuals* to help others in distress extend as far as situations like these? Is individual responsibility mediated through politics, so that government has the direct task of providing relief, while the individual's moral commitment is limited to trying to ensure the democratic election of a government which is responsive in this way?[1] Or do the responsibilities of neither individuals nor of governments extend so far? And what of chronic, rather than immediate distress, either local or more distant? What should one's moral stance be towards poverty, ignorance, ill-health, insecurity – and in what degrees? Again, what should individuals or governments do, if anything, about such things?

Answers to these questions yield a range of different views. At one end, a minimalism which restricts the moral framework to prohibitions plus immediate relief of disaster in the here-and-now; at the other, an insistence on unlimited responsibility on the part of individuals and/or governments to help provide the necessary conditions of personal well-being to everybody everywhere. Most respondents will come somewhere between the two extremes.

This leads us towards another kind of divergence concerning the nature of morality and moral education. These may or may not make room for critical reflection. One can bring children up disposed to do what is required by the moral framework but without questioning whether it is right that they should do it; or one can encourage them to think about this.

Moral education which leaves minimal room for critical reflection can serve religious ends or the secular end of maintaining the social status quo. In a class-divided society, this secular end tends to go with moral minimalism. It is in the interests of the rich and powerful that all children be socialized into *prohibitory* rules or virtues: the few are then less likely to be killed, injured, robbed or cheated by the many[2]; at the same time the few lose nothing in energy, time and money in their own adherence to the prohibitions, since refraining from killing and stealing makes no call on these commodities. But it may not be in the interests of the rich and powerful to insist on the injunction that others should be helped in distress, except where this is severely restricted in its application to, for example, here-and-now catastrophe. It costs nothing to the rich person, and may indeed save him (or her) something, if ordinary people help each other out of serious trouble; if he is in a road accident himself, he will benefit from the precept; if he has to lend a hand in an emergency himself, this will be only on rare occasions. But the more it is incumbent on individuals or governments to provide both immediate relief and more long-lasting welfare provision of all kinds on a massive scale, the more the rich and powerful will feel the pinch.

Critical morality can spring, for example, out of scepticism about religion, or out of a challenge to the hegemony of the rich and powerful. It always faces the problem of what criterion or critical test it can apply to individuals' actions, or the rules which embody them, to judge whether they are morally acceptable. Different forms of critical morality adopt different solutions. Kantian morality asks whether the maxim or rule of the action can be willed without contradiction to be a universal law; utilitarianism, whether the action or rule will lead to more happiness overall than any alternative; contractarianism, which principles a hypothetical group of agents would adopt, perhaps behind a 'veil of ignorance', so as to maximize their own well-being.[3]

As well as positive ethical theories like these, there are also negative theories claiming that objective criteria of moral acceptability cannot exist since morality is essentially subjective, either in the sense that it rests ultimately on the choices, decisions, feelings or tastes of the individual moral agent, or in that it is culture-relative.[4]

This is not the place to launch into a detailed discussion of each of these, and other, alternatives. I wish to make two points. First, their existence adds further answers to the questions 'what is morality?' and by implication 'what is moral education?'. This makes the picture even more complicated and solutions harder to find. If any of the new, critical, perspectives were clearly better founded than the others, things would be different. But, and this brings me to my second point, not one of them, either positive or negative, is without serious logical defects patently evident to all but the most rigid-minded of their partisans.[5]

Critical ethical theorists have been busy since the Enlightenment in the search for objective criteria or the attempt to show this to be fruitless. Over the past 200 years we have seen a succession of powerful objectivist theories countered by equally powerful critiques, some from other objectivist positions, others from the subjectivist side. Subjectivist theories have also been to the fore, especially this century, but apparently irresolvable problems in them have led to new kinds of subjectivism or to yet other reworkings of Kant, utilitarianism and other objectivist theories. Two hundred years since critical ethical theory first got under way there is still no widespread agreement about which kind of theory one should adopt. Not that nothing of any value has been achieved over this period. On the contrary, it has been rich in insights. Yet the absence of progress towards agreed solutions is striking and disturbing.[6]

Law-based conceptions of morality and moral education

When controversies multiply bewilderingly and the prospect of consensus grows less and less likely, it is appropriate to ask whether there may be something fundamentally amiss about how people conceptualize the field in question. Is this true of morality? Several recent writers on the topic have argued that it can be. Where philosophers have taken a wrong turning is in singling out and focusing on 'moral' phenomena in the first place. It is not that these phenomena do not exist or are not an important feature of human life, but that their centrality to that life has been greatly exaggerated.

Central to traditional ways of conceiving morality has been the concept of law. We began our discussion of why morality has been taken to be important by referring to the social necessity of a 'moral framework'. This, as we have seen, is partly embodied in laws against murder, stealing, bodily harm and so on, and partly not so embodied. Where it has gone beyond the legal system, it has still traditionally taken a legalistic form: moral injunctions have been seen as *rules* to be obeyed, as belonging to a moral *code*. Critical moral philosophy has by and large worked within the same thought-horizon. It has conceived its task as trying to provide criteria to determine which conventionally accepted moral rules are reflectively acceptable, or as showing that such criteria are impossible in principle. Not only has it thus taken aboard the legalistic concept of a moral rule, in appealing to criteria (or their impossibility) it has made use of a second such concept, ie the concept of a moral principle. This is a higher-order moral rule whose function is to include or exclude lower-level rules. The legal foundation of critical moral philosophy is at its most explicit in

Kant's theory of the categorical imperative; but the search for high-level moral principles has run through most positive critical theories, from utilitarianism in the nineteenth century through to those of Hare and other writers in our own age. In philosophy of education this has been particularly marked in the work of Richard Peters. Moral education, in his view, is to be founded in the early years on conformity to moral rules, pupils later acquiring the critical equipment, in the shape of rational moral principles, to reflect on those rules, reject inadequate ones, and follow the rest autonomously, not heteronomously (Peters, 1981, especially chs 2, 3, 4, 7).

A law-based conception of morality has been so much part of our ethical outlook, not least for those of us working in education, that it is difficult not to see it as natural and irreplaceable. But recent work in ethics is bringing about a transformation of perspectives. What has long seemed a constitutive feature of morality now appears as a localized cultural phenomenon flourishing over the past 300 years. The Greeks, as can be seen in Plato and Aristotle, did not make laws, rules and principles the heart of ethical life. When Socrates asked 'How should we live?' or Aristotle wrote about the 'moral virtues', their frame of reference was personal well-being as a whole. Intrinsic to that well-being is, as befits the social animals that we are, a lively concern for the well-being of other people with whom we live, work and form communities. Our altruistic inclinations are woven, as elements of our own well-being, into settled dispositions of character, or virtues – eg courage, temperance, friendship, practical wisdom and justice. A large part of 'justice' consists in adherence to the community's laws. Its importance is shown by Socrates' refusal to flee abroad when legally charged with the corruption of Athens' youth. But obedience to law is only one aspect of Greek ethics and other parts of it are not modelled on law but seen more directly in terms of their contribution to personal, and therewith, social, well-being.[7]

The replacement of well-being by law as the central ethical concept marks the dominance of Christian, especially Protestant, ethical thought by the beginning of the modern era.[8] Obedience to God's commands now becomes the guiding principle in human life. Happiness or well-being is no longer something to be achieved, if fortune permits, within our natural life. Blessedness belongs, if at all, to the life hereafter: our concern in *this* life is with the Right, not with the Good. The centrality of law is revealed in more than one way. The laws of the state, first of all, are thought of as backed by divine law. The life of the individual conforms both to these and to an array of further rules regulating attitudes to other people, religious practices, sexual behaviour, work, business relationships, upbringing and so on. Critical moral theory sees the search for a moral criterion in legal terms, looking for a single principle, or a small number of principles, under which to bring lower-order rules. Kant's 'moral law', his categorical imperative, replaces the commandments of an arbitrary God by a supreme principle of rationality, but the underlying notion, of rules or maxims being justified by reference to some higher-order yardstick, remains the same. In the transition beyond Kant from Christian to the wholly secular moral theory of last century and this, the idea has persisted of moral phenomena forming some kind of intelligible system, the diversity and detail of our moral experience being brought into coherent order by higher-level principles. Nineteenth century examples are the utilitarian theories of Bentham, the Mills and Sidgwick; contemporary moral systems are those of Hare (1981), Rawls (1971), and in our own subject, Richard Peters (1967).

From the individual's point of view Socrates' question 'How should one live?' becomes narrowed to 'How ought I morally to behave?'. Obligation now becomes a central concept (Williams, 1985, ch 10). In most if not all forms of ethical life, including that of the Greeks, obligations, together with correlative rights, have played a part, especially in arrangements for making and keeping promises and contracts, as well as, or including, more specific obligations attaching to different social roles. But in Christian and post-Christian ethics obligations move centre-stage. They are now no longer *one* form of ethical consideration among many – and we will say more below about what these others might include – but the very heart of morality. This is true whether we are dealing with morality in its conventional or its critical forms. People have been brought up for centuries to believe it their Christian duty not to lie, steal, fornicate or be idle; in a more secular age their dos and don'ts may be partially different in detail, but they still perceive them as what one morally ought or ought not to do. As for critical morality, nowhere has moral obligation been so prominent as in Kant, for whom the life of highest worth is that founded on duty, conceived as reverence for the moral law. This stern conception of human life, itself a reflection of the Protestant culture in which Kant lived, is also traceable in: more stringent forms of nineteenth-century utilitarian philanthropy; and in our times in certain forms of Marxist and social-democratic thinking, in some types of terrorism and to some extent in versions of pacifism, feminism and animal liberationism. In some of these latter examples *rights* are prominent, whether women's, animals', or those of some oppressed cultural minority or national group; but to highlight moral rights is to highlight moral obligations, for the more seriously rights are threatened the more urgent is the obligation to protect them.

Minimalist and maximalist morality

My reason for introducing the historical perspective has not been academic, but has been to throw light on the complex ethical world in which we now live, as a necessary background to working out which aims should guide us as parents and teachers.

One of the most significant divisions that can be made in this area is between what might be called a 'minimalist' conception of individual morality and a 'maximalist' conception. We have already encountered one example of this division, but I would now like to examine it more globally. The case we looked at arose out of the distinction within the moral framework between prohibitions (eg not to lie or kill) and the positive injunction to help others in need. If along with prohibitions the injunction to help were restricted to emergencies in the here-and-now, the resulting morality would be minimalist; however, it could be given a maximalist interpretation if the positive injunction were extended so as to help provide the necessary conditions for everyone's well-being. (I am here concerned only with moral obligations falling on individuals, not on governments.) I call it 'maximalist' because it fills the agent's life with moral obligations. Unlike minimalism, which, once one has fulfilled one's basic moral responsibilities, leaves one free for other pursuits, maximalism moralizes the whole of one's life.

The case just given is of a utilitarian form of maximalism. Examples of its adherents, familiar to us today, include many people who devote all their free time to politics, animal liberation, famine relief, disarmament campaigns, the women's movement or anti-apartheid. A second type of maximalist creed is found among those Christians and members of other religions for whom every aspect of life falls under some moral duty. These duties could take a utilitarian form in some people, but they might also cover such things as work for one's local church, prayer or self-examination. A third kind of maximalism, which again may or may not overlap with others, is Kantian. Moral duties here again would rule one's life, their content being determined by the requirements of the categorical imperative. Maximalism, as is clear from our three examples, can take a critical or a non-critical form. The same is true of minimalism, which I turn to next.

Moral minimalists are as prominent in contemporary Britain as maximalists, perhaps indeed more prominent. With the ebbing of Christianity, the inclination to moralize one's whole life has receded. For many people their own well-being, however variously they conceive this, is of fundamental importance. They know at the same time that they should respect others' moral rights and lend a hand where required, but may see no reason for extending these moral responsibilities beyond what is conventionally expected. Since most of these obligations are negative, fulfilling them may cost one little in time, energy and resources. It is possible in our kind of society to lead a morally upright life and devote virtually all one's attention to one's personal ambitions and enjoyments.

There are different sorts of minimalist, distinguished partly by the range and type of obligation which each takes as basic and partly by how each relates the moral framework to his or her well-being. On the latter dimension the minimalist who includes supererogatory duties under personal well-being is matched in the opposite direction by the minimalist who sees part or whole of the basic moral framework itself under this heading. Something of the background to this new position needs now to be filled in.

What reason do minimalists have for complying with the basic moral framework? If they are not religious, traditional appeals to God's will do not motivate them. As we saw earlier, it is not necessarily in a person's interests to behave morally, so appeals to their own well-being may fare no better. Some minimalists may have instrumental reasons for acting in accordance with the moral framework – and this only when it suits them to do so. In other words, they may refrain from immoral behaviour in order to avoid social opprobrium or legal penalties, but they do not do so for intrinsic reasons. *How much* they conform to the framework depends on convenience. The more easily transgression is undetectable, the more likely many are to transgress. In modern societies the general prohibition against stealing is a frequent casualty, not only among professional criminals but in the population as a whole: for example, fare-dodging, tax fiddles and illicit share dealings are less and less seen as wrong, and more and more as 'obviously' sensible, provided one can get away with it.

Reasons why people might take this instrumental attitude to the framework can vary. While they are all founded ultimately in what is seen as one's personal well-being, since conformity or non-conformity is related instrumentally to desire-satisfaction, they may be more, or less, related to one's *private* interests. Personal enrichment may be one motive, as in the examples given, but another may be the success of the corporation for which one works.

This brings us to another variation on the theme of minimalism. I said that instrumental minimalists act 'in accordance with' the framework when this is convenient. In the new variation what one finds is the deliberate *appearance* of conformity to the framework, while in reality the person has other goals in mind. Books on management techniques provide endless examples. One I saw recently is devoted to 'controlling conversations'. It describes various ways in which a manager can steer conversations towards the achievement of some preconceived goal, eg to get another employee to comply with one's wishes. One specific tip among a hundred others is to learn to listen rather than talk very much, so that when one *does* speak the other is likely to take more notice of what one says. Using techniques like this one intentionally gives the appearance of being interested in the other's point of view, while not wanting to push one's own opinion, and of trying to improve the other's working conditions, or whatever – at the same time one's real goals remain masked.

In one way manipulation of this sort – and it is found not only in management but in advertising and political propaganda – seems to go beyond minimalism. We saw above that minimalists keep positive rules, ie those to do with beneficence, to a minimum. But if beneficence is merely feigned there is no bar to its enlargement, provided always that its recipients are taken in. In our society we have grown used to living among appearances of kindness, concern, friendship, recognition, tolerance and respect. But they are nonetheless appearances for all that, and not the real thing. That is why I categorize manipulation under minimalism, as a further degeneration of it beyond instrumentalism.

A final twist in the downward spiral is the phenomenon of 'counter-ethical' behaviour, as Bernard Williams (1985, pp 13–14) has called it. This is a delight in maleficence or being ill-disposed to others for its own sake: it comes in different degrees, from the large-scale brutality of Nazis or Stalinists, to wanton physical injury to individuals, on down to wanting to see others as inferior to oneself (Palma, 1988), maliciousness towards colleagues, or domestic needling. Counterethical intentions can be masked by apparent concern for the other, hence a connection between this category and our last, the difference between them, however, lying in the intrinsic motivation of the counterethical as distinct from the extrinsic motivation found in manipulation. Hence, too, a vestigial connection between the counterethical and minimalism: some of the counterethically inspired can work behind a facade of conventional morality, while others will joyously and openly kick it in the teeth.

The cultivation of altruistic dispositions

So much, then, for varieties of maximalist and minimalist. This completes our survey of some of the very different things that can go under the heading of 'morality' and thereby under 'moral education' or the 'moral aims of education'. It is not surprising that many of us are confused about how, or why, we should lead a moral life, or about how as teachers we can set about devising moral education programmes in school. The confusion inside ourselves is an internalization of the fissures in our culture.

None of the moral positions sketched above affords a permanent resting place, each at most only a temporary perch from which to flit on somewhere else. Not knowing where we stand on morality, we do not know, either, how to relate moral considerations in our lives to those of our own well-being. It is not surprising that as teachers we may not know where to begin in working out the aims of education, considering how large a role both morality and well-being must play in any such fundamental reflection.

Where can we go from here? I mentioned above a new direction which philosophical ethics is now taking and would like to pursue this further. Following other writers, I drew attention to the dominance of the connected concepts of law and obligation in our notion of morality, to the culture-rootedness of that notion, and to the alternative picture of the ethical life presented by the Greeks, where altruism, in the shape of the actualization of virtues of character, is taken to be part of a person's well-being.

I wish now to follow up these hints, in two stages. First I shall say something about altruistic dispositions, without taking any stand on the issue of whether or not they form part of personal well-being; and then I shall turn directly to that issue.

Perhaps the most widespread reason for teachers' and parents' interest in the 'moral' side of education is that pupils should grow up attentive to the needs of others, not only their own. It is altruism, then, in the sense just given that educators have in mind. (I am not taking 'altruism' necessarily to imply a *self-sacrificing* concern for others.) In so far as this is so, we will all get further, I suggest, if we address ourselves directly to issues of altruism and its cultivation, than if we continue to talk in terms of morality. The two concepts do not necessarily go together. First, where duty or obligation is the central moral concept, as in Kantian ethics, 'duties to oneself' can appear alongside duties to others, largely as a way of leaving some legitimate room for one's personal projects in a world where obligations towards others seem all-encompassing. An example, found in Kant (1785, ch 2) and quite widely adhered to in popular morality, is the alleged duty not to let one's talents rust. This is held to be a moral obligation, but not an altruistic one. Secondly, according to some conceptions of morality it is sometimes held to be morally right to uphold some rule even when doing so can be seen to benefit no one, including others than oneself.

A big advantage of focusing directly on altruistic, rather than moral, educational aims is that this enables us to take into account types of behaviour, reactions or attitudes towards others which are worth fostering but which are either not normally brought under 'morality' at all, or else accepted as morally relevant on some criteria but rejected on others.

Altruistic dispositions are of different sorts. The following categories are not meant to be exhaustive; there may also be overlaps between them. Several of these we have met already:

1. Being attached to those close to one: parents, spouse, children and other near relations; friends; pets. There can be different degrees of intimacy here.

2. Having less intimate but still warm relationships with those with whom one comes into frequent contact: neighbours, colleagues at work, fellow-participants in non-work activities, more distant relatives. Again there can be different degrees of warmth.

3. Being well-disposed to strangers with whom one has face-to-face contact – eg on buses, in shops, in the street. Intimacy and the kind of warmth just mentioned are out of place, since these depend on a depth of shared experience and knowledge of each other. But there is still room for friendliness and sympathy (in different degrees), tolerance, being ready to help others when they are in distress.

4. Being attached to one's local community, village, town, and more widely, national community, or ethnic or religious community.

5. Being attached to institutions of which one is a member and which one sees as conferring some kind of benefit on others: eg one's school, workplace, a political party, a sports club.

6. Being disposed to fulfil the special obligations one incurs in a social role – eg as parent, as foreman, as policewoman, as goalkeeper.

7. Being disposed to honour the general obligations one incurs in making promises and contracts. This includes being aware of the importance to others' well-being of their being able to rely on one's keeping one's word and of the way their plans can be disrupted if one does not keep it.

8. Being impartial between claims, both between one's own and others' claims, and among those of others.

9. Being disposed to protect others' well-being in general, ie beyond the specific groups mentioned in earlier categories: eg not to lie, harm people physically or mentally, be intolerant.

10. Being concerned to promote others' well-being in general, without restriction to more local categories, eg being attentive to the needs of the sick, poor, hungry and ignorant in the world as a whole.

11. Possessing altruistic virtues. Many of these have been included in previous categories – indeed, all of the dispositions mentioned

so far can be labelled 'altruistic virtues'. Among the virtues of character that philosophers have discussed since Plato and Aristotle are courage, temperance, practical wisdom, self control. It is not difficult to see how some of these can be, even though perhaps they need not be, harnessed to altruistic ends: a soldier's courage, one's control of one's feelings of anger towards others, one's regulation of one's eating and drinking so that one can do one's job adequately, one's using one's intelligence in the service of others. Some of the earlier categories, eg attachments to communities or institutions, may embrace virtues like these.

Most people will agree that children should be brought up with altruistic dispositions of these main types. Differences of opinion will emerge the further one goes into specification: attachment to one's national community, for instance, will not find favour with everyone as an educational goal; but broadly I suggest the list is uncontroversial.[9]

Education in altruism has two components. The first and more basic is acquiring the various dispositions; the second is learning what to do when the values enshrined in them conflict. Conflicts can occur within the main categories outlined and between them. *Within* the categories one might instance the distress suffered by members of ethnic minority communities torn between attachment to those communities and to the national community; or by a person who can only avoid bringing about another's harm by telling a lie. *Between* the categories, there can be conflicts between caring for the well-being of local communities or for humanity as a whole; or between doing what one's job demands and telling the truth or promoting general well-being. Innumerable further examples can be given of both main types.

Learning how to cope with these conflicts does not involve applying rigid rules or an unchanging hierarchy of value. The tension between helping those close to one and helping those in need more generally is not to be resolved by always giving priority to the larger group of beneficiaries or (which may not yield the same result) by appeal to a utilitarian principle of maximizing well-being. Neither do there seem to be any values which are inviolable and so must always take precedence in conflict with others. It is not clear that even killing (or something equally reprehensible) is always to be avoided: for if one's refraining from killing should lead to other people being killed, it seems irrational to insist that one should not kill on the grounds that no one ever ought to kill (Scheffler, 1982, p 82). Resolving conflicts requires flexibility, not rigidity. It necessitates attending to detailed features of opposing possible courses of action, including their possible or likely consequences. Values which weigh more heavily with one in one situation may weigh less heavily in another.

Being able to handle conflicts of value presupposes that one has made the values one's own in the first place. This brings us back to the first of our two types of altruistic aim. The priority here is logical and not necessarily temporal. It certainly does not seem sensible to think of spending children's early years in building up their altruistic dispositions and only later, when all the dispositions are firmly in place, moving on to conflict resolution. For one thing, dispositions continue to be shaped and strengthened throughout our lives. For another, some conflicts can occur when a child is very young, as yet incapable of acquiring some of the more sophisticated dispositions. A child too young to know about poverty in the Third World and hence to possess sympathetic dispositions in that direction may still be torn between visiting her (or his) sick friend in hospital and leaving her sick cat at home.

That said, a major task of early education will still be to form altruistic dispositions, to build these value-commitments into children as firmly as possible.[10]

Beyond moral education?

What is lost or gained by abandoning 'moral education' for education in altruism? Some will repudiate the question on the grounds that what I have just sketched out exactly fits their conception of moral education. But not everyone who uses 'moral' terminology will agree with them; as we have seen, conceptions of morality vary widely. If this were also true of conceptions of altruism, we might find ourselves as confused as we were over morality. I suggest, however, that what altruistic dispositions are is not, by and large, mysterious. If we can attach some determinate and agreed meaning to 'personal well-being', as we tried to do in Chapter 2, we can agree on what it would be in general to be attentive to others' well-being. There will not be agreement on all points of detail or priority, as we have seen, but I suggest that the sketch I gave gives educators a direction to follow which most people will think reasonable. It is, above all, a practicable proposal. All sorts of further things have to be thrashed through to do with how children are to acquire the dispositions, about which dispositions are in particular to be included, and about how children can learn to cope with conflict; but at least this means it is possible to map out the tasks ahead. It was just this sense of knowing where to go from here that we found lacking in the alternative approach, via morality.

How might 'Moralists' – if we can so name proponents of this alternative approach – reply to 'Altruists'? That depends to some extent on what kind of Moralist one has in mind. But are there features of moral education which all or most Moralists would want to retain and think threatened by education for altruism? One source of anxiety, I suspect, is the absence in the latter, at least as outlined so far, of any general hierarchy of importance among the altruistic values spelt out in the list. Individuals are to respond flexibly to conflicts of value and pay attention to particular circumstances; but we need to bring children up with clearer guidelines than this. Unless we do so, they will grow up thinking that it is *up to them* how they establish priorities. Some of them, perhaps many of them, will take advantage of this by downplaying whatever is irksome to them. When values conflict there is nothing to stop their favouring those closer to their own well-being – local attachments to friends and family, for instance, rather than more impersonal values concerning general welfare or impartiality, promise-keeping or truth-telling. But the ethical life cannot be trimmed to one's convenience. In this book it has already been agreed that children are not to be brought up as utter egoists, intent only on their own interests to the exclusion of others'. Both Moralists and Altruists are in accord on that. But if people are brought up to believe that they can weight their altruism towards friends and family, what is this but a kind of extended egoism? We condemn nepotism and other kinds of favouritism towards one's close associates, and rightly so. There need to be bulwarks against egoism, extended or unextended. These bulwarks cannot be left to the play of subjective preferences: children must learn that some things in the ethical life are not negotiable, that their self-concern is hemmed in by impersonal demands whether they are inclined towards the latter or not.

This counterargument of the Moralist misses the mark. It assumes that Altruists want to make prioritizing depend on individuals' preferences. But this is not so. For the Altruist individual *judgement* is certainly important; and different individuals may well respond differently to the same kind of conflict. But all this is against the background of an upbringing which has not only developed various altruistic dispositions but also established certain priorities among them. One of the things which children learn is that friends and family should *not* always come first. They learn this as part of their induction into various social roles, either directly or via the imagination. Part of what it is to be a member of a sports team, a committee member or a bus conductor is possessing a sense of justice, related to the ends which the role seeks to realize, which rules out partiality of this kind.

This example shows that it is not accurate to talk, as I just have talked, of 'developing altruistic dispositions' *and also* 'establishing certain priorities among them'. For acquiring the dispositions *is* to some extent accepting priorities. Learning to tell the truth is in part learning not to lie even when lying would bring one's friends or family advantage. Children come to see that *everyone* needs a reliable environment in which to pursue his or her projects, and that lies, broken promises and the fear of personal injury undermine that reliability. Prohibitions against these things are of great importance because of the fundamental place of reliability as a condition of personal well-being. In acquiring dispositions of this sort, children acquire at the same time a sense of the bedrock significance of these prohibitions to our personal and social life. So the precedence of adhering to the prohibitions over advantaging particular individuals, including those close to one, is grasped *in* learning not to lie or injure people.

Two comments on this. First, grasping this precedence as part of acquiring these dispositions depends on understanding *why* lying and so on undermine personal well-being in the way just described. If children are brought up not to lie without being given such a rationale, then the precedence has to be established in some other way; perhaps it is stamped in, for instance, by a system of sanctions which establishes particularly heavy penalties for transgressing the prohibitions. The second point is that the Altruist will only want to establish a *general* precedence, ie one which leaves room for exceptions when circumstances warrant these. In extreme circumstances the claims of those close to one might outweigh a more general altruism. A parent whose children are starving and who can keep them alive only by stealing from the rich may be sensible to do so. Pupils brought up under Altruism will learn that exceptions may on occasion be justifiable. In doing this, they will need to reflect on the underlying reasons for the values they are taught and to take into account relevant detail about particular situations. Intelligent response rather than blind adherence to rules is the hallmark of this kind of upbringing.

If we turn now to conflicts between attachments to those close to one and one's desire to promote the well-being of everybody, again we see that priorities are not 'up to the individual' in any arbitrary sense. True, different people will come to weight things differently: one brother in a family will devote himself to working for Oxfam while the other spends all his time looking after his invalid parents. But such variations can be rooted in a shared understanding about priorities with which one has been brought up. Both the flourishing of those dear to me and the improvement of the lot of the long-term unemployed in this country, or the destitute in the Sahel are important to me. I can be brought up to desire both, but to see that there are different means of realizing them. With friends and family I share my day-to-day world: not to care for them would be inconceivable to me, for then the foundations of that world would not exist. I cannot feel attached in this intimate way to mankind in the mass, but my sympathies can be so extended that I put myself in the place of the unemployed or starving and am moved to do what I can to help them. Since the scale of assistance required is so vast, I can do little on my own but much more, in theory at least, by lending my weight to collective action. Not all forms of valuable collective action are political, in the sense that they are undertaken by government – witness the success of Bob Geldof's Bandaid in relieving famine – but political action is in principle the most powerful means of bringing about large-scale improvements.[11] Altruists will both bring up children to value their intimate attachments very highly and at the same time will develop their awareness of politics and of the way they can contribute through it to the promotion of well-being more generally. Once again, then, ways of coping with value-conflicts can be built into upbringing from its early days. Although children will still face all sorts of conflicts in their lives, often acute ones, they need not, and should not, grow up bereft of major guidelines.

A reply to Moralists on these lines is not likely to satisfy all of them. Some will still press for a more systematic form of upbringing in which priorities are more sharply delineated. But there is no a priori reason why we should expect ethics to be particularly systematic. Ethical values do not have to form a tight logical system. Their *raison d'être* is practical: they serve their purpose of guiding us in how to live even though they are incapable of exact description and untidily related to each other. This raggedness may indeed be a virtue. Situations in which one has to make choices and decisions are often complex and to some extent unpredictable. A rigid template is likely to be of less practical use than a looser set of values which leaves plenty of room for intelligent judgement. Moral philosophers have usually been tempted to impose more order on our ethical lives than they either exhibit or require. Their theories, whether Kantian, utilitarian or contractualist, have tended to reduce the rich complexity of ethics to a small number of central ideas or principles. In this way certain values – prohibitions, perhaps, or universal well-being – have come to be accorded an unwarranted pre-eminence.[12]

The shift from moral education to education in altruism minimizes the damage which can be done to pupils by moral zealots highlighting favoured values. Our age is full of such enthusiasts, whether left-wing or right-wing, religious or secular, advocates of universal brotherhood, the liberty of the individual, attachment to the law of Moses or Mahomet, anti-permissiveness, etc. The result is often intransigence, an unwillingness to meet others half-way. If ethical values are less hierarchically ordered, children will grow up better able to understand those with whom they disagree, seeing them not as living in darkness, apart from the light of Moral Truth, but as sharing the same values as themselves, only putting different weights on them.

A related advantage of education in altruism is that it reduces the place of guilt and blame in ethical learning. A central concept for the

Moralist is *obligation*, not in the more limited sense in which we speak of ourselves as 'bound' by promises or contracts we have made, but in the more general sense of 'moral obligation' as embodied in such precepts as 'nobody ought to lie', 'it's wrong to steal', 'we all must work for the common good'. Children are brought up to believe that ineluctable duties are laid on them to do or refrain from this or that, the content varying according to the moral system in question. They also learn, as part of this same scheme of thought, to feel guilt and remorse when they fail to live up to their obligations. They come to blame themselves for their shortcomings. And not only themselves. They are trained to see other people, too, through the same reductive spectacles, as abiders by, or deviants from, their moral duties.

The combination of rigid adherence to favoured values, unwillingness to compromise, and the pervasive tendency to blame oneself and others for moral defects is a familiar feature of our contemporary ethical landscape, not least perhaps in Britain. But our ethical life does not *have* to be as unlovely as this. There is a place for obligation, as for guilt and blame. If one makes promises one obliges oneself to keep them. But there is no good reason why these things should dominate over everything else. They are only some among the many elements in our ethical life, but are given a distorted and exaggerated significance in some influential moral systems.

Chapter 4

A Unified Upbringing

How are moral or altruistic aims related to aims to do with the promotion of the pupil's own well-being? Do we have two distinct aims here, steering us in different and perhaps often conflicting directions? Or is there a more intimate connection between morality or altruism on the one hand and personal well-being on the other, such that the promotion of a pupil's well-being already embraces moral or altruistic goals? In dealing with these questions we need to take separately the relationship between morality and personal well-being and that between altruism and personal well-being.

Morality and well-being

Morality, as we have seen, has been conceived in radically different ways. This means that there is no simple answer to the question before us about the relationship between morality and well-being. Different moral theories and different strands of popular thinking about morality point different ways. Some say that moral demands can conflict with self-interest; others that it is in one's interests to lead a morally good life.

The conflict view

The first view embraces several different positions along a continuum of frequency: at one end of it conflicts are rare, but they occur more often as one moves along it, until at the far end one finds morality and self-interest always at odds with each other. Conflict will be least where the conception of morality is minimalist: it may be, but need not be, greatest where it is maximalist. At the infrequent pole, rare conflict can become virtually no conflict, and in some actual lives, perhaps no conflict at all. Imagine a rich person who keeps to all the moral prohibitions against lying, stealing and so on and also gives to charities in order to relieve serious distress. He or she may be able to do all this without having to sacrifice any of his personal goals.

In his (or her) actual life, therefore, there may be no conflict. At the same time, the *possibility* of occasional conflict still exists. As it happens, throughout his life he has never been present at a fire, accident or other emergency where there would have been a clear moral requirement that he should help, and where helping would have jeopardized some project of his own which he was currently pursuing. If he *were* faced with such a conflict, he would recognize it as such and try in some way to resolve it; so the *idea* of conflict forms part of his ethical outlook, even though it is not actualized in his life. It is this last fact that distinguishes him from the person for whom personal well-being *includes* acting morally, since for the latter the idea of conflict is ruled out by definition.

Conflict may be very frequent where moral demands are maximal. If I hold it to be a moral duty, for instance, to do all I can to relieve world poverty, this may seriously get in the way of my personal projects and attachments. A resolution of the conflict is possible if I can come to reconceptualize the moral goal as a personal goal: in this way morality becomes a part of personal well-being *for me*, even though it is not necessarily part of *everyone's* well-being. With some versions of morality, however, no resolution is possible: moral and prudential reasons for action are mutually exclusive, so that whenever one is acting morally one cannot be acting prudentially, and vice versa. This is so, for instance, where acting morally is conceived as acting out of duty and where acting out of self-interest is seen as acting out of inclination, or for pleasure – given, that is, that duty and inclination/pleasure are taken to be incompatible reasons for action (Kant, 1785).

But conflicts can also be frequent where the morality is less demanding. Even the minimal morality which causes few problems for the affluent may often clash with self-interest where the agent is less fortunate. A poor man may well be more tempted to steal or deceive than the rich man.

How can these conflicts, whatever their frequency, be resolved? There are the following three possibilities:

1. reasons of self-interest should always take precedence over moral reasons;
2. moral reasons should always take precedence over self-interested reasons; or
3. neither type of reason should always take precedence: sometimes moral reasons should win out, sometimes self-interested.

Most people will reject point 1. Recognizing the force of moral reasons not to kill, cheat, steal and so on but going on to override these in one's own interests will find few overt supporters, however logically impregnable a position this may be. How many *covert* supporters it may have today, bearing in mind our earlier discussion of pseudo-moral forms of minimalism (pp 44 and 45), is a further question.

What shall we say of point 2? If my ability to pursue a project to which I am highly committed is threatened by having to keep a promise I have made (as in Gauguin's case, perhaps, where his artist's *daemon* was at odds with his duties to his family), do I have good reason to sacrifice the project? As we saw earlier, it is difficult to show that there must always be such a reason. A crucial question here is whether all one's reasons for actions must be 'internal' reasons, ie dependent on one's desires, or whether one can also have 'external' reasons, which are independent of them (Williams, 1981, ch 8). If all reasons must be internal and I have no desire to do what morality demands of me where this clashes with self-interest, then moral reasons cannot weigh with me. The onus is on the supporters of point 2 to show that some reasons can be external. They would then be in a position to argue that in some cases morality makes demands on one, requires one to do such and such, whether one wants to do it or not.

But no convincing argument has been put forward, to my knowledge, to support the possibility of external reasons.[1] It is hard indeed to see how anything could motivate a person to action unless it were at some point dependent on what he or she desired. In this, Hume's dictum that 'reason is and ought to be the slave of the passions' appears to be on the right lines. Until good arguments for external reasons are produced we have no reason to accept point 2. The same is true of point 3, since we cannot say that there must be some occasions when moral reasons should take precedence even though they will not always do so.

If the general line of argument is right, therefore, points 2 and 3 yield no way of resolving the conflicts in question. It should not be surprising, therefore, if, as we suggested in fact quite often happens, people attached to a 'conflict' view of the morality/self-interest relationship, fell back on some version of point 1, covertly if not overtly. There is now no problem of external reasons, since the only reasons which move one, ie reasons of self-interest, are internal.

At the same time the recourse to point 1 is not, as we have seen, an option with wide appeal. Proponents of a 'conflict' view face a dilemma: either they retain the precedence of moral reasons, but then have to give an account of how these can be desire-independent; or they resolve every conflict in favour of self-interest. It is because both choices raise serious difficulties that some thinkers have turned away from a 'conflict' view towards one which makes morality a necessary element in self-interest.

Being moral as in one's interests

The chief problem facing this latter claim has been evident since Plato's treatment of a related issue in Books I and II of *The Republic*. Whatever sanctions are employed to make it in people's interests not to be immoral, some individuals may still find it profitable to be so. Plato described two ways in which one could avoid the pain of sanctions – by becoming so politically powerful that one is above the law, like Thrasymachus; and by making one's misdeeds untraceable to oneself, as in Glaucon's story of the ring of Gyges, which made its wearer invisible. Versions of these two strategies can be found in the contemporary world, in the tyrannies of Hitler or Stalin on the one hand, and in the invisibility which a large-scale, amorphous urban society can afford on the other.

Philosophers have looked for ways of convincing the rational egoist that, despite appearances, it is after all in his (or her) interests to be moral, but none of the arguments put forward seem conclusive. The crux is again the apparent impossibility of external reasons for action. If someone is rich and powerful enough not to fear any personal disadvantages from cheating, lying or killing, and if his major goals comprise, say, the enjoyment of bodily pleasures and being an object of fear and envy among the populace, then he has no internal reason to lead a moral life. If there were external reasons to be moral, this would not of itself show that his being moral was a part of his personal well-being, since the moral reasons might be independent of the latter. But in any case, as already stated, external reasons for action do not seem to be possible. The egoist, it seems, can always deny that it is in his interests to be moral, without being irrational.

Many contemporary philosophers by and large accept the impregnability of this position. Some of them are still tempted, however, by the thought that morality is in one's interests and settle for a modified version of this claim. A recent example is James Griffin (1986). Griffin acknowledges that 'some people are self-interested in a very cramped, crabbed, ungenerous way; nothing much matters to them but their own comfort and safety' (p 128). Working from this conception, Griffin sees no hope of reducing morality to self-interest. With a richer conception of self-interest things are different.

> One has not got a specification of the prudential at all without a pretty full account of what moral demands there are on us and how they are to be accommodated. Prudential value does not stop at the edges of an individual's own private life. Some persons may see their self-interest in a narrow, crabbed way. But anyone with a defensible idea of prudential values can see what he cares about not just as what as a matter of fact he *now* cares about, but as what he *ought* to care about or what he *will* care

about after subjecting his concerns to full deliberation. He will find it hard, therefore, to keep moral and prudential values apart. One of the things he will want is a life of point and substance. What he will see as prudentially valuable, valuable to his own personal life, will to some extent coincide with what he will see as valuable morally. (pp 131–2)

A danger with this line of argument, as Griffin himself notes (p 130), is that one writes morality by definition into this richer concept of self-interest. He seeks to avoid this, but it is not clear that he succeeds. Much turns on the notion of a 'life of point and substance'. He comes back to this later in the chapter. He says then that prudentially speaking we want 'to live a life of substance or value or weight' (p 156). Since we want this, we have to decide what a valuable life is. We cannot lead a life of value 'if we have no regard for, or if we damage, values generally, including the value of other persons' lives' (pp 156–7).

I do not find Griffin's case convincing. Even if one rules out people who have a crabbed picture of their well-being in which comfort and safety are all-important to them, there can be richer conceptions of a flourishing life which still fall short of embracing moral demands. There can be lives of evil grandeur. A rich, politically influential person may lead anything but a narrow existence. As well as comfort and safety he (or she) might prize: being able to control other people's lives on a large scale; making people afraid of him; bestowing and withholding favours in an arbitrary way so that people don't know what to expect of him; going in for costly adventures which keep him in the public eye; and doing things, however outrageous, with a view to gaining a place in the history books. He may do any or all of these things without regard to moral constraints: being wicked on a grand scale may be central to his project. Even though it may be true that non-crabby forms of prudence require one to decide what a valuable life is, one's conception of value could still be within amoral horizons.[2]

We still lack any good reason why one's well-being must include morality, even given all the qualifications and exceptions put forward. If we make the promotion of pupils' well-being a major educational aim, we cannot assume, following the arguments looked at so far, that we need do nothing more to turn them into morally good people. We might be helping them to become moral monsters.[3]

One could obviously explore these various conceptions of morality further. However, in the light of our earlier discussion of morality in this chapter this might well be unprofitable. What I hope to have shown in this section are the difficulties which those who think in terms of morality face in charting its relationship with personal well-being. The 'conflict' view leads one towards either externalism or egoism, while the 'harmony' alternative is open to counter-instances which tempt one back towards the 'conflict' theory. Again, as in our earlier discussion of morality, we find no secure resting place, only an anxious shifting from one inadequate position to another. For this and other reasons we may do well now to leave morality on one side and turn to relationships between personal well-being and altruism.[4]

Altruism and well-being

How are altruistic aims to be related to personal aims? Alasdair MacIntyre (1981) provides an Aristotelian account of the good life for the individual.[5] He sees human well-being as partly embracing the pursuit of what he calls 'practices'.

> By a 'practice' I'm going to mean any coherent and complex form of socially established cooperative human activity through which goods internal to that form of activity are realised in the course of trying to achieve those standards of excellence which are appropriate to, and partially definitive of, that form of activity, with the result that human powers to achieve excellence, and human conceptions of the ends and goods involved, are systematically extended. Tic-tac-toe is not an example of a practice in this sense, nor is throwing a football with skill; but the game of football is, and so is chess. Bricklaying is not a practice; architecture is. Planting turnips is not a practice; farming is. So are the enquiries of physics, chemistry and biology, and so is the work of the historian, and so are painting and music. In the ancient and medieval worlds the creation and sustaining of human communities – of households, cities, nations – is generally taken to be a practice in the sense in which I have defined it. (p 175)

Practices, therefore, contain internal, shared, goods. These include not only the excellence of what is produced – paintings, cities, farms or whatever – but also the virtues necessary to sustain a practice – the courage and honesty, for instance, found in the willingness of a novice to subordinate herself or himself to the best standards available within the practice, or the cooperativeness necessary for working on a common task.

Money, power, fame are not internal but 'external' goods. Unlike the former, they are not necessarily shared but can belong exclusively to particular individuals. Also, unlike the former, the more some individuals possess them, the less there is for other people: external goods are essentially competitive. MacIntyre does not deny that external goods could have *some* place in the good life, but they must be subordinate in importance to internal goods.

MacIntyre's good life does not consist solely in engagement in practices. For one thing, what is required in one practice may be at odds with what is required in another: the demands on one as an artist, for instance, may get in the way of one's duties as a parent. Somehow the different practices in which one engages must be held harmoniously together within one's life as a whole. There must be some rational, integrating structure into which they all fit. The good life is to be understood, once again with Aristotle, as the goodness of a life seen as a whole. For MacIntyre one's life has the structure of a narrative – it is a gradually unfolding story whose future development is unknown and uncertain. The good life has the nature of a quest: 'the good life for man is spent in seeking the good life for man' (p 204). To sustain one in this quest one needs virtues over and above those found in particular practices; One needs a more general form of courage and temperance to enable one to withstand the dangers and temptations besetting one's life as as whole; one needs wisdom and judgement, integrity, constancy and patience.

A third, and final, stage in MacIntyre's account of the good life introduces the concept of tradition. In seeking the good and exercising the virtues one does not do so as a solitary individual but as a bearer of a particular social identity, as someone's daughter or father, as a member of such-and-such a work-group, as a citizen of such-and-such a city or nation. It is as a role-holder that I engage in practices; and what helps to hold my life together in a unity is my progression into and out of a succession of such roles. These roles and practices, and the institutions and communities in which they appear, have a historical dimension: behind them lie traditions of thought and action which must be sustained and cherished – and certainly not in a hidebound way – if they are to flourish.

If MacIntyre is right, an individual's well-being cannot be self-contained, but must embrace the wider well-being of those with whom he or she is engaged in various practices. The question is: is MacIntyre right?

Can one show that the good life for man consists in being the kind of person MacIntyre delineates? A sceptic might argue that he or she cannot see why shared ends must predominate in a person's value-system, while external ends like power or fame must be of secondary importance. No doubt many people will be drawn towards communal forms of life embodied in practices and lives woven round them, but how can it be claimed that this is the good life for all and not only for those who so choose? How far has MacIntyre made the very familiar mistake of objectifying his own personal vision of how life should be led and erecting it into a goal for everybody?

If MacIntyre's theory were true, there would be everything to be said for initiating children into practices and getting them to see that their own good is inextricable from the good of others. But if all we have is MacIntyre's personal preferences, in seeking to base educational recommendations on them we are in danger of imposing these preferences on all those pupils brought up under this aegis. Far from achieving their own good, they may become indoctrinated in somebody else's unfounded vision of it.

MacIntyre's account is attractive, but I cannot see how it can avoid the sceptic's attack. If personal well-being is to be understood in terms of the satisfaction of one's major informed desires, there is nothing in this concept to suggest that these desires must have altruistic objects, among others. A Thrasymachus, who lived only for domination and personal pleasures, could be successful in the pursuit of these ends. Why would his not be a life of great personal fulfilment?

Problems in separatist upbringing

Altruism is thus not a part of the general concept of personal well-being: it is logically possible to flourish without caring for other people and their interests. There is no reason, however, why *educators* should operate with the most bare concept of personal well-being in sorting out their aims. We saw in Chapter 1 that although personal autonomy is similarly not a logically necessary feature of well-being, promoting an autonomous version of well-being is a reasonable educational aim in an autonomy-supporting society. The question now is: are there equally good reasons why educators should build altruism as well as autonomy into their concept?

We can start from the contention, with which all will agree, that education should have *some* altruistic aims. No one would want all – or any – children to be brought up as complete amoralists, and for an obvious reason: if we have no consideration for each other, life is going to go worse for all, or virtually all of us, than if we possess this.

But this contention does not get us very far, because it does not imply that the satisfaction of the altruistic desires which children come to acquire will contribute to their well-being. Their altruism may lie outside this area. Indeed this seems not only possible but also sensible: altruism is directed towards furthering *other people's* well-being; and since other people are not oneself, furthering *their* well-being will be something quite distinct from furthering *one's own*.

If there are good reasons, nevertheless, why educators should build altruism into the concept of the child's well-being, what could they be?

An important consideration is the difficulty one would face in trying to keep the two apart. One's pupils would be brought up to be altruistic, but their altruistic desires would be kept in quite a separate category from those concerned with their own interests. It is hard to see, practically, how one might try to do this; and indeed the enterprise may turn out to be more deeply incoherent.

Activities with shared ends

As MacIntyre's notion of 'practices' reminds us, many of the activities in which we engage have ends which we share with others. This is most obviously true where we co-operate with others face-to-face in a common task – as parents in bringing up children, for instance, or as members of a drama group or hockey team. But there can be shared ends, too, where interaction is not face-to-face. Physical scientists working on the structure of matter can be separated in time and space yet still be engaged on a common pursuit; and so, in a sense, can poets and their readers. Now let us suppose that an individual is pursuing an activity with shared ends that is of great importance to her (or him): satisfying the desires which it brings with it comes high in her hierarchy of personal ends. In satisfying these desires of hers she will also be satisfying the desires of those with whom she is sharing the activity. She is promoting their well-being as well as her own. But if her altruistic desires are to be kept in a separate pigeon-hole from her self-interested desires, how are we to conceive of this?

We would have to say something like this. The agent in question wants something which we shall call 'x'. It may be being in a winning hockey team, for instance, acting in a successful play, or designing a car. X is not the sort of end which she can achieve on her own: she has to share it with other people. She sees the other members of her team as individuals, each, like her, pursuing x and needing the co-operation of others to enable them to do so. She is glad that her pursuit of x helps the others in their pursuit of x. But her own self-interested desire is only that x be achieved: she has not in addition the self-interested desire that the others' desire for x be satisfied – although she *does* have this as a non-self-interested desire.

Is it possible to learn to see things in this highly individualistic way, where one's own well-being is kept strictly free of altruistic desires? I have been assuming so far that the only relevant desire which the agent has relates to the accomplishment of a goal – winning a match, putting on a successful play, discovering atomic structure, or whatever. But people take part in co-operative activities for other kinds of reason than this. For one thing, they like being with other people and doing things with them. Even if the shared goal is not achieved, the fact that they are able to satisfy these social desires contributes to their well-being. Normally the fact that others, too, are able to satisfy their social desires also enhances the agent's own well-being: among her self-interested desires is the desire that the others in her group realize their social desires. For the separatist, who wants to keep altruism apart from personal well-being, this normal attitude is something to be ignored or discouraged. It is hard to see what point there would be in doing this, or, indeed, quite what alternative there could be. The agent would have to have two quite separate desires, one self-interested, the other altruistic – the first of these being the desire to be with others and do things with them, and the second, the desire that others realize their desires to be with others and do things with them. How could these two desires be built into a pupil as separate motivational tendencies? While it is easy to see how children could be brought up with the *single* – ie both self-interested and altruistic – desire that *we* be with and do things with each other, it is difficult to grasp the separatist alternative.

I have described the social desire so far as 'being with and working with' others. But more can be said about it than this. Part of what I enjoy in this is being with people with certain personal qualities. I do not see them only as efficient means of realizing the shared goal. They are not simply, as far as I am concerned, good instruments to help me to get what I want; and I don't simply see myself as a useful tool in *their* service. I enjoy being with them, and they with me, because of what we are in ourselves. We like being with people who are friendly, loyal, independent-minded, entertaining, courageous, co-operative, not too self-assertive or too self-effacing, enthusiastic about common purposes, yet not carried away by their enthusiasm. Most of these qualities are helpful to the group and may thus be said to have an instrumental side to them. But they are far from *purely* instrumental. People who possess them are valued for their own sake and not only as a means to something else.[6]

There is a dual aspect to this. Beyond my general desire to be with people who possess these qualities, I desire two kinds of thing in particular: recognizing or appreciating others' qualities; and being recognized and appreciated by others for the qualities which I possess. For the separatist the former desire would be allocated to altruism, the latter to self-interest. But it is doubtful, once again, whether the two motivations can be kept separate. Recognition within a group is mutual: you recognize me for my qualities and I recognize you, and so on through the whole membership. If I fail to recognize others, to reinforce their perception of themselves as valuable members of the group, then I, too, will fail to achieve recognition.[7] One of the most important personal qualities prized within a group is a propensity to recognize the valuable contributions of others, so my desire to praise or otherwise recognize others' virtues cannot be classified as altruistic alone. In recognizing others I am making it more likely that I, too, will receive *their* recognition. It is in my interests to be altruistic, but this cannot be in any instrumental way. If I were to give recognition solely in order to receive recognition, then not only would I probably fail (unless I could keep my true intentions well hidden), but also, more importantly, I would not be the altruist which it is currently being taken for granted that I am. Granting others recognition is *a necessary condition* of my receiving recognition from them but it is not *a means* of bringing this about.

One line of argument against the ideas in the last paragraph might be to challenge the claim that recognition must be mutual. Is it not possible for me to get recognition from others within a group without my according it to them? Imagine that I manage to become the leader of the group, am looked up to by other members, and know that I can get people to achieve the group's goals without my having to give them any recognition in return.

There can be, and are, groups like this, but I do not see it as a strong objection in the present context as such a position makes it once again difficult to see me as the altruist I am supposed to be. The less I can rely on my recognition of others the more I will have to motivate them to achieve group goals by treating them not as ends-in-themselves but as instruments to this end.

One way in which separatists can try to avoid difficulties over shared ends is to steer the children they are bringing up towards activities which lack these. From the point of view of their well-being, children could be steered towards activities with ends that are not shared with others; and as altruists-in-the-making they could be encouraged to throw themselves into good works which are not intended to help themselves. What might be included? On the self-interested side, perhaps such things as: going for solitary walks; writing private journals; enjoying physical pleasures like eating, drinking and sex, but without the companionship which usually embraces them; taking up watching television or competitive sports, but again as a loner; or climbing up some competitive career ladder for the sake of personal success and not, except instrumentally to this, in order to pursue shared goals with others. And on the altruistic side, where we have in mind devoting oneself to something beneficial to others but not to oneself, examples might be: working long hours for low pay as a coalminer or as a worker on an assembly line.

One *could* bring children up with such dual ambitions, but the point of it would be hard to see. How could one be justified in steering them away from the great range of activities with shared ends, which fall between the two poles just mentioned and which make up so much of people's day-to-day lives?

It is interesting that it is just these two poles which our culture so often highlights, not least in its educational ideas. British secondary education, as David Hargreaves (1982, ch 4) has pointed out, is marked by a 'culture of individualism' in which corporate activities and attachments are given low priority. Although students are present together in the same classes, much of their time is spent not in working *with* others for common ends, but in working atomistically for success in competitive examinations. These examinations are seen as opening doors to a life of greater personal well-being based on continued competitiveness and, often, private or semi-private pleasures. If one fails at the examination stakes, a life of unpleasant toil (if not unemployment) stretches out before one, a life, that is, of diminished well-being, centred around work that may be beneficial to others but has few personal rewards and is relieved largely by the private or semi-private pleasures which a modern economy lays on for its proletariat – television-watching, shopping, drinking and the like.

I do not want to exaggerate. Shared activities are widespread in British, as they must be in any, society. But they are little emphasized in formal education, either in its objectives or in its pedagogy. In these two respects British educational thinking has been different both from Marxist collectivism and from the Deweyan heritage in North America, both of which favour co-operative activities. Separatism has been especially influential in this country.[8]

Character education

Difficulties for the separatist over personal qualities arise not only with regard to shared activities but also more generally. Children are brought up to possess virtues like courage, temperance, practical intelligence, justice, patience, generosity and benevolence. Many of these virtues, and arguably all, are beneficial both to their possessors and to others. Temperance is a good example. In learning to control my bodily appetites I make it more likely that my major desires will be satisfied, since they are less likely to be thwarted by the demands of appetite; and at the same time I make it easier to satisfy my altruistic desires, for the same reason. Similar points could be made about courage: regulating my propensities towards fear and rashness both serves me in good stead and makes me more effective in helping others.

Separatism will urge that the motivations embedded in these virtues be compartmentalized. Children are to grow up not with a generalized desire to regulate their appetite for food and drink, but with (a) the desire to do this for their own benefit, plus (b) the desire to do it for others' benefit. Is there any good reason for bifurcating virtues as a part of upbringing? Is it in any case a practical possibility?

If separatism has problems, conceptually, with educating in virtues, a radical way out for it would be to leave virtues out of education. It might think of the latter in terms of academic learning for its own sake, for instance, or as preparation for work.[9] Each of these, it is true, would bring with them their own virtues – or alleged virtues. On the one hand would be intellectual virtues like a judicious regard for the evidence or the avoidance of self-display, and on the other virtues like punctuality and industriousness. But these virtues, unlike courage, temperance or practical wisdom, are more easily confined to the specific spheres of activity in question. What the separatist would have to avoid is an education in which personal well-being and altruism were taken seriously as aims, for it is here that the problems over education in general virtues of character begin. If aims are to be located elsewhere – in the pursuit of learning for its own sake or in vocational preparation, for instance – these problems evaporate. The fact that actual educational aims are indeed so often located elsewhere may be further testimony to the strength of separatist ways of thinking in the education system as we know it.

Intimate attachments

We have looked at the difficulties which separatism faces in the areas of co-operative activities and general virtues of character. A third area, which overlaps the first two but raises further problems of its own, has to do with one's attachments to those close to one – to one's family, one's friends, perhaps even one's pets. The difficulty here for separatism is this: in so far as children are to be brought up to want to further the interests of those close to them, on a separatist view this desire must belong with pupils' altruistic dispositions *rather than* with their personal well-being. But this is not how things are normally conceived, either by children or by adults. All of us, by and large, see our own well-being as inextricably connected with the well-being of those near to us: we are elated by our friends' accomplishments, depressed by their ill-fortune. As members of a family, the well-being of each of us is affected, for better or worse, by the well-being of all the others; we are upset by the sickness or death of our cat or dog and glad when they are happy and contented. These, as I say, are normal reactions which will be familiar to all of us. The separatist will seek to replace these normal reactions by more exclusively altruistic dispositions. What point there is to this is hard to see.

Once again the separatist cannot cope. It undermines so much of what we take a valuable human life to be, to say that our attachments to family and friends should have nothing to do with our own well-being. As with our engagement in activities with shared ends, we think not about what is good or bad for me on the one hand and for you on the other, but about *our* well-being, about how well or badly things are going for *us*. One way of putting the challenge faced by separatism is that it can make no room for this perspective: how *we* view things must always be reduced to how I see things added to how you or they see things.

Once again, too, all that separatists can do is to make their educational plans in such a way as to demote or exclude local attachments. This would not be difficult within the British educational system. Attachments to one's friends, family and pets are at their most prominent in nursery and infant education, where they are woven into classroom activities at many points. The older the child gets, the less place they find on the curriculum: still important in junior school, they are given less and less attention as the pupil nears school-leaving age. (If literature, the vehicle *par excellence* for exploring intimate relationships, had more time devoted to it in secondary education, the picture would be different.) Close attachments flourish, of course, at all ages and in all sorts of ways; our social life could no more do without them than it could do without co-operative activities. My only point here, by now a familiar one, is that the educational system does not mirror their centrality in our lives. It directs pupils to their own, narrowly understood, advancement at one pole and to the impersonal demands of a universalistic morality or a large-scale economy at the other.

Separatism is a powerful influence in contemporary British education. It turns us away from co-operative activities, from character education, and from intimate attachments, towards ends where answers to the question 'whose well-being is being promoted?' divide neatly into self-regarding and other-regarding.

A unified upbringing

In criticizing separatism I have dwelt on the absence of good reasons in its support and on its possible logical incoherence. I now want to look, more positively, at one benefit of following the non-separatist path.

Whether a separatist or a non-separatist, any educator will want whatever dispositions are being developed to be firmly rather than tenuously acquired. Separatists will want their pupils to be committed, not half-hearted, altruists and at the same time to possess in full measure those habits which underpin their personal well-being. Non-separatists will also favour this, but without any implication that the dispositions be built up along different lines.

One reason for favouring anti-separatism is that it is more likely than its rival to deliver the strength and firmness of disposition required. A child brought up along more separatist lines – and we should remember, here as elsewhere, that separatism can be a matter of degree – will have dual motivations: some of his or her desires will be altruistic but not self-interested, and others vice-versa. There are several reasons why this internal economy of desires is likely to be weaker than its non-separatist alternative.

First, there is the very existence of two kinds of motivation, each pulling one in opposite directions. As long as occasions for conflict between them are minimized, this is not necessarily a defect. But it may be difficult to find such occasions. People could in principle be brought up to spend part of their time on other-directed and part on self-directed pursuits, but in practice it is hard to see how this could work. How, for instance, would one classify what they did at work as part of their job? The first difficulty, then, is the possibility of conflict between one's two objectives. Arising from this is the absence of any guidance from the separatist on how to cope with such conflict. If I am torn on a particular occasion between looking after myself and helping to remedy some social injustice, then which way should I incline? Separatists could at this point seek appropriate criteria from within an ethical theory, eg some version of utilitarianism or Kantianism which weights things on the side of universalistic or impersonal demands. But because all ethical theories are the subject of controversy, the motivational force behind whatever resolution to the conflict is adopted will be unstable: the strength of the agent's disposition will be dependent on his or her not seeing cause to jettison the theory – and this can by no means be guaranteed. A further point: talk of jettisoning a theory implies having assimilated the theory in the first place, and this may impose intellectual burdens on the agent which he or she may find hard to bear. If, on the other hand, they are not initiated into the theoretical considerations but are simply taught rules of thumb for dealing with such conflicts and no supporting rationale, then these may well prove too inflexible to cope with similar but importantly different situations. Again, this is a weakness from a motivational point of view. (It is doubtful, too, of course, whether teaching people rules of thumb without a rationale can be squared with the ideal of personal autonomy.)

A second source of motivational weakness is the lack of clarity within separatism about what counts as one's personal well-being and what counts as others' interests. If one has a desire for x and a clear picture of what x involves, one's desire is likely to be more stable than if one's picture of x is fuzzy or uncertain. Not only is it easier to keep one's target in view, one is also less at the mercy of circumstances, including other people's actions, which cause one to redefine one's understanding of x. Separatism has no clear picture of personal well-being – neither one's own nor other people's. If this is understood in terms of the satisfaction of one's major informed desires, these will illicitly include one's altruistic desires. That apart, the attempt to pare away altruism from one's own self-interested desires leaves the latter so impoverished – denuded as they are of any trace of intimate attachments or co-operative activity – as to be scarcely recognizable as constituting human good at all.

The two obstacles just discussed do not apply to non-separatism, or monism. Monist educators bring children up in such a way as not to make a hard line between altruistic and self-interested reasons for action, but to see these as inextricably interrelated. The first difficulty is less acute because the more the two types of motivation coalesce the less they can conflict. Over large tracts of their day-to-day lives pupils can learn to be guided by desires which are self-interested and other-regarding at the same time: this can be true of their life within the family, with their friends, and – provided that their working conditions allow this – in their job. This is not to rule out the possibility of conflict between what some would call self-interested and altruistic desires. An academic working in a university may be torn between indulging her or his passion for Roman sociology and throwing herself into the anti-racist cause. This is a conflict right enough, but to pin the labels 'self' and 'others' on the opposing sides is to over-simplify: doing Roman sociology is as much a collective enterprise as rowing in an eight, except that the co-operators are not physically co-present; and working for anti-racism is as much a personal project as studying Roman sociology. The conflict now is not between self and others but within the self. One is confronted by two desires, both demanding satisfaction as part of one's personal well-being, and somehow one must find a way of weighing them against each other. In principle, this is the same problem that arises if one is motivated by two conflicting desires that a separatist might call self-interested, eg the desire to overeat and the desire to preserve one's health. Again, it is a matter of weighing one thing against another, depressing one desire so that the other can have fuller scope, or perhaps arriving at some more finely balanced compromise. So this argument for monism rather than separatism is not that monism eliminates all conflict and so brings about a state of perfect psychic harmony. Conflict is endemic in human life and it is a misplaced perfectibilism which would wish to see its annihilation. Rather, the point is that, first, by polarizing sources of motivation separatism increases the a priori likelihood of clashes between them, and, secondly, where conflicts exist they can be reconceptualized not as self-orientated versus other-orientated, but as between two self-interested desires.

The second obstacle can also now be circumvented. Pupils do not need to be brought up with a clearly demarcated picture either of their own well-being or of altruistic ends since there are no such clearly demarcated pictures. They learn instead to see their own and others' well-being as interconnected at point after point. The fact that demarcations do not seem to be available is a source of weakness for separatism, given that dispositions are strengthened by having their related goals clearly delineated (and vice versa). In monist education this last condition is more likely to be met. Its goals may not be clearly *demarcated*, but they may be clear for all that. Children are brought up with dispositions which help them to realize a number of first-order ends. These include:

1. Enjoying physical pleasures – eg, of eating, drinking, sexual activity, the senses or the use of one's limbs.

2. Engaging in personal projects to which one is deeply committed, including under this anything from collecting seashells to looking after animals, studying mathematics, working for a relief agency, teaching children or tending one's garden.

3. Enjoying others' company – eg, as friends, members of a family, lovers, or members of the same club or pub.

4. Protecting and promoting the well-being of those close to one.

5. Working with others for shared goals. This can include specific activities like running a shop or playing a game; and also promoting the well-being of a community – eg, a workplace, city or nation-state. In all these cases one will have sub-goals defined by one's role within one's group – eg, wicket-keeper, finance-manager, elector etc – and connected with the sub-goals of other role-holders via the common support they give to realizing the group's larger purposes.

6. Promoting general well-being. This goes beyond the well-being of intimate acquaintances and members of communities to which one belongs, to embrace people outside these circles and, at the limit, to humanity in general – perhaps even all sentient life. (There is no implication here that it is always better to promote the well-being of a larger rather than a smaller group.)

7. Fulfilling general obligations that one has to be truthful, keep one's promises, be just, refrain from causing injury to others and help others when they are in distress.

(This should not be seen as a hard-and-fast categorization. It draws on, but is broader than, the list of altruistic dispositions in Chapter 3.)

These first-order ends are related to each other in many ways, some of which I have already mentioned. Personal projects can involve working with others for shared ends and enjoying being with them; physical pleasures can be enjoyed in company as well as in private; some physical enjoyments (eg exercising one's limbs) are found in some collective activities (eg playing football); keeping one's promises and telling the truth are important in one's intimate relationships, in co-operative activities and for reasons of general well-being.

As well as being related to each other, first-order ends also subserve one's well-being as a whole, not instrumentally but as part of it: personal well-being depends, among other things, on the satisfaction of one's major first-order desires. First-order goals are the immediate objects of one's desire. In order to achieve a life of well-being, as many philosophers have pointed out, it is counterproductive always to aim directly at attaining such a life. It is ultimately incoherent, indeed, to be intent on furthering one's overall happiness but to have no interest in friendship, accomplishments, physical pleasures or any other of life's components. Direct consideration of one's well-being usually comes into play only when one finds that one cannot follow one first-order end because it would clash with another. One then has to weigh one end against the other and try to resolve the conflict by reference to one's well-being as a whole. (What such conflict-resolution involves will be examined in further detail in Chapter 5.)

The aim of monist education is relatively clear, even if it is not simple. Children are brought up disposed to promote their own well-being. What this well-being consists in is, by and large, unproblematic. It consists in the first instance of realizing one's first-order ends, bearing in mind that these are weighed against each other in hierarchies of importance: the source of the weighing can be the traditions and customs of one's community, or – and in addition – in a society like our own, personal autonomy.

Although the aim is relatively clear – so that people should not grow up in any doubt that it is a good thing for them to enjoy the pleasures of the flesh, exercise, others' company, personal projects and so on, whatever differences of individual weighting there may be – it is complex rather than simple. It embraces, as we have seen, many sub-aims. These sub-aims are intricately related to each other, and by internal rather than external connections: far from being discrete from each other, they interpenetrate and coalesce in the ways I have described. However, they are not merely *related*: the sub-aims can also *come in conflict* with each other, both across the major categories listed above and within those categories. Examples of cross-categorial conflict might be: wanting to get on with some personal project while also wanting to help a friend who has suffered some misfortune; wanting to keep on drinking but realizing that this might jeopardize other satisfactions; or wanting to tell the truth about some malpractice in one's workplace but wanting at the same time to be loyal to one's colleagues. As examples of conflict *within* a category we might take: being torn between taking exercise (because one hasn't been able to do one's jogging for a fortnight) and having a meal (because one has had nothing to eat all day); being true to Lydia and being true to Laura; choosing between a career as a croupier and a career as a locksmith; giving one's money to famine relief and giving it to fighting Aids; or knowing that if one tells the truth this will bring someone great harm. Balances must be struck between competing motivations of both these major kinds, balances which each individual will strike in his or her own way.[10]

All this makes for complexity in the aim of promoting pupils' well-being. Yet the aim is unitary, not two-fold as in separatism. An image which comes to mind is that of a web: one thing, but composed of manifold interconnected parts. Of course the image is inexact in many ways, notably in its suggestion of symmetry and in the possibility of connections only with adjacent parts of the structure, but it will help to bring the advantages of monism more concretely to mind.

A web is made strong by the mutual support that each part gives to each other part. In the same way the mutual reinforcement of one desire by another strengthens our psychic constitution. The reinforcement can take different forms. One desire can be embedded within another, such as when one's sociable dispositions are helpful in one's career as a teacher; or there may be some sort of causal interaction between them – eg, my desire for your recognition in some venture in which we both take part can spring from my admiration of you. Even the all-pervasiveness of conflict between one's desires can be a source of strength and not of weakness, provided that rifts are not too deep. At any particular time each one of us, including the most psychologically stable, has succeeded in bringing his or her desires into some sort of *modus vivendi* with each other – conflicts between them having been resolved into some kind of equilibrium, however liable to further change this might be. This equilibrated structure can vary in its stability from person to person. At the weaker end of the range, someone may be scarcely able to keep under control some powerful desire which threatens to demolish their fragile equilibrium. But the fact that people are normally more stable than this supports the thesis that conflict can reinforce as well as undermine, for in the stable personality it is conflicts themselves which have created the power of the structure: without conflict, desires would not have been brought into weighted relationships with each other. Conflict binds them to each other and this not in any piecemeal or atomistic way: because of the interconnectedness of all our desires, the tension between one desire and another and the resolution of that tension bring with them readjustments through the whole desire-structure; each of our desires is what it is and has the intensity and durability that it has only because of its relationships to other, and ultimately all, of our desires.

I have tried to show why a monistic upbringing is preferable to a separatist one. As will have become obvious, full-blown separatism is not a practical or even perhaps a logical possibility and my description of the contest between the separatist and the monist is not meant to reflect educational realities. That there are *strands* of separatism running through people's thought about education I am in no doubt, but thoroughgoing separatism is another matter. Its invocation here has been chiefly intended to bring to prominence the virtues of monism – and this, unlike separatism, *is* a practically possible, as well sensible, way of bringing up a child.

Chapter 5

Education for Personal Autonomy

The upbringing of a radical chooser

It is time to pull threads together. Our central topic in this book is education for personal autonomy. In Chapter 1 we saw how the ideal of personal autonomy lay behind neutralist accounts of the role of the state and suggested that government should actively encourage education for personal autonomy rather than restrict its educational aims to the spheres of morality and basic needs. In Chapters 2 to 4 we began to build up a fuller picture of the relationships between personal autonomy, personal well-being and morality. Since education for personal autonomy involves aiming at promoting the autonomous person's well-being, it was important to become clearer about the concept of well-being in general. This enabled us to tackle the question of whether morality or altruism are essential elements in personal well-being. Although conclusive arguments were found wanting and doubt was cast on the very propriety of talk of morality, it was claimed, nevertheless, that educators have good reason to bring up their pupils with a view of their own well-being that includes altruistic concerns of different kinds.

We now need to come back and to focus more on personal autonomy. In this chapter we shall see a more rounded delineation of the auto- nomous person and the dispositions and understanding which he or she possesses. Later we shall come back again to the role of education *vis-à-vis* basic needs.

Autonomous people need not be altruistic but this is not true of the kind of autonomous person we now have in mind. What distinguishes autonomy from heteronomy is that autonomous people choose their major ends themselves rather than leaving them to tradition, religion or others' domination. So while the autonomous egoist chooses major ends which are in his or her interests alone, *our* autonomous person chooses ends in which personal and altruistic interests are inextricably involved in the way described above.

But what is it to choose one's major ends? There are different ways of understanding this and some of them are misconceived. It will be helpful to clear these out of the way before turning to a more adequate account.

A first picture of autonomy is as follows. One is more autonomous the more one's life is not determined by factors outside one's own choices: the more one can minimize the role of such factors the greater one's autonomy. Examples of these, as just mentioned, are tradition, religion and others' domination, all of which are social constraints. As well as social constraints there are natural constraints: one's autonomy is weakened the more one is under the unwelcome sway of bodily appetites, drugs, some kinds of physical defects or certain primitive emotions. Those committed to autonomy will try to diminish as far as possible such social or natural constraints: their ideal is that *they alone* should shape the way they are to live.

I would by no means want to dismiss all attempts to escape the natural and social chains that bind us, but the attempts can go too far. Human beings cannot make themselves into whatever they like. This is not only for practical reasons, but because the ideal carries with it an inadequate picture of the choosing self. If the self is to determine what it is to become, it can have no fixed dispositions. These would limit it in advance, obliging it to stay forever within certain tracks. With this conception of autonomy character itself becomes another form of constraint: one must be free to make and remake oneself at will.

It is doubtful whether any coherent sense can be attached to this ideal. Dispositions seem to be the very girders of human life. We possess virtues and we are attached to other people, to our projects and to wider causes; we have and express attitudes and reactions to people and events. If proponents of autonomy accept any of this, they can only do so half-heartedly, watching out for any disposition which threatens to gain too firm a hold. This is not only a curiously unattractive ideal of life, amounting to a kind of wilful self-destruction in the name of self-creation; it also seems logically incoherent, since the agent in question is left with one firm disposition when all the others have been weakened, namely vigilance in monitoring all other dispositions.

What has happened here, as I see it, is that personal autonomy has failed to detach itself sufficiently from a certain conception of freedom. Positive liberty, in the terms used in Chapter 1, has become over-impregnated with negative liberty. We saw in that chapter how freedoms from different kinds of interference – from coercion or manipulation by individuals or institutions – are not self-justifying, but derive their value from the ideal of self-determination: to live autonomously there must be no constraints on one's chosen ends. There are, as we have begun to see and shall see more fully hereafter, other facets of autonomy than this: negative liberty is one necessary condition only and there are others. In the radical version, negative liberty has become too prominent. It is almost as if there were nothing more to autonomy than to challenge or escape restriction. Negation becomes our *raison d'être*.

To return to dispositions. It is characteristic of radical choosers, as portrayed in literature and philosophy, that they are mature persons. Little is said about how they came to become what they are, about their upbringing. What kind of upbringing would be most appropriate for them? Character-education is suspect for reasons already mentioned: children are not to be moulded into possessing the virtues, attitudes and other dispositions which their educators favour.

Should the education be based on knowledge, since among the impediments to adequate choice are ignorance, false beliefs and muddled thinking? But if character-education is to be avoided as a form of constraint, then are pupils to grow up without any personal qualities at all, but only with various kinds of knowledge and understanding? It is hard to make sense of this. Again, it would be wrong to think that by concentrating on knowledge one has turned one's back on dispositions altogether, for intellectual activities bring with them intellectual virtues: the teacher of physical science, either as a major form of knowledge in its own right, or as a necessary background to understanding science-based life options, wants his or her pupils to develop a judicious regard for evidence, a willingness to have their ideas challenged, a pertinacity in dealing with difficult material.

To sum up this part of the discussion. Radical choosers are usually portrayed as mature persons. Presumably they have had some kind of upbringing which has made them what they are; but it is hard to see what this might involve.

Early education and the handling of conflicts

Another way of assessing this version of autonomy is to start not with the mature end-product but with its raw material, the young child whose upbringing is just beginning. If the line of thought in the final part of Chapter 4 was broadly acceptable, then education for autonomy must be rooted in the cultivation of a number of complexly related desires. The task of early education is to form children as people with certain sorts of personal qualities: pleasure-loving; closely attached to a few people and with a weaker but more general altruism beyond this circle; committed to personal projects; and disposed to work and play with others in the pursuit of shared ends. Society, mediated by parents and teachers, steers children in these directions, taking into account their biological nature. If personal autonomy is to come out of this, it cannot run counter to all social constraints since these constraints are built in from the start.

Autonomy must be founded on dispositions which are firmly and securely acquired; the more they reinforce each other the better. Educators need to work confidently on laying these foundations, untroubled by the thought that they are illicitly moulding children after a preconceived pattern.[1] Not that it is easy for them to be confident, since ideas associated with radical choosing are so prominent in our culture and have left many of those concerned with child-rearing uncertain about what to do and anxious about being too restrictive.

How can autonomy be built on the foundations suggested? What kind of autonomy will it be? A first step on the way to an answer is to turn again to the phenomenon of conflict. We saw in Chapters 3 and 4 how conflicts can occur between the major categories of desire and within these categories. Children have to begin to learn how to cope with these conflicts by weighing one desire against another. The more firmly their desires are established, the clearer the conflict between them can be expected to be. This is important because clarity about the alternatives that are at stake is a necessary condition of resolving any conflict. This is a logical point. Conflicts may *come to an end* in all sorts of ways: mortal enemies may be physically separated; wars may finish through the depletion and exhaustion of both sides; and internal clashes between different parts of the soul may be terminated, at least temporarily, by repression or by mechanisms of defence. But in none of these examples is the conflict *resolved*. For this to happen whoever resolves the conflict must have a good understanding of what is at stake on both sides. This is familiar from examples of arbitrators of all kinds: international peace makers, ACAS officials or schoolteachers. The more sharply they can bring into focus what divides the two sides, the easier it is for them to see what might bring them together. Conversely, the more the conflicting values are blurred, perhaps because one or more of the parties are not too sure what they want or where they stand, the more difficult it is to see what might be done. This is also true of internal conflicts. Suppose I want to get on with some writing project to which I am very attached and at the same time badly want to visit a sick aunt. Because the two values at stake are relatively clear, I am in a good position to weigh them against each other. But imagine now that I am much more half-hearted about my project, that I have vague doubts about how worth while it is which I have not articulated to myself and that I am easily put off when I suffer some reverse. Imagine, too, a similar embroidering of my desire to see my aunt. It will be much more difficult for me now to bring the two desires into relationship with each other because it is harder to get each one separately into focus: I do not know in each case quite *what* I want. I am not implying that it is always preferable to have clear-cut wants than fuzzy ones: there may be all sorts of cases where fuzziness is desirable. The claim is, rather, that *from the point of view of conflict-resolution* the more sharply focused a desire is, the better.

It should go without saying that children need to be brought up with firm rather than weak dispositions. This would be assented to in *any* society, whether the upbringing were autonomous or heteronomous. But the truism is especially important for the cultivation of autonomy. This is ultimately, as we shall see, a matter of coping with desire-conflicts of a certain sort. The more strongly children come to desire things, right from the start, the more easily they will be able, in time, to understand what is involved when their desires conflict and so be in a position to resolve these conflicts.

Insight into conflicts between one's desires is not easy to achieve. This can be true for anybody, not only for children. It is difficult enough, sometimes, to grasp what is afoot in *external* conflicts, ie between my desire and yours, or between hers and his. But at least in external conflict the opposing desires are located in two separate persons. It is that much more difficult to gain a purchase on internal conflict, because it takes place within one's own soul. If this introspective awareness is hard to achieve for adults, how much harder it is going to be for children! How are they to begin to make sense of what is going on in their own minds?

There are good philosophical reasons why inner understanding in general cannot come about through wholly private operations on the part of the subject.[2] The concepts required (eg the concept of desire), like other concepts, belong to public conceptual schemes and the criteria for their application must be interpersonally agreed. One learns how to use the concepts through interaction with other people who are already adept in their use.

It is not an empirical point, therefore, that children first learn about desire conflicts and how to handle them from their parents (or whoever else is responsible for their upbringing).

It is parents who first get children to understand what they want, through initiating them into the correct use of 'want' and words which imply wanting. They do this by themselves identifying the desires that inform children's overt behaviour. A parent sees her two-year-old rubbing her eyes and yawning and says 'You're sleepy' (= 'You want to sleep'). Through repeated encounters of this kind the child comes to understand these words and use them, suitably modified, of herself ('I'm sleepy').

Wanting to sleep is a desire that is part of our biological constitution, like wanting to eat, drink, move our limbs and so on. Natural desires are shaped into culturally acceptable forms and a superstructure of wants of increasing complexity is built up from these foundations within the categories outlined in the final part of Chapter 4.

The more desires children come to have the more occasions there will be for conflict between them. These conflicts will be of different sorts. I have already mentioned the distinction between conflicts across desire categories and those within them. Another type of distinction is that between desires present in one's consciousness and desires which may or may not be present but which exist in one dispositionally. I may want a cup of tea in the first sense if I am thirsty. However, I may want to travel around the world even if I feel no desire to do so at present, but if it is a longstanding ambition of mine, for example. In this case I have a dispositional desire to travel round the world which is not manifested, unlike in the tea-drinking example, in any present desire. Children's desires can conflict in this dimension, too. Sometimes this might involve two present desires (wanting to stay on the swings versus wanting one's tea) or a present desire and a non-present desire (wanting to punch someone in the face and wanting to be a good Christian).

Parents must not only help children to identify desires: they also have to show them how conflicts between them may be resolved. The less mature the child the less he (or she) will be able to understand how he is to go about this. Once again, the progression must be from the public to the private: he has first to learn how these situations are normally handled within the culture before he can independently handle them himself.

At first parents have every reason to *defuse* conflicts rather than engage with children in resolving them. Conflicts can be painful and parents naturally often prefer, especially with very young children, to remove them as soon as possible. This is part, indeed, of establishing that firmness of disposition already mentioned: removing a conflict is allowing desires to find satisfaction unfrustrated by others.

As time goes on parents will involve children more directly in resolutions. This will become possible as the latter learn to tolerate the pains of inner conflict, to live with them for a while. Given this, defusion will not always be the parents' overriding priority. It may be more important to take time to talk things through, to suggest ways in which compromises can be reached and problems overcome. Parents can initiate children into a variety of solutions, spacing out satisfactions over time, for instance, or not satisfying one desire at all, as to do so would be inappropriate in this situation. They can enable children to understand the causes of their desires and the consequences of acting on them, thus helping them to judge the relative importance of trying to satisfy them rather than others. As well as with conflicts between present desires, they can induct them, too, into coping with conflicts involving non-present desires. They can remind them, for instance, that something they badly want to do (as a present desire) is at odds with some higher-order desire they non-presently have to be a person of a certain sort (cf 'Act your age!'). Conflicts of this sort are not felt, of course: the parents' role is both to bring them into consciousness and also to guide children towards one desire rather than the other.

In these various ways parents and children co-operate in focusing on the children's inner conflicts and their resolution. The ideas must come first from the parents since the children do not have enough understanding to cope. This is why adherents of autonomy should not bristle at every instance of parental directiveness. It is good for children to see that conflicts can be sorted out, and when they are too young to do the sorting out themselves it is good for them to see that someone else can do so. But parental directiveness must subserve the children's own self-directedness. As they learn how to go about things, children must be left increasingly to solve their conflicts in their own way, and where higher-order, non-present desires are concerned, learn to take over their parents' role in reminding themselves of what they want to be.

I mentioned earlier the distinction between internal and external desire-conflicts. The growing child has to learn to deal with both – not only with her inner conflicts, but with those between what she wants and what someone else wants, and with those between what two or more third parties want where her desires don't come into the picture at all. On the separatist account of upbringing examined in Chapter 4, inner and outer conflicts might be seen as rigidly separated and each requiring its own kind of learning. In rejecting separatism we thereby reject this rigidity. If I am closely attached to you and your desire for X clashes with my desire for Y (you want to go to MacDonalds and I want to go to Pizzaland), then the external conflict can become internalized because one of my desires may be to do what you desire. Third person conflicts can also become one's own: think of a child who is very close to both her father and mother who for some reason do not see eye to eye over some matter. Interconnections between internal and external conflicts are a rich field for investigation elsewhere. I mention them here as another dimension to the story of how children learn to handle their inner conflicts. To think of these conflicts as exclusively inner is to misunderstand them.

Taking over responsibility for one's life

Personal autonomy is born out of the ability to handle conflicts, but one can possess this ability in many respects and yet not be autonomous. Conflict, as has already been said, is a feature of human life that cannot be eliminated. Every human society must have ways of coping with it built into its child-rearing practices. This is as true for the least autonomous society as it is for the most.

A heteronomous society can put a high priority on the cultivation of virtues. Its children can be brought up, for instance, to be temperate in eating, drinking and sexual activity. This can be represented as their learning to resolve conflicts between different types of desire. They have a natural inclination, for instance, to eat when hungry – a permanent dispositional desire. This disposition is allowed legitimate manifestation within the food mores of the culture. But not all manifestations, that is not all instances of present desires to eat that are felt, are culturally approved. Sometimes children will eat too much for their own good, and the community will try to cultivate in them some other desire connected with their larger well-being, which conflicts with their present desire to overeat and which they must be brought to weigh more heavily. Children may also want to eat at the wrong time, or eat the wrong things, or eat in the wrong place (where 'wrong' here is to be understood in terms of the norms of the community); here, too, their elders will implant in them and strengthen the countervailing desire to become a good member of the community in these respects. Gradually the two desires will be brought into a proper relationship with each other, backslidings will become less frequent, and children will learn to become temperate (in this respect) as the community conceives this virtue.

It would be wrong to imagine that all this must happen in some mechanical way which minimally engages children's intelligence. Acquiring good eating habits requires the exercise of judgement, as Aristotle pointed out with regard to the virtues more generally in his *Nicomachean Ethics* (Book 2, ch 6). It is not reducible to learning to follow some simple rule or a collection of simple rules ('Never eat more than two pieces of fruit at a single meal', 'Never eat between meals'). There may be occasions when it is all right for temperate people to eat much more than usual, or to eat at unusual times. Those people have to then bear in mind not isolated rules but the overall point of temperance and its connection with good health, their own well-being and the well-being of their community. Thus they adjust their behaviour intelligently to different circumstances in the light of these larger ends.

We have concentrated on eating, but similar points could be made about the regulation of other bodily appetites, like drinking and sexual activity, which also fall under temperance. The discussion could also be extended further to other virtues. Becoming autonomous is not *simply* a matter of learning intelligently to resolve one's conflicts of desire. The acquisition of virtues involves learning of this sort, and virtues can be acquired in heteronomous as much as in autonomous societies.

Yet although one can be temperate, brave, just, patient and so on in a heteronomous society, one's intelligent choices are confined to decisions about what to do in particular circumstances. The larger ends within which one lives are fixed by the mores of one's society.

Autonomous individuals live self-determined lives. They choose their major ends and decide what relative weight to give to each. In an autonomous society like our own people choose what job they will do, where they will live, whether they get married, how to spend their free time, whether to give to charity, what clothes to wear, etc.

If people choose their major ends, what distinguishes them from radical choosers? The answer should now be clear. Personally autonomous people have been shaped from birth onwards by their parents and other teachers and by the cultural values which inform their child-rearing. They have acquired sets of interrelating dispositions to satisfy types of socially approved desires. Included in these dispositions will be virtues of various kinds: temperance, justice, benevolence, courage, practical intelligence, etc.

Their upbringing will have helped them to resolve conflicts between these different desires, both those associated with virtues, as in the extended example of temperance just given (for part of these children's education will include elements also found in traditional societies), and other conflicts within and between desire categories. At first their parents will have played the leading role in conflict resolution, but gradually the children will have come to be able to work out their own solutions for themselves.

As they grow up children are involved in the weighing of one desire against another. They construct within themselves some kind of system, or hierarchy, in which these desires are graded in relative importance. I mean by this nothing exact, or mathematical – and nothing that can be pictorially represented. I mean only that as they grow up children form a relatively settled, though shifting, pattern of preferences. These vary in content from child to child: one is more closely attached to her mother, another to her father; one becomes passionately committed to acting, another to CND.

In this way children will gradually take over responsibility for their own value-systems until as mature beings (and there is no cut-off point between maturity and immaturity) they are more or less self-determining. They are by then very different from radical choosers. They far from feel that their autonomy resides in doing what they freely will to do – in the ability radically to change direction, abandoning everything that they have valued up to now for the sake of some quite novel enterprise. I do not mean that they have become set in their ways. They might change tack, even dramatically, but this will be because of major adjustments they make in weightings between different values, not because they start from scratch on something new.

The notion that one chooses one's values is mistaken. Sartre used his famous example of the anguished choice facing a young man in the war, torn between going off and fighting for the Resistance, or staying with his widowed mother as her sole support, to illustrate the doctrine of radical choice. But it fails to do so. Whichever way the man decides, he cannot be represented as choosing values. Both values, the one to do with an intimate attachment and the one to do with a more general well-being, are part of him already. He has at no point chosen them, having been brought up in them, along with others. If, all things considered, he decides to go off and fight, this means that he has, on this occasion, pushed the claims of intimacy into second place. This is far from an arbitrary decision or 'criterionless choice'. He does not *relinquish* the value of intimacy; it still weighs heavily with him and continues to do so once he has made his choice. To make this choice he has had to engage in complicated reflection about the likely consequences of doing one thing rather than the other and about which elements are most fundamental in his scheme of values. If on balance he comes out against intimacy on this occasion, this does not mean that he has made a decision that the general well-being should always outweigh it: in another situation, with different patterns of probabilities and different factual circumstances to consider, his preference might tilt the other way.

★ ★ ★

It is not easy to characterize the autonomous person we intend our child to become.[3] Autonomy has many faces. It is easy, as we have seen with the radical chooser, to exaggerate the importance of one of these while failing to give due consideration to others. The task of a philosophical delineation of the autonomous person is to keep the different aspects in proper relationship with each other so that something like a rounded picture can be constructed. In what follows I shall try to do this, revealing on the way the points at which one might be tempted, as many writers on education have been tempted, to exaggerate, but also pulling us constantly back towards a more judicious account.

As our pupils learn to become autonomous persons they come to make choices of wider and wider scope. Earlier, they chose within more tightly circumscribed frameworks; now they are beginning to make more global choices. As they have grown up, their desires have become organized into some kind of hierarchy of importance. They have learnt which desires it is more important to them to satisfy and in which contexts. One should not exaggerate the systematic nature of such a 'hierarchy'. Some of the dispositions which children have acquired will have been relatively isolated one from the other. Dream ideals of themselves as journalists or singers will have coexisted with fairly self-contained desires to make models, go roller skating, bake fairy cakes or read stories; to these have been added the pleasures of company, of family life, and desires to behave and refrain from behaving in such and such ways towards other people. In some ways these desires will have been bound together through differential weighting in different circumstances: but in many ways, too, they will have coexisted in mutual independence from each other.

As pupils gradually take over responsibility for their own lives, they learn to give more cohesiveness to their desire structure. They find themselves endowed through their upbringing with dispositional desires of all kinds. Their educators, with an eye on their autonomy, will encourage them to impose their own order on all these, the more global, or comprehensive, desires subsuming the other lower order desires beneath them. So children build up pictures of themselves which are no longer the disconnected dream pictures of an earlier period. Their self-pictures are now more closely connected with their more determinate desires, and are in this way more realistic. The child who saw herself (or himself) in a vague way as a journalist without much conception of what this way of life involves has later given up this wish and now, at fifteen, has no specific career in mind at all. But she feels she would like to do some kind of job, whatever it may be, that is absorbing in itself as well as in some way socially useful. She likes art and she likes mathematics and would like to do something involving these two. She has also recently become interested in left-wing politics and has joined CND. Social injustices weigh very heavily with her. So do other things, like friendship, for example. She has had friends in the past, but largely as pleasure-sharing companions. She now prizes more intimate attachments, of the kind Aristotle (*Ethics*, Bk 8) referred to as character-friendships rather than pleasure-friendships. Many of her more specific interests – in pop music, swimming, shopping – are now closely connected with her friendships and other central values. Some of her earlier interests – in eating, or in spending whatever money she had on clothes, records, magazines – are now kept more under control, being regulated by her picture of herself as sexually attractive, financially responsible and politically sensitive.

Autonomous people learn in this kind of way to bring their lower-order desires under higher-order and more global desires of their own choosing. As we can see from our example, this choosing is a form of putting weight on and shaping dispositions which one already to some extent possesses. The girl's determination to avoid a boring job, the importance for her of intimate attachments, her wider concern for social well-being – all these are continuous with desires with which she has been brought up in earlier years. Her choosing is still within a framework of values which she has not chosen, but taken over from her culture.

Talk of global choices leads us into two interrelated aspects of personal autonomy about which more must now be said: life-planning and self-knowledge.

Doubts about life-planning

The autonomous person has been represented, both in general philosophy and in philosophy of education, as a planner of his or her own life. One can see how this thought arises. To be autonomous is to be self-directed. This means that one chooses the main directions in which one's life is to go, rather than following tradition, being coerced or manipulated, or drifting along aimlessly. Building on such a thought, various writers, notably Rawls in his *Theory of Justice*, have seen autonomy as residing in making rational plans of life (Rawls, 1971, Ch VII). In my own earlier ideas about educational aims also, this concept has been of pivotal importance (White, 1973, 1982). More recently, however, I have seen reason to question and qualify these ideas.[4] If one is not careful, talk of life-planning can soon become one of those forms of exaggeration earlier mentioned. Everything depends on how one understands the term.

An excessively crude picture of education for autonomy is this. Education is upbringing. It ends when pupils become mature. They are mature when they are capable of self-determination. To be self-determined is independently to choose one's plan of life, having been acquainted with the full range of options from which one may choose.

There are difficulties regarding what counts as this 'full range of options'. These apart, is this 'choice of a life plan' meant to be a once-for-all-time event occurring during adolescence? Certain pressures within our society may chime in with this. It is during adolescence that young people are sorted out into different occupations and into the lifestyles that go with them. As things are, many of them do find themselves having to look at their possible future life as a whole and decide, broadly, how they would like to fill it. They may or may not have very specific ideas about what job they would like to do, but they have narrowed down the options: they want a well-paid job perhaps, a job that can build on their academic strengths, a job that involves working closely with others. Pressure is put on adolescents by parents, careers advisers and teachers to decide on lifetime occupations. One reason for this pressure is fear of the child's having to make do with an ill-paid, boring or unpleasant job, or perhaps no job at all, and the diminished chances of a life of well-being that flow from this. Long-term life-planning is seen as some bulwark against this.

Whether it is prudent for young people to go in for long-term planning, given existing social conditions, I shall leave on one side. It is the conceptual issue that is of greater interest at the moment, that is, whether personal autonomy necessitates life-planning. Any temptation that educators or others may feel to answer that it does may be the product of the kind of society in which they live. For, once one brackets off conventional expectations, there seems good reason to deny any logical connection. Suppose we imagine young people in a much more fortunate position than those just mentioned. They have plenty of inherited wealth, so they know they don't need to compete for jobs in order to be able to do more of what they want in life; and their parents put no pressure on them to follow a career but only encourage them to live as they please as autonomous beings. Is there any reason why they should go in for life-planning?

That they will do *some* planning in their lives is undeniable. They all have, and must have, purposes to be realized in the future; and they must all give some thought to how those purposes might be achieved. Some of their plans and purposes may stretch further into the future than others. Some of them may indeed have life-long plans – to make a career in art, politics, the church. But others may take life more as it comes. Their self-directedness will still be revealed in the central role played by their global desires in their day-to-day lives. These global desires need to be seen not as indelible, but rather as replaceable in time by others as priorities and interests change. All this is a far cry from aimless drifting. Neither does it imply any frivolous attitude. At any one time these young people will live by global desires which, by definition, are of great importance to them. They may well have friends and lovers, projects and causes, to which they are closely, perhaps passionately, attached.

Autonomy does not imply life-planning. Neither does it imply that modification which I proposed in earlier books, that the life-planner need not draw up an unchangeable blueprint for the whole of his or her life, but may well modify and adapt his or her current plans as circumstances change. Still implicit in such a softening is the idea of plans projected into the far future, even though particular plans may be replaced by others. This is a long way from taking it as it comes.[5]

One's urge to soften a too-rigid doctrine of life-planning may have all sorts of causes, including perhaps the desire to make some kind of gesture towards spontaneity. But it is interesting, once again, to reflect on how this softening is in line with current perceptions of economic demands. We hear on every side these days the propositions that the workforce of the future must be flexible, that everyone must be prepared to change jobs several times in the course of their lifetime, and so on. Flexible, rather than blueprint, life-planning is what such advocates might favour.

We have stressed socio-economic motivations for writing life-planning into autonomy; but there may be others. Or perhaps the socio-economic reasons should not be seen in any isolated way, but as linked, via common historical roots in our culture, with metaphysical considerations which also favour life-planning. What I have in mind here is our Christian heritage, especially the puritanical strand in it which dates from the sixteenth and seventeenth centuries and which has been so closely interwoven with the rise of capitalism and its attitudes towards work (Tawney, 1926). It has been characteristic of Christianity, at least this sort, to urge us to see our lives as it were from the outside – from God's perspective – as complete entities, for the adequacy of which, in religious terms, we are to be held to account. Religious adequacy came to be associated, in puritanism, with economic success. The latter was taken as a sign of salvation, an indication that one belonged to God's elect. A late twentieth-century shadow cast by this doctrine is selection in and via the educational system, with the parental anxiety it engenders that one's children should find a place among the professional élite and thus be rescued from a proletarian existence.

This external point of view is in conflict with the view from within. In our day-to-day existence we are not detached spectators of our lives, but are engaged in activities and experiences within it. The object of our attention at any one moment is not our life itself, taken as a whole, but something more local: eg the signs of rain on the way, arrangements for next Christmas, the contretemps at breakfast. Our perspective is, as Bernard Williams (1981, p 35) remarks, 'from here'. We focus on what is happening, what will happen and what has happened.

Life-planning may sometimes give rise to disappointment and frustration. The further one's plans extend into one's future, the more chances there are of their going adrift. To have plans that stretch throughout one's whole life maximizes this likelihood. One's preferences might change; war, economic collapse or radical changes in the socio-economic structure may blight one's hopes; one might fall ill, lose one's powers. If personal well-being involves overall satisfaction of one's central desires, a more tightly planned life might leave more of these desires unsatisfied. Life-planners are more at the mercy of good or bad fortune than their more spontaneous counterparts. They are also more likely to feel frustration – not only because large contingencies may ruin their plans, but also because the people with whom they interact in their various activities may often, and unintentionally, get in their way. Where these people are themselves life-planners the risks of mutual frustration are intensified – along with the anger, more subtle forms of retaliation and heavier demands on one's self control which might ensue.

Whether there are any more solid foundations for life-planning I shall have to leave others to decide. But all this has been in the abstract. If we come back now to our own society and to educators' tasks within it, what role, if any, should life-planning have in their conception of educational aims?

If we are talking about the education of particular individuals, then, given the big differences in overall well-being that different occupations can bring with them, it seems rational for *parents and teachers* to engage in at least *some* life-planning on behalf of their pupils. They have good reason to help them, for instance to lay the foundations for a career with greater possibilities in terms of well-being. At the same time, educators would do well not to emphasize life-planning at the cost of their children's failing to respond to the appearance in their lives of unplanned experiences – self-reflective, aesthetic or interpersonal – which they might find very rewarding. As the children grow older, they will take over responsibility for their own life-planning, bearing in mind the limitations to it just mentioned. Considerations to do with their autonomy also make it important to make children aware, when they are mature enough to be so, that the planned life is not necessarily ideal, but forced on us in our particular socio-historical circumstances.[6]

These may be rational strategies, given things as they are, but the status quo itself is difficult to support. It puts too much weight on life-planning as a component of the good life. It encourages people to compete with each other in order to escape a life of limited fulfilment. Those who succeed in the competition find themselves endowed with dispositions towards life-planning which they may have needed earlier but may now be counterproductive. Those who fail not only live a life of lesser well-being but also suffer the added displeasure of having failed. There must be saner ways of organizing our society so as to maximize everyone's chances of a happy life. One final point. We saw above that wealth can free one from the need for long-term planning. If everyone, and not only a few, were rich this would be ideal. However, something of the same end can be achieved in less ideal circumstances. The concept of the welfare state is under heavy attack today in some quarters; it would be a pity if its virtues came to be forgotten. For welfare services, like inherited wealth, can free people for a more spontaneous life-style if they wish to choose it. They are less constrained to make long-term plans to earn enough money to cover housing, medical services, education, provision for old age. Rather than cut down the welfare state, we could expand it, guaranteeing everyone not only the benefits just mentioned but also a job, not necessarily for life, in which working conditions and remuneration were arranged as far as possible to promote rather than obstruct the personal well-being of everybody.

Self-knowledge and its acquisition

That personal autonomy in some way involves self-knowledge seems intuitively obvious. Our task now is to give defensible shape to this intuition and to dissociate it from various misconceptions.

As our pupils have become more autonomous they have learnt to organize their desires hierarchically in the ways earlier described. Some things they want as means to further ends; other things they want as ends in themselves. Some of their desires are first-order, others second-order. At the top of their desire-hierarchy are global desires to do with the overall pattern of their life. They are increasingly able to cope with the conflicts that may arise between their desires on particular occasions by reference to such priorities.

All this presupposes some understanding on the pupils' part of what their desires are and which are more important to them than others. The more these desires and priorities are hidden from themselves or the more confused they are about them, the less self-knowledge they have.

Lacking self-knowledge can threaten one's well-being. Suppose someone wants to make a fortune in the mistaken belief that this will gain him (or her) others' respect. If he had seen clearly that he had these two instrumentally related desires, he would have been in a position to reflect on the soundness of the connecting belief. As it is, however, he is much more dimly aware of his desire for respect than he is of his desire to make a fortune, which is always in his thoughts. If he succeeds in the latter, he does not, let us suppose, increase his well-being since his major desire, for respect, is still unsatisfied. Another way in which one could lack self-knowledge is through self-deception. Someone may hide her (or his) desire for power over others from herself, believing herself to be wholly motivated by benevolence. She tries to satisfy these different desires, one consciously, the other unconsciously, but each inclination gets in the way of the other.

Being clear about one's desires, then, is a necessary condition of satisfying them. The practically orientated self-knowledge which every autonomous person needs is for the most part knowledge of the particular and local, rather than of oneself in any global sense. A particular incident in one's life can make it clear to one how much one values something. Enobarbus' desertion of Antony makes him realize the paramount importance to him of loyalty. He comes to grasp something about one element in his desire-hierarchy, not about himself as a whole. As one proceeds through life, occasions for particular self-knowledge multiply. One reflects now on this desire, now on that. A person who 'really knows himself' is someone who has had many experiences of this kind, has clarified different desires and their relationships on innumerable occasions. But he may well not be able to give you a description of his value-hierarchy in general.

There are many ways of attaining practical self-knowledge. Coming to a decision, for instance. This can reveal to one very sharply two opposing values and oblige one to balance them against each other. Left-wing parents facing secondary transfer and having the chance to send their clever child to a selective school rather than a mediocre local comprehensive may have to weigh their concern for their child's well-being against a more general benevolence. Not only the process, but also the aftermath of a decision can bring about a revaluation, as the example of Enobarbus shows.

One's emotional reactions are another source of self-knowledge. 'Why do I so often feel angry these days?' one might ask oneself. And one might trace things back to the high value one has put on realizing the rather inflexible life-plan that one has devised for oneself: this has multiplied the occasions when one has felt, rightly or wrongly, that people have been frustrating one, hence the anger. Feelings of guilt can make one aware of the conflict between the actions and associated desires about which one feels badly and one's desire to live up to the code against which one has transgressed. Other emotions – shame, fear, joy, remorse, envy, contempt – can give one similar insights into one's values and may lead one to confirm them or to question them.[7]

Literature can be useful here. It often portrays fictional characters discovering things about themselves via their actions and reactions. In identifying with the characters, one comes to know in imagination what it is like to experience this self-discovery. This can make one more conscious of its possible role in one's own life. And sometimes literature's influence can be more direct. If its characters feel things and do things which one does or feels oneself, this might trigger off reflections in oneself of the kinds just indicated.

One way of attaining self-knowledge has been described philosophically, notably by Aristotle, and portrayed in innumerable works by novelists and dramatists. I refer to what Aristotle called 'friendship' but which stretches beyond what we normally include under that term to embrace close relationships of other kinds of varying degrees of intimacy – within the family, for instance, or in shared activities of all kinds, such as colleagues at work, fellow-members of a pottery circle, political associates. The more a relationship is founded on shared values, the more one can see one's own values mirrored in the other person. Since one is more likely to be objective about other people's characters than one is about one's own, this might in some circumstances be a more reliable avenue to self-knowledge than direct reflection on oneself. But perhaps the most important benefits of close personal relationships arise out of conversation and out of non-verbal cues.

All these points about how one may attain self-knowledge can be put to good use educationally. If self-knowledge is educationally important as a necessary component in personal autonomy, then reflection on one's actions and experiences, as well as literature, philosophy, conversation and personal relationships, can all play their part in promoting it. This is to say nothing about where or at what age such education should take place. In particular, there is no implication that all this will be occurring in children, or at school. Acquiring self-knowledge of this sort will, in any case, continue beyond one's upbringing – ie beyond one's education, as I am using the term – and throughout one's adult life, often being informally woven into the texture of that life and deepening in sophistication as one grows older. But the seeds need to be planted in childhood, especially among older children who have developed something of a settled value-hierarchy and are now in a position to improve its coherence and the soundness of its foundations. It would be good to see conversation, shared activities and private reading (not in lockstep with one's school class, but more freely chosen, perhaps with guidance, so as to be more closely attuned to one's own situation and concerns) occupying a more prominent place in the upper secondary school, along, perhaps, with elementary philosophy in some cases. Here and there provision is made for them, in classwork under the umbrella of 'Personal and Social Education', for instance. But the pressures on pupils to move in quite other directions at this age are too well known and too much with us to need underscoring here.

Insight into the origin of one's desires

Self-understanding is different from understanding the physical world in that it can change what it reveals. Reflection on one's desires and the priorities among them can lead to the elimination of a desire or its promotion or demotion *vis-à-vis* others. Part of one's becoming aware of a desire is attaining insight into how one came to possess it. Some of the desires we acquire have been bred into us by our parents and teachers, or picked up imperceptibly from our culture. When we come to reflect on these we find some of them unacceptable and desire no longer to desire them. Higher-order desiring of this sort enables us, if it is successful, to rid ourselves of our unwanted desires and thereby to make our desire-structure more authentically our own. Personal autonomy requires us not to be imprisoned by desires which we have not freely accepted in this way.

Exaggerations can slip in here. If autonomy is held to demand the removal of *every* desire that has been implanted in us by other people, then we will be left with very little. This demand is too strong. We may want to retain many of our socially received desires: it is only the unacceptable ones which we need try to extirpate. But what counts as 'acceptable'? Is this wholly up to the individual to decide? If this is held to be so, a second exaggeration arises. Autonomy will then reside in the arbitrary will of the individual. If he (or she) wishes, he may try to rid himself of whatever desires he likes – his altruistic desires, for instance. He may harden his heart against the needs of strangers, and perhaps, if his misanthropy goes far enough, against his more intimate relationships. There is no good reason why we should work with so individualistic a concept of autonomy. If earlier arguments in this book are accepted, we are now taking it as read that the pupils whose education we have in mind are being brought up within a value-framework which is not negotiable. Close personal relationships, bodily desires, personal projects, co-operative activities, respect for others and the desire to promote forms of general well-being will all be accepted by them as of permanent value, albeit in varying orders of importance.

This non-negotiable framework apart, some of one's desires may be unacceptable to one once one reflects on how they originated.[8] In many societies it has suited dominant groups to try to get others willingly to accept subordination. In our own time we have become familiar with many examples: white South Africans *vis-à-vis* the black majority; men *vis-à-vis* women; authoritarian parents and teachers *vis-à-vis* children; British racists *vis-à-vis* a black 'underclass'. Perhaps the most pervasive form of this indoctrination, both in capitalist societies and in certain non-capitalist countries like Stalin's Russia, has been traditionally directed against those in subordinate positions in the economic structure. Educational planners have tried to use schools to accustom future workers to be obedient to authority-figures; they have cocooned them in religious or psychological ideologies which make them believe that it is better to be poor and humble, or that professional careers are out of the question for them because their innate intelligence is too low.

Because these many-sided pressures on people to be happy in their subjugation are so strong, it is especially important for teachers to try to combat them, both by keeping horizons broad and encouraging dispositions towards independent-mindedness, and by helping pupils who do possess submissive desires to reflect on their acceptability once they know more about how they have originated.

Ironically one of the weapons used to manipulate children has been self-knowledge itself, or, rather, what has passed for it. One of the aims of personal and vocational counselling in secondary schools has often been to give young people a 'realistic' picture of their own abilities and potentialities. In the heyday of intelligence testing it was thought important to acquaint those with lowish IQs with the fact that they were of limited innate intelligence, so as to turn their sights away from careers held to be too intellectually demanding. Although the term 'self-*knowledge*' was used in this connection, it seems clear that the most that pupils could have acquired were *beliefs* about themselves and sometimes, as with their innate intelligence, false or unfounded beliefs about themselves. In earlier generations children came to 'know' about themselves that they were essentially immortal souls: then, too, the implanted belief helped to demote certain desires (eg to enjoy the 'things of this world') and to elevate others (eg 'to do God's will'). Residues of these religious and psychometric 'self-knowledge' aims are still with us. A more up-to-date example comes from profiling. Several writers have recently drawn attention to the 'hijacking' of liberal or radical educational ideas by policy-makers wedded to the maintenance of the social status quo.[9] One of these ideas is pupil self-assessment. While in liberal hands this is a means of boosting self-confidence and self-esteem, it is not difficult to grasp its more reactionary potential if pupils learn to think of themselves as possessing dispositions thought necessary in a modern workforce – 'co-operativeness', punctuality, honesty, orderliness.

[Whether the kind of knowledge of their dispositions that pupils may acquire through self-assessment is desirable is uncertain. With some – modesty, for instance – the difficulty is notorious. But with any there will be problems of self-detachment. Benevolent people are motivated by a concern for others' well-being. Their knowledge that they are benevolent may contaminate this motivation: they may give the beggar money not just because he needs it, but because this is what a benevolent person does. Difficulties over detachment may apply not only to the more dubious kinds of self-assessment associated with manipulation, but also to self-assessment more generally. It is certainly a central educational task to cultivate various desirable dispositions in pupils; and while it may well be important for *educators* to assess how well they have succeeded, it is not clear that it is always good for *pupils* to know this.]

★   ★   ★

Autonomous persons need, then, to reflect on the origins of their desires so as to see whether they still find them acceptable in the light of this new knowledge. So far we have concentrated mainly on manipulation. But some of the desires we come to question have not been deliberately implanted in us by others but have been appropriated more impersonally from the culture. Reflection on the cultural origins of some of our desires can help us to liberate ourselves from them. Desires to do with male or racial superiority are possible examples.

Cultural awareness is important to us not only so that we can free ourselves from unacceptable desires. All our desires have come to us through our culture – which is not to say, of course, that they belong exclusively to it. Autonomy is as much a matter of grateful acceptance as of questioning and rejection.

In Britain today we are heirs of manifold influences – of Christianity in its many different forms, of the philanthropic rationalism and utilitarianism of the Enlightenment, of the expressionism of the Romantic reaction, of myths of national and racial superiority, and of civic values traceable back to the Greeks.[10] To these mainstream influences we should add the cultural traditions of our many ethnic minorities. The more we understand these unseen backgrounds, the more we understand ourselves. I mentioned earlier the educational part that literature and philosophy can play in enhancing our self-knowledge. To these we should now add history and sociology for the further appreciation that they can give us of the cultural sources of our values.

Where other tools of self-understanding may equip us to grasp more clearly our individuality – the unique form that our value-structure takes that renders us, no less than do our fingerprints, different from every other person – literary, philosophical, historical and sociological studies help us to see what we have in common with those others with whom we share a culture. These embrace not only our fellow-countrymen but, increasingly, owing to the confluence and complexity of cultural influences all over the world, human beings everywhere. Once again, it is important not to fall into one-sided exaggeration. Achieving autonomy and therewith self-knowledge is not wholly reducible to living a life of authentic uniqueness, or true individuality; and neither does it mean merging oneself wholly into the culture which surrounds one. Both elements are essential. Self-knowledge is at once self-creation and self-discovery.

Chapter 6

Justifying Personal Autonomy as an Educational Aim

Personal autonomy, in the shape of self-directedness in the conduct of one's life, is a central value in a liberal democratic society. But how can its promotion be justified as an educational aim? In this chapter we come back to this unanswered question, left hanging from Chapter 1.

I shall look first at a recent discussion of this question in Eamonn Callan's book *Autonomy and Schooling* (Callan, 1988). Then I will go on to examine Joseph Raz's account of the value of personal autonomy (in general, not specifically as an educational aim) in his *Morality of Freedom* (Raz, 1986). Finally, I will take up the issue of the education of children in minority communities which do not value the autonomous life.

Callan's argument

Callan looks at a number of arguments for the value of autonomy.

In the first, he examines an *instrumental* justification, that autonomy is desirable because it leads to happiness. His objection is that it does not always do so. In a society with extensive freedom, where people have the opportunity of creating the meaning of their lives, 'their happiness is likely to be fragile at best if they have little realism or independence of mind' (p 41). But we can still ask if this kind of society is desirable. In tradition-directed communities people can lead contented lives with very little room for individual discretion. 'The development of tradition-directed communities which fit that description does not seem to be an unfeasible aspiration' (ibid).

Callan seems to be assuming here that a valid justification must apply *universally*, ie across tradition-directed and non-tradition-directed societies. Otherwise he could not appeal to the experience of people living in a tradition-directed society as a counter-example. But is this so? Need the justification of autonomy show that it is valuable for *every human being*? He also claims it a feasible aspiration to develop tradition-directed communities. Is it? We shall be returning to both these points later.

Second, he then turns to an argument *from the absence of ethical experts*. The argument runs like this. There are no experts on what the good life should consist in, so no one is in a proper position to lay down to other individuals how they should lead their lives. People should, therefore, be left to lead their own lives, ie autonomously. Callan's objection to this is that if one accepts the premiss that there are no experts on the good life, it does not follow that autonomy is a good thing: 'we have no reason to believe that pupils who become highly autonomous will be better placed to make the right decision than those who unthinkingly follow orders' (p 41). So there is still something arbitrary about acting autonomously.

Callan is assuming that there *is* a right decision to be made. Is there? Is it indeed appropriate to talk of a 'right decision' here? What does it mean? Further, Callan has already conceded that in a non-tradition-directed society like our own autonomy may well promote happiness. So it may not be arbitrary in our context to urge autonomy, if, that is, the promotion of happiness is an acceptable reason.

Third, Callan's positive argument begins from the claim that autonomy is intrinsically valuable, but that not all intrinsically valuable things in life are experiences. He refers to Nozick's example of a machine that stimulates in the brain whatever experiences we desire, eg the experience of scientific discovery, winning a match or making love, claiming that we would regard these experiences as a poor substitute for the real thing (Nozick, 1974). As he says, this shows that experiences alone are not intrinsically valuable, but it does not show that autonomy is. At this point he refers to Nozick's further idea of a transformation machine which can turn us into whatever kind of person we wish to become; and a results machine that changes the world in any direction we wish. We still would not want to live our lives plugged into these machines, because they would be leading our lives for us: we would not be living our own lives. 'We live our own lives to the extent that the experiences we have, the kind of persons we become, and the changes we make to the world flow from the exercise of personal autonomy.' (p 44)

How far does this justify personal autonomy? Suppose we agree that everyone would prefer a life that they led themselves to a life plugged into Nozick's machines: this does not imply that all who so choose will be personally autonomous. Callan contrasts the autonomous person with the tradition-directed person. But a tradition-directed person may well also reject the machines. He (or she) may want his life to flow from his own choices. True, what he chooses to do will be in accordance with tradition, but even so, his life is governed by his choices, not by a machine.

Following Gray (1983, p 74), we need to distinguish what has been called the *autarchic* person from the *autonomous* person. An *autarchic person* enjoys negative freedom from force and coercion, and is also rationally self-determining, in that he (or she) has engaged in rational deliberation on the alternatives open to him. One can be autarchic, at least to some extent, in a tradition-directed society. Traditions do not always minutely specify what one should do: there is room for rational deliberation and choice. An *autonomous person* has the features of the autarchic person, but 'must also have distanced himself in some measure from the conventions of his social environment and from the influence of the people surrounding him. His actions express principles and policies which he has himself ratified by a process of critical reflection.' (Gray, p 74)

Callan may have given us grounds why autarchy is valuable – ie that no one would want to live without it since the desire for it is deeply embedded in everyone's desire-structure – but this says nothing about why autonomy is desirable. Why is it a good thing to distance oneself from conventions, to live a critically reflective life?[1]

The basic problem in Callan's positive argument is echoed in the account of the pupil's good that I spelt out in an earlier book (White, 1982, ch 3). I claimed there that personal autonomy is a necessary feature of human flourishing and that its promotion is required in any education which seeks to cultivate the pupil's well-being. But my argument for this was weak. Just as Callan begins from Nozick's experience machine, I focused on Huxley's *Brave New World*. If we reject the picture of human flourishing given in that book, why do we do so?

> But what, after all, is wrong with *Brave New World*, if anything is? Many would say it is that its inhabitants have not been given the autonomy to determine their own lives for themselves: they have been *conditioned* to lead a life of constant pleasure and have not chosen this themselves. (p 39)

But the rejection of *Brave New World* does not necessarily spring from considerations of autonomy. For the autarchic member of a tradition-directed society would also oppose it – just as he would spurn the experience machine.

To return to Callan, we may conclude that his positive justification for autonomy does not work, except by weakening the notion of autonomy so that it is no more than autarchy. In addition, the justifications he rejects have not been conclusively shown to be inadequate. Taken together, his arguments raise the question: how far should we be looking for a justification of autonomy of a universal type, ie one which shows it to be a good for every human being? If we take this line can we get farther than justifying autarchy rather than autonomy?

Raz's argument

We need a new starting point. Joseph Raz (1986, pp 390–395) also discusses the value of personal autonomy, but in general, not in relation to educational aims. Earlier in the book he argues, convincingly in my view, that personal autonomy is not a necessary feature of personal well-being in general. He defines personal well-being partly in terms of a life (or part of a life) in which one's major goals have been realized – ie those desires which are most important to one in the hierarchy of one's desires. So a person in a tradition-directed society could lead a life of great well-being. Suppose he wants above all to be a good carpenter, a good father, to be highly regarded in the community, generous, temperate, etc, etc. If all this comes to pass, he may be said to have achieved a high measure of personal well-being according to this view.

Raz sees personal autonomy as having to do with a particular ideal of the good life. He writes

> In western industrial societies a particular conception of individual well-being has acquired considerable popularity. It is the ideal of personal autonomy. It transcends the conceptual point that personal well-being is partly determined by success in willingly endorsed pursuits and holds the free choice of goals and relations as an essential ingredient of individual well-being. The ruling idea of personal autonomy is that people should make their own lives. The autonomous person is a (part) author of his own life. The ideal of personal autonomy is the vision of people controlling, to some degree, their own destiny, fashioning it through successive decisions throughout their lives. (p 369)

He goes on to say that

> It is an ideal particularly suited to the conditions of the industrial age and its aftermath with their fast changing technologies and free movement of labour. They call for an ability to cope with changing technological, economic and social conditions, for an ability to adjust, to acquire new skills, to move from one sub-culture to another, to come to terms with new scientific and moral views. (pp 369–370)

Although there have been autonomous people in past ages, autonomy is an ideal of life particularly favoured in our own culture.

Attending to the kind of justification of the ideal that Raz provides, we see that, unlike Callan, he does not try to show that it is good universally, ie for any human being: in a tradition-directed society it is *not* a component of individual well-being. Raz wants to argue that for *us*, in a non-tradition-directed society, autonomy helps us to flourish.

How does Raz deal with the objection that this is only true of those of us who make autonomy one of our major goals in life? How can it be good for those others of us who do not include it among their major goals? He replies that this assumes that autonomy is one goal among others: writing poetry, bringing up a family, making a fortune. . . . being autonomous. But, he argues, it is not like this. Being autonomous is not one goal among others, it is tied more closely to features of the kind of society in which we live. His general conclusion is

> For those of us who live in an autonomy-supporting environment there is no choice but to be autonomous: there is no other way to prosper in such a society. (p 391)

This introduces the notion of an 'autonomy-supporting environment'. I need to say a few words about what Raz takes this to be. His point is that the social institutions among which we live are constituted on the assumption that people will be leading a broadly autonomous life (given that the latter can be a matter of degree). They may have their counterparts in tradition-directed societies, but the latter are not built on the assumption mentioned. Take marriage as an example. In our society marriage is built on the assumption that people will independently choose whom they will marry, rather than on the assumption of pre-arrangement. Similar points can be made about choice of occupation or place of residence. Generally, we are brought up in a culture whose major institutions are premised on the ideal of personal autonomy. Within this framework there may be variations in the extent to which people welcome making choices; some may 'base more of their lives on those aspects, such as parenthood, where choice is more limited' (p 394). So some people may lead less autonomous lives than others, but broadly speaking, 'ultimately those who live in an autonomy-enhancing culture can prosper only by being autonomous'. (ibid.)

Raz's account of the value of autonomy is attractive, but I have one reservation. Recall Gray's description of autonomy, quoted above: 'an autonomous agent must have distanced himself in some measure from the conventions of his social environment and from the influence of the persons surrounding him' (p 74). Now it is true that people in our kind of society are not directed by convention or authority in the selection of marriage partners, occupation or place of residence. (And we might add to these the selection of types of food or domestic goods, non-work activities, etc.) But the institutions concerned with marriage, work, residence, consumer-choice etc within which we flourish, themselves embody conventions. It would be quite easy for people in our kind of society to make choices within these areas, yet never to reflect on the conventional structure itself.

I heard the other day of a young woman who works as a home help in the day and as a security officer in a company at night, snatching a little sleep in the afternoons. She is saving up for her wedding in December. Her dress will cost her £1000 and she is inviting 700 guests. At the same time she has cut herself off from all interest in the outside world beyond her immediate family and friends. She has no idea what is going on in the wider world and does not care. As she says, she lives only for herself and sees nothing wrong about this.

Although the details of her case may be unusual, there are many people in our society, I suggest, who have broadly the same attitude to life. They delight in the fact that they can make their own choices about how they are going to live – about their marriage-arrangements, jobs, even patterns of sleeping and waking. But are such people autonomous if they simply accept the conventional structures around them and never question them? It is possible to imagine a version of Huxley's *Brave New World* in which people are not genetically programmed and conditioned as in that book, but are encouraged to live a life of abundant choice-making, yet are still manipulated by an élite to be docile and unquestioning.

We seem to be dealing with a weaker and a stronger sense of 'personal autonomy'. The difference between them is that the stronger sense, but not the weaker, requires critical reflectiveness about basic social structures. If this is so, then Raz's argument for the value of autonomy certainly seems to work for the weaker sense, in that in order to flourish we must (broadly) make various choices in our lives as encouraged by the choice-supporting institutions among which we live. But does his argument support personal autonomy in the stronger sense? Has he shown that it helps us to flourish and to be critically reflective about our basic social institutions? This is where I am more doubtful.

In Raz's defence one might point to other institutions than the ones he has concentrated on, like marriage and work, to political institutions and perhaps to the education system, which might be said to be autonomy-supporting in the stronger sense of the term.

Take the political system. We live in a liberal democracy. This implies that citizens do not simply accept whatever government happens to rule over them, but that they choose what they consider to be the best government in the light of critical reflection on the various alternatives. Similarly, it may be argued that part of our understanding of what our educational system is about is that it helps to produce critically reflective people. For some thinkers, John Anderson, for instance, this aim is written in definitionally into the meaning of 'education'.

How powerful is this possible defence of Raz? One might reply that it is not impressive as an account of what our political and educational institutions are actually like – as distinct from some idealized picture of what they might be.

When people vote, is this in the light of critical reflection on the kinds of social institutions they want? According to a Schumpeterian account of democracy, there is certainly choice involved – ie autonomy in the weaker sense. But the choice is between competing élites, all of which are committed to the maintenance of the social structure as it is. So there is no support here, from this viewpoint, for autonomy in the stronger sense. As for the educational system – as it is, not in an idealized sense – there is no need to outline the evidence that while pupils are certainly encouraged – at least in many instances – to work hard at their science, maths, languages etc so as to promote their life-chances – and hence their autonomy in the weaker sense – there is not generally the same pressure to encourage them to be critically reflective about their society as a whole. Political education has not the same status within the system, to put it ludicrously mildly, as science or mathematics.

Can we conclude, then, that we do *not* live in an autonomy-supporting society in the stronger sense? Not so quickly. We cannot assume that the character of our political and educational institutions is manifested only in what happens within them in practice. On the political side, it is often said that we live in an imperfect democracy. Perhaps many voters *do* choose among party-élites according to which can best produce economic goods, but this is not all that those who over the centuries have forged our democratic system have had in mind. They have had something more like the stronger autonomy ideal in mind – a vision of self-determining citizens, aware of ideological obfuscations which can make them *seem* independent agents, even though they are victims of subtle manipulation.

The case of education is similar. It is part of the liberal democratic ideal in general that young people are brought up equipped and disposed to play their part in a democratic society. This would involve their acquiring a good deal of knowledge of their society and other societies, as well as various virtues, like independence of thought, political courage, concern for others in the community etc. From this point of view a school system which paid no attention to this, or made it harder for pupils to acquire these achievements, would be a perversion of the democratic ideal.

Following this through, one must attend to, as it were, the inner logic of our political and educational institutions, not just their outward forms. They go with a picture of a society in which these logical requirements are more fully realized. This would be a society in which citizens voted in full understanding of the issues at stake, were roughly equal in political power, and exercised their democratic dispositions not only in national and local government but in all aspects of their lives, including their workplaces. It would be a society in which part of everyone's education would prepare them for life in liberal democratic institutions of these sorts. If it is allowed that our political and educational institutions carry with them such a social vision, it makes much more sense to see them as autonomy-supporting in the stronger sense.

If it is allowed . . . the question remains, how far is it legitimate to extrapolate in this way from the actual to the ideal? Certainly, if we come back to the central issue of whether individuals need the stronger kind of autonomy in order to flourish, we have to take them as we find them, shaped by the avowedly imperfect political and educational institutions among which they have grown up. It is still not at all clear why they cannot flourish if they lack reflectiveness about their society. If flourishing has to do with fulfilling one's major goals in life, then why must such fulfilment bring with it this reflectiveness?

Let us try one more way – not, at least initially, based on Raz's argument about an autonomy-supporting society – of showing that personal autonomy in the stronger sense is a condition of flourishing. Strong autonomy can make one alert to possible ways in which one's flourishing may be frustrated – by manipulation, for instance, or political tyranny. But is being autonomous helpful to *everyone* in this way? Much may depend on how one construes personal flourishing or well-being.

Suppose this is conceived in a highly individualistic way, such that, in order to flourish, the individual need not be concerned with promoting others' well-being. A person may, for instance, be interested in pursuing a musical career and be quite prepared to work within the social framework in which she (or he) finds herself: she simply doesn't want to think about this. Is it necessarily in her interests to become reflective about social institutions? She is certainly concerned about removing obstacles to her well-being, but these are things like not having enough to live on, falling ill, having too little time to practise. Need she go further than this?

Suppose, on the other hand, we are working with a conception of personal well-being that embraces concern for others, at both intimate and less intimate levels: it is now part of my own flourishing that I promote the flourishing of my friends and of others – strangers – within the groups and communities in which I find myself. Here I do not know what might be obstacles to these people's flourishing. I have a far less determinate picture of this than the musician had in the earlier example. Among the new obstacles may be political ones, like manipulation, authoritarianism, the power of sectional interests: the broader concern for others' well-being leads one thus to have a broader view of possible obstacles.

As far as the value of autonomy in the stronger sense goes, the conclusion is that this is more clearly visible if one works with the wider rather than the narrower conception of well-being. It *may* be true that one is also better off in the more individualistic sense if one is autonomous, but this is less clearly apparent.

But let us press this last point further. Could the musician in our example flourish, after all, without social reflectiveness? Flourishing is a matter of degree. Would she flourish more with reflectiveness? How far is it true that she can identify obstacles to her well-being without it? The difficulty is that whatever category of obstacle we think of, it is hard to seal this off from wider social and political concerns. Understanding what might promote or harm one's health, for instance, cannot but lead one, in our kind of society, into considerations of public health policy, pollution, advertising and food-processing methods. Similar points could be made about other vital needs – for shelter, clothing, security against personal injury, theft or deceit, freedom of thought and action, social recognition, etc. There is no consensus in our kind of open society about how such conditions of flourishing can best be guaranteed. Given that it is in anyone's interests to think about such matters, it is impossible to avoid the controversies that abound in all these areas. Reflectiveness is, after all, unavoidable.

Bernard Williams (1985, ch 9) makes a related point in his discussion of 'Relativism and Reflection'. He draws attention to the 'growth of reflective consciousness' which has typified the modern world over the past century or two: 'the urge to reflective understanding of society and our activities goes deeper and is more widely spread in modern society than it has ever been before'. (p 163)

Williams argues that

> there is no route back from reflectiveness. I do not mean that nothing can lead to its reduction; both personally and socially, many things can. But there is no *route* back, no way in which we can consciously take ourselves back from it. (pp 163–4)

This line of argument gives further support to Raz's view that we live in an autonomy-supporting society and cannot help seeing our well-being as involving autonomy. It enables him to be able to defend autonomy in the stronger as well as in the weaker sense.[2]

Children from minorities not valuing autonomy

I turn, finally, to the education of children from minorities who are living in the midst of an autonomy-supporting society like our own but who do not themselves favour autonomy. Examples would be some religious communities, whether of Christian, Moslem or other persuasions, whose members are not encouraged critically to reflect on the basic assumptions of their belief-systems. Should the autonomy aim be imposed on children who belong to such communities?

We have seen that personal well-being is not always served by autonomy. This is true of tradition-directed societies. Could it be argued that children's well-being within the minority communities in question, is better served by a non-autonomous upbringing? This is an argument which may lie behind demands for separate schooling. (There can also be other arguments for separate schooling; some West Indian children, it has been urged, may gain in confidence if educated away from white children, to whom they are often made to feel inferior.)

This argument does not work if children are going to spend their life, at least partly, within the wider open society as well as within their community. Here the autonomy aim still stands. Suppose, though, they are brought up wholly within their community: they can then hope, it may be said, to lead a flourishing life without being autonomous.

But there is an important difference between them and children brought up in a tradition-directed society *not* within an open society. In the latter, their educators have no awareness of any alternative way of life, but in a minority community there *is* this awareness. This means that the educators and other community leaders of the tradition-directed society have to take steps to keep their children within the fold, to prevent their being influenced by the values of the wider society. This means that forms of indoctrination are required; these are aimed at a deliberate sequestration from the wider society and a restriction of attention on to the values and traditions of the community. (I am taking 'indoctrination' here to mean the intentional prevention of reflection.)

How might this be justified? Can it be justified in terms of the children's well-being? But might it not have been better for them not to be indoctrinated but to be brought up as autonomous persons? Doesn't the recourse to indoctrination suggest that if the child could choose between the values of the closed and of the open society he or she might well choose the latter? The community leaders might appeal here to internal religious arguments that personal well-being is only possible via the religious belief in question. Things tend to get complicated at this point: there is usually no short way of settling disputes on this topic.

But even if it is difficult to show quite conclusively that a child's flourishing *cannot* depend on his or her being indoctrinated into a set of religious beliefs, does this imply that the community leaders should be left alone to indoctrinate? Surely no one – and this includes the community leaders – would want to say that *anyone* has the right to bring up a child according to their own conception of human flourishing, whatever form this may take, and however convinced they are about the truth and unassailability of their conception, and willing to back up their position by acres of theological or other argument. A fundamentalist Christian, for instance, would not readily allow that a true believer of some other faith or a homespun ideologist of more idiosyncratic views had the right to impose his own conception of the good on children in his, the Christian's, community. Why, then, does the Christian think he has the right to do this? If he appeals to the truth and unassailability of his beliefs and to the inexhaustible arsenal of arguments to support them, he is in no different position from his opponent, for the latter will do exactly the same.

In an autonomy-supporting society *all* children must be protected against true believers who wish to impose on them a non-autonomous conception of the good life. How this is done is a further question. It does not necessarily mean open conflict between different cultural groups. Consideration for the integrity of the child's psychological development is enough on its own to point to the desirability of gentler methods.[3]

Chapter 7

The Place of Knowledge in Education

Critique of the knowledge-centred tradition

It may seem surprising that in a book about the purposes of education so little has been said so far about the acquisition or pursuit of knowledge or understanding, especially because many other writers have made variants of this aim central to education. In many ways, I, too, would accord this aim a high priority. I am very ready to agree that, if we are talking about schools, teachers' time should be very largely taken up with imparting knowledge or extending understanding. Outside the classroom – in the home for instance, especially, but not only, for the pre-school child – aims in this area are of fundamental importance. The issue is not *whether* knowledge-aims come into education, but *how* they come into it.

Knowledge-aims in general, I would hold, are to be justified in terms of underlying ethical values. More specifically, as I shall now spell out, the kinds of knowledge and understanding which are educationally important are to be seen as derivative from the substantive values discussed in previous chapters.

There is, indeed, a more general link which was made in Chapter 2 between knowledge and values. In discussing personal well-being I suggested that this is to be understood in terms, *inter alia*, of the satisfaction of *informed* desires. Promoting pupils' well-being, therefore, involves not only extending and helping them to organize their desires, but also equipping them with knowledge about the objects of their desires.

This way of thinking about education is apparently at odds with the view that education is *basically* concerned with knowledge. (For the moment I shall use the term 'knowledge' as a shorthand for 'knowledge and/or understanding'. It can also cover 'experience', bearing in mind those educationists who want to base their more detailed prescriptions on the delineation of 'areas of experience'. Also, for now, the differences among aims to do with knowledge, understanding and experience will be taken to be less important than the relation or lack of relation of any of these aims to ethical values which may underpin them.) There are many variants of this view, which, I would argue, has been the dominant force in thinking about education over the last two decades, certainly in Britain, and I think also elsewhere. It has been held by influential educational philosophers like R S Peters and P H Hirst; by curriculum theorists like Denis Lawton; by writers of recent HMI papers; by thinkers of the 'new right' like Roger Scruton; and by the drafters of the new National Curriculum. Even those sociologists of education who have been most critical of knowledge-based accounts, including some of those just indicated, have tended, when adumbrating their positive views on what education should be about, to emphasize intellectual liberation or 'consciousness raising'.[1]

I said that knowledge-based views are *apparently* in conflict with the claim that educational aims should rest on ethical values. When one examines these views, however, one typically finds that they do rest on such values after all. This is only what might be expected, for the question can always be asked 'Why is the acquisition/pursuit of knowledge taken to be important as an educational aim?'; and it is hard to see what answer can be given to this except in terms of some kind of benefit to someone – whether individuals, societies or the human race taken as a whole.

Difficulties here are that knowledge-based views sometimes contain an ethical rationale which is either implicit or stated too embryonically; or is attached to a small selection of ethical values, without giving a comprehensive picture of how ethical values, taken together, generate knowledge aims; or is so illogically tied to the knowledge aims which allegedly flow from it as to make one suspect that it subserves other interests which its authors want to keep out of the light of day. There are no sharp divisions between these views, as we shall see.

★   ★   ★

Accounts which leave their values implicit include those whose understanding of education makes its nature *essentially* to do with the achievement of cognitive ends. An example would be the theory of the Australian philosopher John Anderson, for whom 'education as the development of judgment or of criticism is the development of an objective view of things' (Anderson, 1980 p 117). In one sense Anderson's claim cannot be questioned, since its grounds are definitional. One cannot ask, in the hope of uncovering supporting ethical values, *why* the development of an objective·view of things should be the aim of education: that it is, is already written into Anderson's understanding of the term. The same is true of R S Peters'

(1967, ch 1) claim that education has essentially to do with the acquisition of a body of knowledge, an understanding of underlying principles for the organization of facts, and a 'cognitive perspective' which enables one to see the various parts of what one knows and understands in relation to each other. In another way, however, views like Anderson's or Peters' *do* rest on ethical assumptions. Of each, one can ask 'Why does he want to define "education" in this way? Why does he see cognitive ends as important?' In Anderson's case the answer is reasonably clear. His work is powered by a Millian commitment to freedom of thought as a condition of general social well-being. As might be expected from this, when Anderson thinks of the role of education in encouraging critical judgment, it is especially *universities* that he has in mind.[2] Peters' reason for adopting the concept of education that he does, puts more emphasis on the intrinsic value of the pursuit of knowledge for the individual. Where Anderson's preoccupation is with preserving the open society and preventing its domination by blind tradition, economic objectives or totalitarian creeds, Peters' concern is with contemplative activities as essential ingredients in a rational person's well-being. Both writers, it seems to me, look at education from the perspective of the university, the one starting from its critical function *vis-à-vis* current social assumptions, the other from its role of supporting scholars in their disinterested pursuit of truth. (I do not want to imply that there is no overlap between these two ideals in these writers: I am sure there is).

Most books about education and its aims have probably been written by people who work in universities. It would not be surprising if some of them have tended to write about the world they know best. There is nothing wrong with that, of course, but confusion may arise if they are taken to be making more general prescriptions about upbringing. To say that the essence of education has to do with the disinterested pursuit of truth or with critical judgment is straightforward enough within a university framework, but it makes little sense to a primary teacher or to the parent of a pre-school child. There has to my mind been a lot of unnecessary confusion in this area over the past two decades, springing from this dual use of the word 'education' to refer to children's upbringing on the one hand and university-type learning on the other. It has been an unintended consequence of the otherwise laudable involvement of universities in the education of all teachers via PGCE and BEd courses which began in the 1960s. Primary teachers are not dealing with undergraduates or college dons; and neither is their work essentially to do with *laying the foundations for* the academic way of life in its contemplative or social-critical variants. I think most people will take this as a statement of the obvious. What is less obvious is how far these university ideals should provide the basic rationale for *secondary* education. The closer in age a secondary school student is to an undergraduate, the more purchase these ideals are likely to have. This has been especially true of the sixth form, at least in its traditional, A-level orientated, shape; but universities' participation in public exams at 16+ has extended their influence even further down the secondary school. There is nothing necessarily reprehensible about this, especially because as children grow older *part* of their education in the 'upbringing' sense should be to do with introducing them to different ways of life, including the contemplative or scholarly life, and *part* of it should help them to become critically reflective about their own society. The trouble comes, once again, if the two senses of 'education' get blurred together, so that the university ideals are no longer seen as having *some* place in a more global picture of upbringing, but come to dominate one's perception of what upbringing should be about.

★ ★ ★

To return to our general argument about knowledge-based views of education. Anderson's and Peters' theories have been chosen to illustrate the category of views *implicitly* based on underlying ethical values, ie where the ethical foundation has been obscured because the link between education and knowledge has been made true by definition. In other recent accounts the ethical foundation has been stated explicitly, even though – in various ways – the argument to that foundation has been inadequate.

Probably the most influential knowledge-based theory of education in the last 20 years has been P H Hirst's account of a liberal education built around seven 'forms of knowledge'. 'Education', writes Hirst, 'being a deliberate, purposeful activity directed towards the development of individuals, necessarily involves considerations of value. Where are these values to be found?' (Hirst, 1974 p 32). He goes on to say that values have in fact often reflected the interests of a minority group in a society and been religious, political or utilitarian in character. But 'is there not perhaps a more ultimate basis for the values that should determine education, some more objective ground? That final ground has, ever since the Greeks, been repeatedly located in man's conception of the different forms of knowledge he has achieved'.

Hirst's argument makes a necessary link, therefore, not between education and knowledge, as do Anderson and Peters, but between education and value. The link with knowledge comes later in the argument, as we have seen, in that if we are looking for an objective basis for the values underpinning education we can find this only by referring to the different forms of human knowledge. The argument begins acceptably enough but just how values are meant to rest on the forms of knowledge is left obscure. The more obvious way of taking the relationship between knowledge and ethical values would be by reversing this order of dependence. Mathematics, for instance, may be worth pursuing as an end-in-itself within an individual's conception of the good life; or instrumentally, as an ingredient in some socially beneficial activity like engineering or accountancy. It may be justified by reference to other values, too. (Similar arguments can be provided, of course, for other forms of knowledge.) It is easy to see how knowledge-aims may be justified by reference to ethical values; but what would it be to justify ethical values by reference to knowledge?

It seems clear, for all Hirst's disagreements with Greek philosophers, that he shares the view of Socrates and Plato that personal well-being is to be found in the flourishing of the mind and that the latter consists in being in a state of knowledge rather than mere belief. Putting things this way preserves, *contra* Hirst, the more familiar dependence between knowledge and value: acquiring knowledge is desirable because this is in what one's own good consists. If this point about the dependency relation is right, ethics, not epistemology, is the more fundamental branch of philosophy when it comes to justifications of education – even for Hirst: his implied suggestion that things are the other way round, rests, I think, on a confusion.

Once one isolates the claim that personal well-being consists in the acquisition or pursuit of knowledge, one is then in a position to ask for supporting arguments. Hirst does not, as far as I can see, provide any such grounds himself; and it should be clear from previous discussions of personal well-being in this book that the claim would be very difficult to defend. One reason for this is its excessive simplicity. As we have seen, personal well-being is a multi-faceted notion, relying on not one but a number of ethical considerations, balanced against each other by higher-order ethical considerations to do with the integration of an individual's desires within a settled hierarchy of value. To assert that the acquisition of knowledge – *or any other single phenomenon* – is the only thing in which personal well-being consists flies in the face of this complexity.

The question remains: why does Hirst believe that personal fulfilment – and therewith education – have to do with the *possession of knowledge*? If I may hazard a guess, based on the many sceptical remarks he makes in various writings about the pretensions of religion, I would say that this is counterpoised to the Christian view that our well-being consists in *possessing faith*. This Christian conception, too, manifests extreme simplicity: the good for man consists in one thing only, faith in our Lord. In rejecting this form of religion as a guide, Hirst rejects its assumption that ethical values are backed by faith. For faith he substitutes knowledge.

If this line of thought is right, we can now see that Hirst's difficulty is that his non-acceptance of Christianity has still left him operating partly in the same conceptual framework as Christianity. He has taken over from it the proposition that human well-being consists in the soul's (or the mind's) being in a certain proper state – in the case of Christianity, belief in God, and in Hirst's case, that true, well-founded belief which we call knowledge. In both views, the conception of well-being that they contain is altogether too narrow. Here, as elsewhere, we need to jettison if we can the Christian assumptions which still condition – albeit in disguised forms – so much of our thinking about the good life and about education; and in their place we would do well to reinstate the broader, more comfortable, ways of conceiving these things that we find above all in the Aristotelian tradition.

Critique of recent developments

Hirst's approach to the content of education became politically influential in the late 1970s with the new interest in the shape of school curricula for the nation as a whole in the aftermath of the 'Great Debate' of 1975–6. The 1977 HMI paper *Curriculum 11–16* suggested that the secondary curriculum should be based on eight 'areas of experience' – the aesthetic and creative; the ethical; the linguistic; the mathematical; the physical; the scientific; the social and political; the spiritual. Although the list differs somewhat from Hirst's, there is also considerable overlap between the two. The HMI list is of 'areas of experience', not 'forms of knowledge'. This may reflect to some extent philosophical criticisms which had been made about Hirst's theory, that not all his 'forms' were strictly forms of *knowledge:* 'literature and the fine arts', in particular, had to do with an enjoyment and appreciation of the arts which were not basically, if at all, to do with the pursuit of truth. The Hirstian forms of knowledge came to be described more broadly, therefore – in Hirst and Peters' (1970) recasting of the original theory – as 'modes of knowledge and experience'. The HMI's preference for the term 'experience' owes something, I suspect, to these internal philosophical debates, at least in so far as they implied that knowledge alone was too narrow to encompass all desirable educational objectives. But it may well be that the HMI use of 'experience' is broader than that used in the Hirstian debates. If 'the aesthetic and creative' area of experience is meant to suggest as an essential curriculum objective that pupils learn how to create their own art as well as enjoy and appreciate other people's, then this is wholly outside a Hirstian framework. The difficulty about interpreting what the HMI have in mind is that they give us so few clues as to their meaning: in particular the central term 'experience' is left undefined.

For present purposes, however, this may matter less than the relation between the areas of experience and ethical values. How far do the

HMI follow the logical route of beginning with ethical values and then showing how these are to be realized through the areas of experience? There is, as far as I can see, no evidence that this is how they have proceeded. The document includes *both* an account of the areas of experience *and* an account of underlying educational aims – to do with such things as preparation for autonomous citizenship, leisure, work, parenthood, etc; but these are not brought into relation with each other. There seems, rather, to be an *assumption* that an education within the eight areas of experience will help to achieve these aims.

Further evidence that the relation between content and aims has not been sufficiently thought through comes from the HMI's – unsubstantiated – insistence that all the areas are of equal importance. The areas include 'the ethical' as well as 'the social and political' and 'the spiritual'. Leaving aside the difficulty that these terms are left undefined, it seems odd from the perspective of the general thesis of the present book that ethical objectives (including, perhaps, some of what falls into the social/political and spiritual areas as well as the ethical area as such) are placed on a par with, say, mathematical, physical (which I take to be to do with the body), or scientific objectives. What does it mean to say that ethical experience is no less and no more important than mathematical? I doubt whether the HMI thought this question through. If they had done, it would have been difficult for them not to see that once one asks *why* it is essential for all secondary children to have mathematical experience, answers can only rationally be given in terms of some benefit which someone – they themselves, their society or whoever – might be expected to receive from this. This would immediately make ethical considerations *more fundamental* than mathematical and destroy the claim that they are 'equally important'.

The HMI's egalitarianism about the areas of experience mirrors a similar egalitarianism in Hirst's theory, and I take this as further evidence that they are working in the same broad tradition as the latter. For Hirst, too, all the forms of knowledge are on a par, including also in his case 'moral knowledge'. Again, as with the HMI, one might have thought Hirst would accord priority, when it comes to levels of justification, to moral (or ethical) considerations. But from what we have already seen above of Hirst's way of arguing, it is understandable why he did not do this *within the forms of knowledge themselves*: for he had *already* done it *outside* the framework of these specific forms. Recall his way of proceeding: education must rest on (ethical) values; if they are to have an objective basis, these values must be justified by reference to knowledge in its different forms. Since one of these forms is 'moral knowledge', reference to moral knowledge *comes into* the objective justification of ethical values, but only alongside all the other forms of knowledge, and with no privileged position among them. To look at the same point another way, if moral or ethical considerations *were* given justificatory priority within the forms of knowledge, so that mathematical, scientific, philosophical (etc) knowledge were justified by appeal to ethical values, then the question would arise how the ethical values themselves would be justified. From a Hirstian perspective, the search for an objective basis for such values would lead – once again – to knowledge in its different forms; so according priority to 'moral knowledge' within the forms would lead him towards a vicious infinite regress.

It is understandable, therefore, why Hirst is egalitarian *vis-à-vis* the forms of knowledge. Understandable, if not acceptable, for reasons by now sufficiently clear. But there is no such theoretical backing behind the HMI's egalitarianism. No argument at all is given why 'the ethical' is on a par with 'the scientific', 'the physical' etc. We can only conclude, I think, that HMI unreflectively took over the egalitarian framework from the Hirstian tradition, without seeing the consequences of this for their ability to give a satisfactory justification of curriculum objectives in terms of deeper values.

★ ★ ★

The tradition which we have been exploring has accustomed us to focus on taxonomies of types of knowledge and/or experience which have become disconnected from underlying aims and values. Although not embedded within philosophical or sociological theories, the National Curriculum enshrined within the British Government's 1988 Education Reform Act shares this feature with the accounts at which we have already looked.

The National Curriculum is based on ten compulsory 'foundation' subjects – English, maths, science, a modern foreign language, technology, history, geography, music, art and physical education, the first three of which are given priority as 'core' subjects. As we have seen in Chapter 1, no justification of these subjects is provided. Exceedingly brief mentions are made of educational aims, but no attempt is made to relate the ten subjects of the National Curriculum to any of these.

It is disturbing, but not altogether surprising, given what I have said about our recently developed tradition of thinking about the curriculum, that the first British attempt at a national curriculum for over half a century has been made with so little attention paid to underlying aims and values and to the justifiability in terms of them of the areas of knowledge/experience selected for the curriculum. The National Curriculum has underlined yet again the traditional prejudice that knowledge is what is central to education

– that curriculum planning begins with some kind of carving-up of areas of knowledge, considerations about aims and values being relegated to the periphery. The more rational way to construct a national curriculum is to *begin* with aims and *then* to ask how best these aims might be realized. Different types of knowledge would no doubt now come into the reckoning; however, there is no reason to think that acquiring these would constitute the only such sub-objectives or necessarily the most important among them. Virtues, attitudes and other dispositions would be likely to be among their competitors.

★ ★ ★

The assumption that education has first and foremost to do with knowledge (still using this term to embrace 'understanding' and 'experience') is thus held by many writers on education and educational planners, despite ideological and other differences between them.

Other examples also come to mind – and from both extremes of the political spectrum.[3] The right-wing Hillgate Group, whose main intellectual drive comes from the philosopher Roger Scruton, has been pressing for a 'traditional education' based on 'real skills and genuine knowledge' (*Whose Schools?* p 1) and beginning from a 'sensible and tried curriculum, including reading, writing and mathematics' and later including 'as central disciplines, history, science, mathematics, foreign languages (ancient and modern), the lore and literature of our country, and some of the technical skills which will fit children for participation in a modern society'. They speak of 'an increasing displacement of the traditional curriculum in favour of new and artificial subjects, with neither method, nor results, nor real utility to the child – subjects such as 'peace studies', 'world studies', 'life skills', 'social awareness', and the like, whose purpose is sometimes transparently political and whose effect is to distract the child's attention from serious forms of learning'.[4]

On the extreme left wing we may single out Kevin Harris (1979) whose book begins with the words 'Education is centrally and necessarily concerned with the transmission of knowledge' (p 1, see also pp 128–9). In a liberal democratic capitalist society, Harris claims, this aim is distorted:

> Education, then, in a capitalist liberal democracy is a deliberate systematic process that aims to get people to perceive the world in a certain way that favours the ruling class, while at the same time having them believe that they are seeing the world objectively, seeing it as it really is . . .

As for what might replace capitalist education, Harris pins his money on 'consciousness-raising', which 'can now be seen to emerge as a viable alternative to education, allowing as it does for people to gain undistorted knowledge by interacting with the world in terms of their *own* interests (rather than in terms of other social interests) . . .' (p 176).

★ ★ ★

Other accounts of education, while highlighting, like those above, objectives concerned with knowledge or understanding, connect these explicitly and to varying degrees convincingly with deeper-lying aims. I have in mind Dearden (1968), White (1973) and O'Hear (1981). All three theories share the belief that the acquisition of different forms of understanding is a necessary prerequisite of becoming personally autonomous. Dearden holds that the exercise of rational choice which he sees as an aspect of personal autonomy presupposes 'a well grounded understanding of one's situation in the world' (op. cit., p 60), an understanding that divides into different forms along roughly Hirstian lines; while I claim, having in mind the pupil's making autonomous choices of a way of life, that this requires that 'he must know of all the possible things he may want to choose for their own sake' (op. cit., p 22); and O'Hear writes that 'academic study should form the core of education, because it is here that pupils will be given the general understanding of man and the world, to enable them to make important life choices in an informed and responsible way' (op. cit., p 50).

Critical comments could be and indeed have been made about all these views, but I am less concerned with these here than with what seems to me the well-founded belief they all share – that if you hold personal autonomy to be an aim of education, this brings with it certain requirements to do with knowledge and understanding. Autonomous people are able to choose their major goals in life from various alternative options. This presupposes that they have some understanding of what these alternatives are. Whether they need to know of *all* possible options, as I suggested – if indeed any sense can be attached to that suggestion; and whether the kinds of understanding required are furnished by, or limited to, the academic disciplines that O'Hear picked out; are both further questions which we need not pursue here. The main reason for introducing these theories is to illustrate how knowledge-aims can play a legitimate part in educational programmes once they are displayed as logically derived from more deeply underlying values.

The three theories just mentioned are to this extent, it seems to me, on the right lines; but they are all lacking in comprehensiveness when it comes to the values from which one should start. It should be plain from earlier chapters of this book that these values are manifold and complexly structured. The concept of personal autonomy from which these writers begin is too narrow; it is associated with an ethical dualism which opposes moral claims to those of self-interest – a dualism which has been rejected in this book.[5]

Motivations for knowledge-centred education

In a moment I will turn to what I hope is a more satisfactory account of the relationship between knowledge-aims and ethical values. But why do so many accounts of education and its aims, coming from many different ideological and other directions, focus narrowly on knowledge and seem to eschew beginning with wider ethical considerations?

We have already uncovered some possible motivations. Writers may be thinking of education from the perspective of the university; they may be reacting against a religious conception of education based on faith in God. Other reasons may play a part, including institutional reasons like the traditional association which the public has always made between education, schooling and knowledge-acquisition; and political reasons, to do with basing school curricula on easily testable material (see Chapter 8 below). One could go into further detail on all these, but I would like to say rather more here about a subject that has already been touched on – the philosophically based grounds for concentrating on knowledge-aims concerning the objectivity and subjectivity of ethical values.

Many people – laymen, including teachers, as well as philosophers – are attracted by something like the following line of thought. Although some ethical values may rest on others – the more determinate value of keeping one's promises, for instance, may rest on the more general one of not hindering others in their pursuit of their well-being – at some point one is going to end up with values for which no deeper justification seems possible. In a secular age we can no longer appeal to theological underpinnings. But if there is no foundation for values, they can only express people's preferences, whether individually or collectively. But preferences, and therewith ethical values, will differ from one individual to another and from one collectivity to another. So if one starts one's educational planning from conceptions of personal or social well-being, one cannot help imposing one's own values, or the values of some social group to which one belongs, on others who may not share one's preferences. This is arbitrary and illegitimate, because there is no good reason why one's own preferences should win out over others'. Thus educational planning should start from some other point.

As to what that point should be, one finds a major division of opinion between those teachers and theorists who conclude that *any* external direction of the pupil is suspect, and those who do not go along with this. The first group look for a solution in some version of 'progressive' or 'child-centred' education in some sense of these terms: they see children developing wholly from within, their guiding values somehow written into their natures. The second group rightly reject this viewpoint, arguing perhaps that the notion of innate values is incoherent or that to try to let children grow up without *any* adult guidance courts obvious disaster. Instead of this they seek some *objective* form of external direction which avoids the arbitrariness of beginning with ethical values. Knowledge is by definition something objective: if one claims to know a proposition, but that proposition is not true, one does not *really* know it. So knowledge is the obvious starting-point for education.

This second line of thought is also often accompanied by considerations regarding indoctrination. If one starts from values which guide us, one cannot help but impose them, as we have seen. But this, it is said, is to indoctrinate others into accepting one's own values, perhaps consciously, perhaps not. The only way of avoiding indoctrination is by excluding value-judgments from one's teaching altogether. One can do this by concentrating on subject-matter which does not have one's value-judgments written into it – like language, mathematics, science, physical geography or French, but unlike political education, say, or personal and social education.

The second conception is no more watertight than the first. As 'progressives' are among the first to point out, centring education on knowledge does nothing to deflect the charge of imposing values. If one goes for science or mathematics, one is assuming that the teaching and learning of these subjects are for some reason *desirable* and is thus in danger of transmitting this belief to pupils. There is an illegitimate slide from the fact that *knowledge* is necessarily objective, in the sense that what the knower believes must accord with what is the case, to the conclusion that *a decision (or recommendation) to base the curriculum on knowledge* is similarly objective. If all ethical values, and therewith all decisions or recommendations about what to do, are held to be subjective (in this sense), then a knowledge-based education is as subjective as any other.

There is no reason, then, why one should begin with knowledge-aims rather than aims of any other sort. If the latter fail to be objective and involve the imposition of, and indoctrination into, values, then so do the former. Knowledge-aims do not get one off the ethical hook.

This kind of argument for knowledge-aims assumes that if ethical values are subjective, and if, as such they come to be imposed on pupils, this is somehow unfortunate or undesirable. But this assumption needs to be challenged.

If the values on which we based educational decisions were wildly arbitrary, one could understand anxieties about their imposition. But 'subjective' in the present context carries with it no such connotation. As used in the argument above, 'objectivity' has been understood in terms of a belief's correspondence with what is the case. For objectivity to be possible in any domain, it must be possible to make a distinction within that domain between the order of beliefs and the order of reality in virtue of which true beliefs are true. We can thus talk of objectivity in the area of physical science since we can distinguish between statements made about the physical world and the physical world itself. The present claim that ethical values are subjective may rest on the thought that no such distinction can be made in the ethical area. If I claim to know that acid turns litmus paper blue, this can be tested against the facts: we take it that there is an order of physical reality independent of our beliefs and against which they can be assessed to be true or false. But there is no corresponding reality independent of our ethical beliefs, according to the ethical subjectivism now under discussion. We are talking about beliefs about *basic* ethical values, beliefs for which no further justification can be given in terms of other values. At this point, the subjectivist argues, there is no sense in which our beliefs can be true or false, since there is no objective order outside them. Unlike physical science, ethics is not something that human beings have discovered about the world: it is, rather, their own creation.

Questions arise here about whether the ethical subjectivist is correct. From some points of view there *is*, after all, an objective order standing behind our ethical beliefs. Ethical naturalists identify this with the same world which stands behind our scientific beliefs, seeking perhaps to ground ethics in a deeper understanding of human nature; while intuitionists have posited a *sui generis* world of ethical facts, in which ethical values exist as phenomena independent of our beliefs about them. This is not the place to examine the credentials of such views, and I must limit myself here to saying that arguments which have been put up for them seem to me to be unconvincing.[6]

The central issue relevant to our main argument in this section is this. Suppose the ethical subjectivist is right and there is no way of founding beliefs about basic values on any independent order of reality, because no such order exists: what undesirable consequences follow from this? I am not sure that *any* necessarily do. It need not follow that we are at liberty to change our fundamental values according to our whim or fancy – whether individual or collective – as those who speak of the 'arbitrariness' of values may be implying. For our basic values may have – and, I would argue, do have – to do with deeply embedded features of our common life without which that life would be inconceivable. Attachment to one's friends is one such value. If you asked me why friendship is a good thing, I would not know how to reply. I could not point you to any more fundamental value on which it rests; and neither would I want to say that the value of friendship has an existence of its own in some Platonic world of values. It does not seem to be a necessary part of our biological nature – as it is, for instance, that we breathe and eat – that we are bound together in friendship relationships. Yet friendship is an ineluctable part of how we live together.

The same is true of other values which we looked at in earlier chapters. If these values are 'subjective', that is no reason for dismay. It simply reflects the fact that we have the values that we do, not because they fit some alleged reality, but because they provide the framework for our common life. We have indeed created them and refashioned them – on a long time-scale, of course – so as to make this life less vulnerable and uncomfortable, and to enable us the better to flourish. This does not mean that we can change this value-structure as the fancy takes us – which is not to say that it must never be altered.

As far as worries about imposition and indoctrination are concerned it is important, I think, to separate the two. Imposing one's values on another person is not necessarily a bad thing: it may, on the contrary, be highly desirable. However, we think of imposition in a negative light when it is a question of trying to force mature people to hold others' values when there is no good reason for this – such as when, perhaps, a group of religious fanatics sets out to recruit outsiders to their faith. This is because we take it for granted that mature people should be treated as autonomous beings who make up their own minds about how they will live: being pressed into another's mould runs counter to this. But very young children are not yet autonomous beings. They have to be brought up in the basic values of our way of life – and these will have to be imposed on them by their educators. If we want to avoid all imposition, we shall have to set ourselves against inducting little children into caring for those close to them, avoiding physical harm to themselves, not hurting others, enjoying activities with shared ends, controlling some of their desires so that others may be realized, and so on. This makes no sense.

Imposition of this sort need not involve indoctrination. Indoctrinators want their pupils to possess beliefs in such a way that it is very difficult or impossible for them to reflect on them and thus be in a position to give them up. Whereas this might be true of the group of religious fanatics just mentioned, it need not apply to those who bring young children up in basic ethical values. It is quite possible to induct children into friendship, refraining from harming others and so on, while at the same time welcoming questions which they may later raise about whether these are values to which they should remain committed.

Knowledge-aims and ethical values

Acquiring knowledge is an indispensable part of any education. However, its connections with the values which form the starting-point of education must be made clear. What kinds of knowledge-aims are derivable from the account of educational aims presented earlier in the book?

Before we look in some detail at this, it will be helpful to make a distinction between what I shall call 'constitutive' and 'instrumental' knowledge. Knowledge can relate to ethical values in different ways. Coming to value something presupposes the possession of knowledge of a certain sort. This is because, as we have seen, coming to value x is coming to have an informed desire for x. If one values working with others for shared goals, one needs to know what these goals are. One also needs all kinds of other knowledge – about what people are like, about how the shared activity fits into one's culture, etc; but there is no need to go into this long and complicated story to make the conceptual point in question. Knowledge that is presupposed in this way to the values which guide us, is what is what I am calling 'constitutive'. 'Instrumental' knowledge, on the other hand, is not presupposed to possessing a value, but is helpful in realizing it. Suppose I want to eat a pleasurable meal. Knowing about restaurants and what is on their menus may be useful here. Useful, but not necessary: I may know nothing about restaurants but a lot about cookery, so if I cook my own meal rather than going out and getting it, I can draw on this other kind of instrumental knowledge. Neither knowledge about restaurants nor knowledge about cookery is presupposed to my coming to value the pleasures of eating, so neither can be called 'constitutive': but if I am attending to means of realizing this value on any particular occasion, one or the other or both may be useful to me.

There can, of course, be degrees of usefulness. In an advanced industrial culture knowledge about restaurants can be very important, at least for those with the means to eat out; for members of an Amazonian tribe living far from any town this knowledge is perhaps – at least from some points of views – not worth having; and a range of intermediate cases lies between them. The educational relevance of this should be fairly obvious, but I will spell it out rather more at a later stage.

A further distinction, this time between two kinds of instrumental knowledge, will also be valuable. Sometimes this knowledge is 'attached' and sometimes 'unattached'. The first sort is tied to a value or values included in a person's desire-structure. The second sort is not so tied.

Examples may be helpful to an understanding of this. Given that I desire my own physical well-being, it is useful for me to know about safety in the home; for me, therefore, knowledge of safety in the home is attached instrumental knowledge. Suppose, to take a fanciful example, that a fourteen year old at school in this country is learning how to harpoon whales in one of her (or his) compulsory courses. If this knowledge is not helpful to her in realizing any of her current desires, it must fall into the 'unattached' category. It is still instrumental knowledge, since it *can be* useful to a person; but the fact is that it is not helpful to *her*.

As I have described it, attached instrumental knowledge depends on values which a person *already* possesses. Given, then, that babies have not yet learnt to desire their physical well-being, were they now – *per impossibile* – to acquire knowledge about safety in the home, this knowledge would remain 'unattached'. However, babies can be looked upon not only as babies, but also as mature-persons-in-the-making: one can see them as potential possessors of complex value-hierarchies, not only in some abstract way, but also concretely, as beings who will grow up to be prudent, sociable, autonomous, considerate and, pleasure-loving. In this way knowledge about home safety can be seen as 'attached', even for infants – provided that one sees them not simply as existing in the present, but also has in mind an ideal picture of what they will become. This general point is as true, of course, of the 14-year-old pupil just mentioned as it is of a baby. *If* our ideal picture of the older child included her becoming a whaler, or perhaps a world expert on *Moby Dick*, then her knowledge of harpooning would become attached to this picture. But it would be silly to have such a determinate picture – whereas it would not be at all silly to think of the baby growing up to value his or her bodily well-being.

Let us now go back to the values enshrined in the educational aims outlined earlier, and see what kinds of knowledge-aims they bring with them. It was suggested there that children be brought up to desire such things as: physical pleasures – of food, sex, exercise; close personal relationships; the avoidance of pain and injury to themselves; the protection of their own and others' moral rights, both universal rights, like non-injury or freedom of expression, and rights attached to specific roles; benevolence extending beyond their intimate circle and embracing at the limit humanity as a whole; personal projects pursued for their own sake; co-operation with others for shared goals; virtues like courage, temperance, patience and practical wisdom; the coordination of lower-order values within a coherent value-structure; and personal autonomy.

Producing anything like a comprehensive account of all the kinds of knowledge connected constitutively or instrumentally with these values would be a massive task. What follows is intentionally sketchy: it merely indicates a certain way of proceeding. (Most of the headings below come from the list of values in Chapter 4).

Physical pleasures

I shall take as an example the pleasures of eating. Just how much constitutive knowledge is necessary from an educational point of view in this area depends on how specific one wants the values to be. Does one want children merely to desire the pleasures of eating in general; or those of eating bread, vegetables, fruit, meat; or those of eating artichokes, hamburgers, sauce tartare or nectarines? We generally take it, from a hedonistic rather than a dietary point of view, that our pupils' lives will be better, other things being equal, if they include a wide range of enjoyable foods from which to choose. This value-judgment seems to rest on considerations of autonomy. If it is accepted, it presupposes that all children are equipped with a range of knowledge – its extent left so far indeterminate – about different types of food and the sensory delights, to do with smell and sight as well as taste, which accompany them.

What about instrumental knowledge? Is there any attached instrumental knowledge in this area which we should want all children to acquire? There must surely be *some*. It would be a bizarre upbringing which revealed to children all sorts of eating pleasures but gave them no indication at all of how they might go about getting them. At first, of course, they don't need to bother, as their food arrives, often literally, on a plate. But as children grow older, they will need to know about the major means within their culture which they can adopt in order to realize these desires. British children, for instance, will need to know something about buying and preparing food or about eating out.

I have focused attention on a very narrow field – the pleasures of eating. There are other values, of course, which come into eating-education – considerations of what promotes or detracts from health, for instance, or those of participating in shared social activities to do with the preparation and consumption of food. These values will bring other knowledge requirements with them.

These general points about the pleasures of eating can easily be extrapolated to other physical pleasures. It would be tiresome in the present general survey of education and the good life to go through the knowledge-requirements of each form of physical pleasure – important though this would be for someone writing about the content of early education in the home or about curriculum planning in school.

Close personal relationships

People are to be brought up to take delight in the company of friends, family, pets, lovers. This presupposes constitutive knowledge both of a specific sort – about friendship, for instance – and of a general sort – about other people and (still more generally) about human beings in general.

Each type of knowledge-requirement can be spelt out further. Specific knowledge to do with friendship, for instance, includes understanding something about what loyalty is and what place it has among friends. It also covers some understanding of the distinction between relationships based on mutual utility, like those between two businessmen; those based on the shared pursuit of physical pleasure, like those between boon companions or casual lovers; and those based on a deeper affinity of character. Friendships can be of all these sorts, as Aristotle pointed out (*Nicomachean Ethics*, Bk 8), and it is important for people to come to distinguish them.

Knowledge of other people, and about human beings in general, is also presupposed. Close relationships necessitate some understanding of: others' desire-structures; their biography, current situation and future plans; behavioural indications of their moods, feelings and intentions; the culture in which they live; and their biological make-up.

Attached instrumental knowledge may not seem so important in this category as in some others, since if they are fortunate children will grow up among intimates and not have to seek them out. But not everyone is so lucky and some will need special help in establishing relationships in general. In addition, virtually everyone has difficulties in forming – or breaking – sexual relationships. Some understanding of how to go about such matters is a vital part of anyone's education, whether it comes through discussions in a PSE class, through talking with one's friends, through reading literature or magazines, or in other ways.

Avoidance of pain and injury to oneself

One needs, constitutively, knowledge of types of pain and injury, interpreting this broadly to cover major threats to one's well-being such as sickness, poverty, hunger, lack of shelter and loss of reputation. Instrumentally – in an attached way – one must become acquainted with the main ways in which these misfortunes may be caused – eg inadequate health care; accidents; personal attacks; the breakdown of law and order through war or civil disturbance; profligacy; economic and social causes of poverty; etc etc – and with ways in which they can be avoided – to do with care for one's health; prudence in financial matters; self-defence training; political action in preserving internal and external peace and reducing poverty, etc etc.

Protection of rights

This category covers such things as: refraining from harming others' interests by eg murder, injury, cheating, breaking promises, lying, intolerance, cruelty, constraints on liberty; and protecting oneself against these things. It also applies to behaviour as role-holders, as well as more generally. People must be brought up so as not to cheat or break their contracts as members of work-groups, sports clubs etc, as well as to be aware of the harms others could cause them.

This brings with it constitutive knowledge of what these harms are and how they threaten personal well-being. It also requires some grasp of what different social roles involve and of the rights and obligations which go with them.

One also needs attached instrumental knowledge of how to go about protecting one's and others' rights. This will give pupils some insight of such things as: law in general and its relation to the protection of well-being; major specific laws; the legal service in its main different branches; the police; legal punishments and penalties; protective devices of democratic government like secret ballots, limited terms of office, universal franchise, freedom of the press and freedom of association; the role of trades unions and professional associations; and voluntary organizations protecting civil liberties and the rights of specific groups.

Wider beneficence

Here we are dealing with bringing children up to be concerned about the well-being of people not only within their immediate circle but also more widely – of everyone within their locality, their national community, in other countries, in future generations. This beneficence can take the form of seeking to ensure that everyone's basic needs are met. These basic needs, at least as far as we are dealing with autonomous persons, include the following:

1. what is necessary for healthy biological functioning;
2. freedom and time;
3. education;
4. availability of a wide range of options;
5. a minimum income;
6. democratic government and institutions;
7. company;
8. financial security;
9. self-esteem and social recognition;
10. luck.

Beneficence cannot do anything to minimize ill-luck, beyond what it can do within the other categories.

In order to be beneficent in these ways one needs, first, some understanding of who these people beyond one's immediate circle are.

This points towards the human geography of one's own locality, one's own country and of other countries. Secondly, an understanding of basic human needs in general and their connection with personal well-being. Thirdly, some knowledge of the main groups of people in the wider societies whose basic needs most want attention, and in which areas. Human geography is again important here.

Attached to this value will be the following sorts of instrumental knowledge:

(a) An appreciation of distinction between what one can do as an individual to satisfy these needs – as a worker in a garment factory, for instance; what is being and can be done by political institutions of which one is a member, eg one's national political democracy; and what is being and can be done by other agencies over which one has less or no control – eg foreign governments, and domestic and international firms of which one is not a member.

(b) A broad understanding of the chief ways in which basic needs can be met, both in general and in relation to different localities and cultures. Biological needs in general, for instance, can be met by such things as: farming, clothing manufacture, the building industry, water purification, anti-pollution policies, health services, fuel industries – together with the infrastructure of transport, financial services, etc which go with them.

Also to be included under the umbrella of attached instrumental knowledge is an understanding of the kinds of obstacles that can prevent the satisfaction of basic needs, and how they may be overcome. These obstacles can be treated, as before, both generally – eg those to do with skewed distribution of goods in favour of a minority, religious or racial oppression, or poor natural resources; and specifically – so that pupils come to know something of the problems of drought-afflicted countries like the Sudan, the effects of the caste system in India and the privileges of the bureaucratic elite in the USSR. Among ways of overcoming such obstacles, they need to know about such things as the role of education; irrigation; overseas aid; democratic procedures; revolutionary strategies; international agencies; and diplomacy. Important specific examples of these would also be necessary.

Activities pursued for their own sake

As we are assuming that pupils should be personally autonomous, they will need to know something about the different things they could choose as ends in themselves. This overlaps previous value-categories, since one can come to enjoy physical sensations for their own sake (although to want *just* this is not so common – there is more to enjoying a drink in a pub than bodily pleasure); or the company of friends; or working in a shop (this can have an intrinsic side to it as well as springing from motives of earning one's living or helping to meet people's needs). But it goes wider, embracing, for instance, artistic activities (creating, performing or enjoying works of art); travel and holiday-making; sports of all kinds; other games; gardening; physical adventure; the pursuit of knowledge in one or more of its forms for its own sake; inventing things; non-artistic forms of making (knitting, cooking, building radios etc); reading detective stories.

Once again, attached instrumental knowledge is also necessary – in this case of how to go about engaging in intrinsically desired activities, of obstacles in one's way, and of ways of overcoming them. Since the main educational task so far mentioned under this heading is to acquaint people with the broad range of possible interests they might follow, this instrumental knowledge would remain at a fairly general level and not go into specifics to do with particular activities.

There is another aspect to activities pursued for their own sake. Since children are also to be encouraged to develop particular commitments – eg to get drawn as deeply as they wish into playing the cello, studying physics, making radios or swimming – they will also need to acquire more detailed knowledge of their specific field, as well as relevant instrumental knowledge connected with it.

Higher-order integration of lower-order values in an autonomous form of life

This includes both particular virtues, like temperance, and the more general operations of practical reason in establishing priorities among values, both continuing priorities and those established in cases of actual conflict. Much of the knowledge-requirement for this category has already been covered in Chapter 5 when self-knowledge was discussed. In its more general aspects, this knowledge is important for understanding the psychic constitution of *any* human being, not only oneself. It is thus necessary in the realization of any ethical value of an altruistic sort.

One's own needs as an autonomous person

So far we have dealt with the superstructure of well-being, that is, with its constituents. But pupils need knowledge, too, of its infrastructure – of their basic needs relative to this superstructure. To some extent – that is, once again, in its more general form – this knowledge will overlap that knowledge of others' needs required by the value of beneficence. (See above where wider beneficence was discussed.)

★   ★   ★

This completes our sketch of types of knowledge derivative from ethical values, whether 'constitutive' or 'attached instrumental'. It will have become evident how rich and many-sided this array of knowledge is. Which parts of it are best covered by home education and which by school, including the timetabled curriculum (but not limited to this), is a question I leave for resolution elsewhere.

An important conclusion drawn from this sketch challenges a current orthodoxy about educational priorities. This is that science, mathematics and technology should have a privileged place among areas of knowledge. It is reflected, for instance, in the designation of science and mathematics as 'core subjects' of the National Curriculum, along with English. The sketch certainly has room for these, both as activities pursued for their own sake and as entailed by beneficence aims; but it does not set them above other kinds of knowledge. On the contrary, what it emphasizes, if anything, is the pupils' need to understand themselves, human nature more generally, and the structure and culture of their own society.

The sketch has deliberately excluded *unattached* instrumental knowledge – that is, knowledge which *could* be used as a means to some end or other, but which is not useful to a person in realizing any of his or her current desires or desires which it is intended that he or she will have as a result of being educated. The notion is person-relative, therefore, since what may be useful in this way to you may not be so to me. In the account of education put forward in this book, which makes pupils' desire-structures central, there is no room for this type of knowledge.

This has implications for the content of school curricula. For, as things are at present, much of what children have to learn falls into this category. Sometimes this is because, although the knowledge to be acquired could be and should be attached to a mature desire-structure, in fact it never gets so attached. Although, for example, some understanding of history or physical science is important for participation in the wider community, these subjects can be taught in a hived-off way, never becoming linked to one's personal values.

With some other types of school knowledge it is not even clear how they might be linked to mature desire-structures. This is especially true of foreign languages. These are generally assumed to be staples of a compulsory curriculum: in Britain they now feature as one of the ten foundation subjects of the National Curriculum. But do they really have a place there? They are not attached to pupils' *present* desires: 12 year olds do not need to speak or read French to accomplish any of their purposes. But neither do languages seem necessary to any desires intended as acquisitions in the longer run. Britain may be unlike other countries in this respect. In Kenya children learn three languages. These are all important in maintaining community life in Kenya at local and national levels: knowledge of these languages is attached to the values of those communities. There is a parallel between this and Welsh, Urdu, Gaelic, Greek etc, in addition to English, for some British children, but it yields no reason for compulsory French/German/Spanish for all. Neither do considerations of 'world citizenship'. Suppose we take it as desirable that children are brought up in our shrinking world equipped to communicate with other individuals in other countries: since English is the chief international language, they are equipped for this already. British governments out for value for money in public education can find far better uses for the millions they now spend on compulsory languages for all. (In a BBC radio interview in August 1989, Angela Rumbold – the minister in charge of school education – was pressed on whether modern languages should be compulsory since English was so widely used. She asked us to suppose someone who speaks only English selling goods to foreign businessmen: he might be able to do a deal with them in English, but would not be able to understand the remarks which they were making to each other in their own language and this might put him at a disadvantage. This is true, but it hardly constitutes a reason for compulsory languages for all children, since only a small minority of them are likely to find themselves in such a position.)

This still leaves room for enlarging opportunities to learn modern languages elsewhere than at school. Intensive courses for adults to meet business and other needs make good sense: the knowledge involved is here attached to the satisfaction of current desires.

Unattached instrumental learning is also widespread within other subjects. There is no need for it. One of the most useful functions of national curricular guidelines could be to try to ensure that every bit of knowledge which pupils are expected to acquire is firmly attached to, or constitutive of, the values in which they are being brought up.

Chapter 8

The 1988 National Curriculum

Its relation to ethical values

How far is the education policy of the present British Government guided by the aims and values argued for in this book? How far do the National Curriculum and other provisions of the 1988 Education Reform Act aim at promoting the personal well-being of every child in something of the same sense in which I have been advocating this? Do they see well-being as including autonomy? Or altruism? Or the satisfaction of basic needs? Or as requiring the kinds of knowledge we earlier picked out?

We saw in Chapter 1 that the stated aims of the National Curriculum are excessively sparse and general, that how the ten foundation subjects are supposed to help realize these aims is unexplained, and that no reason is given why school subjects should be thought to be the best way of doing so. We will not get far in understanding the rationale for the National Curriculum until we look at this in the framework of the government's education policy as a whole. But first a few words about some of the topics of earlier chapters, so as to see how far the National Curriculum is in line with or diverges from conclusions there reached.

Personal well-being

The substantive version of personal well-being which was proposed is complex and manifold, presupposing on the part of the individual a hierarchy of values; these include altruism and autonomy and, being not wholly commensurable, cannot be regimented into a monolithic value-system. It was also claimed that education should seek to promote the personal well-being of *each pupil*.

The aim of the National Curriculum as expressed in the Education Reform Act is to promote 'the spiritual, moral, cultural, mental and physical development of pupils'. These terms are left unexplained and it is impossible to discern any picture of well-being which may lie behind them. Neither can it be assumed – although it may be true – that the government has the good of *each pupil* in mind. Governments here and elsewhere have often used the educational system for other ends – to promote the well-being of some of the population at the expense of the others; or of future generations at the expense of the present – and this government may be no exception.

Morality and altruism

'Moral development' is a stated aim of the National Curriculum, but no indication is given of how its ten subjects contribute to this and there has been no broad look at what other vehicles might do so. Aspects of personal and social education, together with gender and multi-cultural issues, although not included in the National Curriculum, have been referred to in later documents. *National Curriculum: From Policy to Practice* (DES, 1989) states that 'these areas of the curriculum are not separately identified as part of the statutory National Curriculum because all the requirements associated with foundation subjects could not appropriately be applied to them in all respects' (para 3.8). This is left unexplained.

There is no sign that the framers of the National Curriculum have dwelt on what might be meant by 'moral development' as an educational aim or that they were ever aware of the bewildering lack of agreement about the nature of morality which we explored in Chapter 3. No attention has been paid to how 'moral' aims are related to the promotion of personal well-being.

Many Conservatives – as well as some socialists – have traditionally closely associated morality and religion. Contrary to the argument of this book, they have seen moral rules, like injunctions not to lie or break one's promises, as based on the word of God. There are well-known philosophical difficulties about this type of reasoning, centring around (a) whether any sense can be attached to 'God' and (b) how, if so, one can derive conclusions about what ought to be done from premises about what is the case – eg about what God has commanded us to do.[1] Leaving these problems on one side, what position do those responsible for the National Curriculum take on the connection between moral and religious aims? How, if at all, is 'spiritual development' related to 'moral development'? How far have decisions to maintain religious education as a statutory element in the curriculum and to make daily collective acts of worship 'wholly or mainly of a broadly Christian character' been motivated by considerations about the 'moral health' of the nation? We know that this was a factor in the provisions of the

1944 Act about religious education, but how far does it still weigh with legislators today?[2]

Personal autonomy

There is as far as I am aware *no* reference in any of the documentation about the aims of the National Curriculum to personal autonomy or self-determination. A curriculum which promotes spiritual, moral, cultural (etc) development, or which 'prepares pupils for the opportunities, responsibilities and experiences of adult life' could be as much at home in a country where social roles are assigned by tradition or by dictatorial fiat as in one where people are encouraged to give shape to their own lives. A reply might be that it is of course taken as read that Britain is a nation of self-determining individuals and the aims-statements should be read in that light. But Conservative educational policy has traditionally *not* assumed this and has always put more emphasis on meeting the needs of industry than on developing a taste for the autonomous life.

Although there is no evidence to my knowledge that the National Curriculum has been designed to promote autonomy, there are indications – if no more – on the other side. One facet of the ideal of autonomy is political: everybody should have an equal right to as much self-determination as possible in the conduct of collective affairs, from national level down to the workplace or leisure group. There is nothing in the National Curriculum about preparation for democratic participation of this sort. 'Political and international understanding' is indeed mentioned in *National Curriculum: From Policy to Practice* (DES, 1989)) as another 'cross-curricular issue', but no substance is given to this.

Neither does the system of national assessment seem to fit comfortably with autonomy for all. One can see how it might go with autonomy *for some* if, as some critics claim, it is a part of a battery of devices, including City Technology Colleges and opting-out, designed to identify pupils to be creamed off into higher-status schools which will open the doors to managerial and professional careers. That apart, it is hard to see how pupils pigeonholed in a lowly intellectual station by the national tests will easily be able to maintain the self-esteem and self-confidence necessary for autonomy.

It remains to be seen whether the detailed content of the National Curriculum as the government reacts to the conclusions of the various subject working groups, puts more weight on critical reflectiveness than on the learning of more easily assessable facts. First signs are not encouraging. Both Kenneth Baker and his successor John MacGregor have pressed for more weight to be given to the latter.

We also need to monitor how much autonomy teachers will be left with to shape National Curriculum requirements to their preferred modes and content of teaching. This is relevant to the issue of pupil autonomy, since we know that children learn by example and are more likely to acquire a taste for the autonomous life from people who themselves embody it than from hemmed-in functionaries within an authoritarian system. Again, all the indications are that the bureaucratic demands on teachers to meet the byzantine requirements of the national assessment scheme are likely to make them more like the latter than the former.

One's needs as an autonomous person

How far does the National Curriculum equip pupils to understand and satisfy their own needs and those of other people? The government has always urged that schools should do more to improve the country's economy, even though it is not immediately clear why a curriculum of traditional academic subjects is thought to be the best means of doing this. Improving the economy may help more people to acquire the material prerequisites of autonomous well-being, such as adequate food, shelter and health care. Whether it makes this easier for *everyone*, or whether in a more affluent society some people will still be as badly off as they are now – or even worse off – are further questions.

However, people have other needs as well as the above biological ones. Autonomous people must also have such things as freedom, time, education, democratic institutions and social recognition. Nowhere in the National Curriculum proposals is there any acknowledgment of these.

Knowledge

Knowledge is an important educational objective, but it derives its importance from underlying ethical values. The ten subjects of the National Curriculum put great weight on certain kinds of knowledge, but, as shown in Chapter 1, the reasons for this are not spelt out: there is no clue in the sparse statements of aims that the government has given.

The prominence given to 'core subjects' – English, mathematics and science – seems to show that knowledge of the physical world is rated more highly than that of the human world. Again, no grounds have been given in support. This last fact is further evidence that preparation for personal autonomy is not part of the agenda. For reasons spelt out already, autonomous people need to know a lot about themselves, other people, their society and its institutions, and about other societies. They need in this connection some understanding of the workings of an industrial society, and for this a grasp of science is desirable. But they do not need science *more than* a knowledge of the human world. The priority goes, in fact, the other way. Someone who has had a thorough grounding in science but has next-to-no self-knowledge, understanding of others' motives or of the make-up of their society, might have their uses as a boffin, but would not get far in directing their own lives.

Why are knowledge objectives so prominent in the National Curriculum? In his reaction to the interim report of the working group on history, Mr MacGregor is reported as saying that he wanted more emphasis on the learning of historical facts, otherwise there was the risk that 'pupils' grasp of the substance of history will not be clearly established or assessed' (see his letter to the Chairman of the National Curriculum History Working Group in their *Interim Report*, (DES, 1989)). The implication seems to be that what is of prior importance is that what is learnt should be assessable. This bears out those who have alleged that the National Curriculum subordinates curriculum to assessment whereas the dependence should be the other way. What they have in mind is that its content has been chosen partly as a means of bringing about an assessment system designed to select people at an early age for different slots in the economy. Are they right? Certainly if you want educational selection, whether to limit those going on to higher education, to sort out 11 year olds entering selective secondary schools, or for whatever other reason, you need some means – preferably simple rather than complex – of doing this. What is more, you need some means which people can accept as *objective*, rather than based overtly on, say, class or income. These two criteria, simplicity and (apparent) objectivity, point most obviously towards *amount of factual knowledge* as a yardstick of selection. Suppose that discussions about a National Curriculum had gone a very different way in 1987–8 and ministers had decided that moral courage and loyalty to their friends should be among the accomplishments which they wanted all pupils to possess. Whether it is possible in principle to devise nation-wide tests to assess such qualities I do not know; but it is clear that as soon as one tried to do so, one would have major problems with the two criteria. The National Curriculum excludes what has been the fastest growing area of the comprehensive school curriculum in recent years – personal and social education; it includes the fact-rich requirement of a foreign language for all – a subject long under fire as part of a compulsory curriculum. As already indicated, ministers have given no reasons for the inclusion or exclusion of any curriculum area. But on the face of it it looks as if there may be some truth in the charge that this is an assessment-led curriculum.

Its relation to wider government policy

In 1988, following a dozen years of public debate on the issue, England and Wales established a National Curriculum for all state-maintained schools. For many years before 1976 they had been out of line with most other countries both in Europe and in the wider world, in leaving the determination of school curricula largely to schools and teachers. Only religious education was a compulsory school subject, having been made so by the 1944 Education Act.

Educationists from abroad, oppressed by the inflexibilities of their own state-determined curricula, had often looked to the autonomous English system as a model. Many of them believed, as did a number of their British counterparts, that this system had always existed, that it had been part and parcel of our age-old libertarian tradition to leave schools free to decide what they should teach.

However, this is a myth. There was until 1926 a centrally laid down set of curriculum subjects that elementary schools, who catered for nearly all children, had to teach; and the curriculum of secondary grammar schools was centrally prescribed until 1945. In each case the deregulation had come about under a Conservative government.

This last fact is worth dwelling on. Why should it be Conservative policy in the 1920s and later to *remove* school curricula from state control, but Conservative policy in the 1980s to *bring them back under it*? My suggestion is that the party was following the same broad objectives at both times, but that diametrically opposed means were thought appropriate on the different occasions.

Conservative education policy in Britain has been remarkably consistent since the beginning of the century. At that time the Conservative government then in power lopped off the 'tops' that elementary schools had been sprouting: throughout the 1890s they had been growing beyond the three Rs and teaching more advanced subjects. After 1900 a divided system was introduced, with élite secondary schools teaching a grammar school curriculum and elementary schools now forbidden by law from teaching science and foreign languages, but obliged to teach, among other things, various manual subjects (Eaglesham, 1967).

The rationale for this move is clear and familiar enough. It corresponds with traditional right-wing educational objectives all over the world: to shape pupils for their destinations in the socio-economic system, whether in managing/professional roles or in some kind of subordinate position.

The Conservatives denationalized school curricula in 1926 as a way – a subtle and imaginative way – of furthering the same objective. Their immediate motive was to prevent an incoming Labour government from introducing a national curriculum of a non-divisive and more liberal sort according to the official Labour policy of 'secondary education for all'. It was universally held at that time that support for the Labour Party would continue to grow apace and that it would not be long before it came to office again, perhaps for a long time. The removal of elementary curricula from parliamentary control in the very month of the General Strike was a brilliant way of foiling Labour education plans. At the same time, *administrative* rather than parliamentary ways were devised of making sure that the elementary schools continued to teach the lowly curriculum that they had taught since 1904.[3]

There is every indication that the real aims behind the reintroduction of a national curriculum in 1988 have to do with the traditional right-wing educational objectives mentioned above – ie to prepare children to fill certain slots in the socio-economic order. The links which this government have constantly made between Britain's poor economic performance and alleged low standards in schools point in this direction. So do calls from the Department of Education and Science for a selective education system 'because we are beginning to create aspirations which increasingly society cannot match . . . People must be educated once more to know their place.' (Chitty, 1988, p 88) So does the absence from the National Curriculum of any form of political education or reflective enquiry about the adequacy of current social arrangements.

In addition, the National Curriculum and the assessment system that goes with it must be taken in conjunction with other parts of government policy – with its heavy emphasis on parental choice of schools, with allowing schools to opt out of local authority control, with the introduction of expensively appointed City Technology Colleges for a minority of favoured children, and with the encouragement of private schooling. Not all these are overtly selective devices, but the overall pattern is unmistakable. With pupils' attainments in National Curriculum subjects being tested at 7, 11, 14 and 16 years old, it will be possible for parents to pick out schools with better and worse results. The 'better' schools are more likely to be selected by middle-class parents. The latter are also more likely to press for their children's schools to 'opt out' of local authority control into direct funding by the state: this is one way by which after a few years a comprehensive school can become a selective grammar school. All the signs are that the different aspects of government policy cohere together in the promotion of a divided system whereby, excluding the privileges accruing to the independently educated, a favoured minority of state school pupils are taught together in schools which steer them towards managerial and supervisory jobs, while the opportunities for the majority to aspire to such careers and lifestyles are reduced, both by excluding them from the élite schools, and by habituating many of them to think of themselves as inferior beings, as the low public levels of attainment they reach in the 7 year olds' assessment are confirmed at 11, 14 and 16.

The more closely a system aims at fitting people for different socio-economic strata, the less it is likely to promote personal well-being of an autonomous sort as a universal ideal. This is because the latter includes choosing one's own mode of life from a wide range of options. In a hierarchical society this will still be possible for those at the top of the pyramid, becoming less and less possible as one descends. Rich people can have innumerable life-options; and their (independent) schooling can make the range as wide as possible. High-fliers from maintained schools are more likely to be restricted to ways of life dependent on earned incomes, but even so have more options open to them than those much further below them on the social scale.

It is not only the *number* of options open to one that is significant. If one were brought up to belong to a social stratum where options were few, but whichever option one chose left one adequately provided with the prerequisites of autonomous well-being, one's chances of attaining a reasonable level of personal well-being in one's life might still be high. But, as already remarked, as things are in a society like the British – and there are many such – the lower one's position on the social pyramid the less likely one will be to possess the wherewithal for the good life: good health and living conditions, income, security, negative liberties, recognition, education and political power.

An educational policy which fits a proportion of the population for jobs and ways of life towards the lower part of the pyramid cannot legitimately claim to be acting in these pupils' interests, to be promoting their well-being. It is likely to make things worse for them, not better. This would seem to contravene a basic assumption on which this book's whole argument rests: that *in every case* education should aim at promoting, and not detracting from, the pupil's well-being.

Can this charge be answered? Different ways of doing so are commonly attempted. These days one does not often come across the *explicit* claim that the rich and powerful are in some way more important in themselves than the poor and powerless, being used as a premiss for the conclusion that their interests deserve greater attention – although this implicit message, pumped into us daily through the media, is ubiquitous enough. But other kinds of élitism than *social class élitism* are currently rationally defended, notably what one may call *intellectual élitism* and *utilitarian élitism*.

The former is found among certain right-wing academics like David Cooper and Oliver Letwin. The central purpose of education, according to this view, is to foster academic excellence on a broad intellectual front, including in David Cooper's case artistic achievement. I will not spend much time on intellectual élitism, since although it has its own counter-suggestion to the view that education should promote the well-being of all, it does not tie it closely to the needs of the economy. On the contrary: it sets its face against such instrumentalism and emphasizes intellectual excellence for its own sake. It still favours stratification of a sort, but in a more global way. Education, strictly speaking, is only for those capable of excellence. As to what should be provided for the rest, little is usually said. In favouring intellectual ideals, this kind of élitism appears to offend against the liberal principle that each person's life is of equal intrinsic importance and that, taking the desirability of autonomy and altruism for granted, the state should not privilege one version of the good life over another. (See Chapter 1.)[4]

Utilitarian arguments seek to justify stratified objectives by the general prosperity their satisfaction will help to bring about. They are very familiar to us these days, whether coming from politicians or from businessmen. A commonly heard line is this: Britain is falling behind as an industrial nation; for this the education system must take a lot of the blame; its ethos has tended to be anti-industrial.[5] The system must now be geared to industrial demands. We need better managers and more flexibly skilled workers: schools, colleges and training schemes can play a major role in producing them. In a few years, when British industry is thriving again, we will all be better off.

We are so used to this kind of appeal these days that we do not always stop to look at its ethical implications. The good which is aimed at is increased general prosperity as measured by, say, GNP or average income per head. Means have to be devised for realizing that good – hence better prepared managers and workers, hence schools etc which will help to provide them. The difficulty with this line of thought is that it puts all the weight on a single good and fails to do justice to other values which may conflict with it.

To take an analogy, familiar from textbook discussions of utilitarianism. Suppose a certain political programme could be guaranteed to bring about vastly increased prosperity for 80 per cent of the population at the cost of imposing great hardships – including slavery, say – on the other 20 per cent. Would it be justified? For a thorough-going utilitarian it would be a matter of seeing whether overall benefits outweighed overall dis-benefits: if they did, the policy would be the one that should be followed.

The problem with this is that it fails to do justice to the 20 per cent whose well-being has to be sacrificed for the good of the 80 per cent. It fails to treat them as individuals, each with his or her unique life to lead. It sees them all merely as means to general economic prosperity, and not as ends in themselves.

Considerations to do with the general well-being do have a place in ethical thinking, but they need to be weighed against other values: I hope the arguments about the plurality of values and conflicts between them, spelled out in earlier chapters of this book, will have made this sufficiently clear.

To come back to current British educational policy. In so far as it is guided by utilitarian principles, it runs the danger of ignoring Kant's principle, just referred to, that one should never treat persons merely as means to ends, but always as ends in themselves. There is no question, of course, of using people as slaves; but the principle still holds good if some people are disadvantaged, in whatever way, and however few of them there are, for the sake of others. If, as I have been suggesting, present policies merely strengthen stratifications into more favoured and more deprived groups, they still offend against the Kantian principle of respect for persons. Stalin justified the liquidation of the kulaks in terms of general economic prosperity. A stratified education policy is not so brutal; but its utilitarian rationale is of the same form, and the Kantian objection to it equally telling.

Utilitarianism brings with it its own form of élitism. It presupposes a division between the utilitarian planners, who are supposed to have a clear picture of the future general good to be achieved and know how to operate the causal levers to bring it about, and the rest of the population whose behaviour is to be shaped in accordance with that goal.[6] In this way it can be used to justify not only what we might call education for ill-being for the lower strata, but also a more general division between education for the managers of society and education for the managed (who are likely to contain more than the really badly off in terms of basic goods). By 'managers of society' I do not mean all managers in enterprises, although some of these may qualify. For many industrial managers are themselves managed from above and seen largely as instruments of 'efficiency': they are hired as possessors, and they see themselves as possessors, of technical expertise only, not of ethical/political insight. The 'managers of society' I have in mind are politicians, industrialists, financiers, newspaper owners, trade union bosses and so on who make or influence high-level political decisions. This division, between a utilitarian élite and the rest of the population, itself divided into different levels of managers and managed, is instantly recognizable in current educational policy-making.

There are difficulties with this utilitarian position over and above its instrumental attitude towards people. Does the notion of an élite of moral experts with special insight into the good life make sense? As we have seen earlier in this book, what personal well-being consists in is both complex and controversial. For reasons already given, I argue for a concept of it which reflects a rich plurality of values, to be weighed against each other in different ways in different circumstances. These include considerations of general welfare, but do not accord these any privileged place.

I do not believe that utilitarian planners in this or any other government's ranks have the ethical insights required. (No one has.) In particular, it will not do to define people's well-being, and increases or decreases in this, in economic terms. Economic growth can give us comforts and physical pleasures. It can help to provide some of the basic goods we need: housing, clothes, food, clean water and so on. It can, in its own way, bolster self-esteem, through providing one with goods that others envy. (Whether this latter is *really* a good depends on what one is writing into the contested notion of well-being: the altruistically orientated conception of it which I have embraced will find this kind of self-esteem harder to rate positively than a more atomic/individualistic version will.) But simply possessing goods that can be bought or sold does not give one such things as intimate relationships, courage, altruistic dispositions towards the community, self-understanding, autonomy, equality of political power, freedom of speech and experience of art.

It may be objected that, even so, the materially richer a society becomes, the more it will be able to provide the conditions in which non-economic values can flourish: the utilitarian planner is not obliged to work with a narrowly economic concept of well-being.

This may be so, but the point cannot be used to justify adopting a stratified, economy-directed educational policy, where this is seen as helping to bring about greater and more extensive personal well-being, generously conceived, some time in the future. Not only are the future benefits uncertain – since economic growth is compatible with all sorts of societies, including those where the benefits just mentioned are not prized – but also, and more importantly, the Kantian principle of treating everyone as an end in himself or herself is contravened.[7]

Chapter 9

Towards an Alternative
National Curriculum

Signposts from the USSR

In the very year that England and Wales shifted to close governmental
control of curricula, the USSR, for half a century dominated by Stalinism
and its legacy, moved decisively in the opposite direction. The Teachers'
Congress in Moscow in December 1988 overwhelmingly approved
the document *A Conception of General School Education* produced by a
working group of the USSR State Committee on Education.[1] Its main
points are now official policy.

This booklet firmly rejects the role of the Soviet school in the
'administrative-command' system of pre-perestroika days. Schools
then were conceived as mere instruments of government policy, as
'closed institutions of the regime': 'children's interests and social needs
did not cross the school's threshold'. 'Teachers and pupils were turned
into cogs of different dimensions in the educational machine'.

But 'the school is not an organ of government, but a social institution'.
Government and society need to work closely together for it to flourish.
'The school cannot live on government air alone. Sooner or later it will
begin to suffer from oxygen deficiency. And sooner or later society will
have to come to its rescue again'.

In its educational aspects perestroika means a shift away from
the 'bureaucratic, closed, monolithic school to one which is open,
democratic and diversified'. Reminiscent of the English National
Curriculum, *A Conception of General School Education* states that the
central aim of such education is 'to promote the intellectual, moral,
emotional and physical development of the person'; but unlike the
British document, it spends some time filling out this general description, so that it is clear that it is to be understood in a liberal rather than
an authoritarian way. Even in this bare statement, the word 'emotional'
– which does not appear in the British prescription – gives an indication

of where the priorities lie. The flourishing of individual children is the central objective. This comes out in several ways. In the emphasis on the need to 'uncover their creative abilities', for instance, and on preparing them 'to take part in democratic self-management'. Education in the arts is seen as having an especially important role in the development of personality. The diversity of children's needs, abilities and inclinations should be matched by a diversity in the content of the curriculum and in teaching methods. For older children only 75 to 80 per cent of timetabled time should be devoted to compulsory courses: the rest is to be taken up with 'supplementary subjects chosen by pupils in accordance with their inclinations and interests'. Children should have the right to go to the school of their choice; 'to move from one school to another in the course of the school year at whatever level of teaching'; 'to choose individual programmes of study'; 'to determine the rates and times at which they will cover their courses'. 'The cultivation of the pupils' self-determination in life is the most important aim of their upbringing'.

A central theme in the document is the democratization of education. 'Democratization is the aim, means and guarantee of the irreversibility of perestroika in education. It not only leads to changes in the way schools are administered, but also penetrates every aspect of school life, its ethos and internal organization.' One of the aims of education, as we have seen, is to be a preparation for democratic self-management. The school is also to be run as a workplace democracy. Detailed arrangements are suggested for this in the document. These include a governing body meeting at least once a year and drawn in equal numbers from (a) older pupils, (b) school staff and (c) parents and representatives of the community; and a school council composed in a similar fashion meeting more frequently throughout the year. Among its duties the governing body will choose the headteacher by secret ballot.

Many of the ideas in the document were incorporated in a shorter paper which in 1989 became official Soviet government policy. Leaving its fate on one side, what is striking to a British reader is its contrast at point after point with the British Government's provisions for the National Curriculum. Liberation, openness, respect for the dignity of the human being pervade the former; restrictiveness, the proliferation of bureaucracy, and the subordination of individual well-being to economic demands, the latter. Ten years ago one could not have predicted that Moscow would be the most passionate advocate of John Stuart Mill's democratic liberalism in the educational sphere, while London turned its back on this tradition for the sake of a more entrenched capitalism.

What can one predict for ten years' time? I will not risk attempting to answer this, but will at least express a hope – that British thinking about a National Curriculum will move closer to the new Soviet model; that in both countries the paramount aim of education will be to promote the autonomous flourishing of each individual and not to subordinate this to the growth of state or capitalist power; and that we can work together on elaborating and applying the 'universal human values' that *A Conception of General School Education* mentions, and that should underlie the education systems of the twenty-first century.

A democratic framework for a national curriculum

What might replace the English National Curriculum to bring it more in line with the values advocated in this book? As opposed to some of its critics, I shall argue that state control over the content of education needs to be *extended* beyond what is covered by the National Curriculum – in two ways. First, the content of education embraces more than the timetabled curriculum. At its broadest, it includes what children learn at home from their parents and the media; even if we restrict ourselves to formal education, the ethos and organization of a school can play a part in transmitting values, as can styles of pedagogy. I shall argue that there needs to be state regulation not only of timetabled activities, but also of educational vehicles such as these. The second extension is to take in schools outside the maintained sector. Under the Education Reform Act independent schools are not obliged by law to conform to National Curriculum regulations. I shall try to show below that there is no good reason why they should be excluded. Controls should apply not only to their timetabled curricula, but also, in line with the first extension just mentioned, to other aspects of school life.

At the same time as controls are extended, they need to be made *less detailed*. As things are now, the demands of national testing at 7, 11, 14 and 16 years have created an extraordinarily complex system of specific objectives, whose burdens on the classroom teacher are every day becoming more apparent. I shall argue that there is no need for such specificity. State control should have to do with more general matters only – with basic principles and values and their broad embodiment in institutions and practices.

In backing this dual claim, for extended but less detailed state control, I need to appeal again to the requirements of a liberal democracy. The leading idea behind this form of government is that each citizen should be equal in the exercise and control of political power. This rests on an underlying belief that everyone should be self-determining in the conduct of their lives as a whole, ie on a commitment to universal personal autonomy. Democratic government thus comes out as a prerequisite of the autonomous life: if decisions significantly affecting one's life are made by an autocrat or a group of oligarchs, one's ability to be self-determined in one's life is diminished.

Criteria can be worked out in accordance with this conception of democracy which can help to determine:

1. what the content of education should be;
2. who should make decisions about the content of school education and at what level;
3. how those aims can best be realized
   (a) via timetabled curricula,
   (b) via pedagogy, including assessment, and
   (c) via school organization and ethos.

These criteria generate democratic constraints on national curriculum planning. My main task now will be to outline these criteria and to show their power and utility in educational planning, whether in the UK or other democratic countries – including, now, it is to be hoped, the Soviet Union and other countries in Eastern and Central Europe.

What should the content of education be?

The central aim of education in a liberal democracy should be to prepare its citizens for a life of autonomous well-being. I have spelt out in earlier chapters how this ideal needs to be understood as entwining personal and altruistic goals and also something of the personal qualities and kinds of knowledge and understanding it requires. This can help us to determine more specifically what the content of education, including the content of school education, should be.

In working this out one will have to start from the top and work downwards. The way to begin is to work out sub-aims derivative from the most general aims of education. Sub-aims themselves can be of different orders of specificity: one can have sub-aims of sub-aims, and even minuter divisions. I do not intend this to be understood rigidly. It is not as though one could operate with a simple branching model, with general aims at the top, neatly subdividing into ramifications of derivative aims, yielding at the bottom specific objectives for particular courses or for particular lessons. What I have in mind can best be brought out by examples.

Starting with the most general aim of all on the current scheme – the promotion of every child's autonomous well-being – we see that this involves the cultivation of certain dispositions – such things as valuing sensuous pleasures, intimacy, beneficence, commitment to personal projects, various virtues and reflectiveness about value-priorities. One reason why the simple branching model breaks down is that these dispositions are not discrete but interpenetrate at point after point.

Within each of these dispositions one needs to think in more specific terms. A generalized beneficence, for instance, is not what is wanted, but rather a concern for others' well-being at the level of: friends and family; wider face-to-face relationships; local communities; the national community; people elsewhere in the world; human beings as a whole, future as well as present; and sentient creatures as a whole. These categories, too, will need to be rendered more specific.

Next, one has to ask what kinds of more specific learning are presupposed for the acquisition of such and such a disposition. In Chapter 7 we saw something of the kinds of propositional knowledge required. Suppose we take, as one example of beneficence, concern for others in the national community. This requires extensive knowledge of such things as: geographical facts about one's country; its major industries; its social stratifications; its sub-communities; its political structure; the major values of the community as a whole and of its sub-communities; and something of the historical background behind the foregoing.

Yet further knowledge may be presupposed at this point. Knowing about the country's major industries, for example, requires some understanding of science and technology, and these themselves depend on knowing some mathematics. There is no need to proliferate further examples.

Other things than knowledge may be needed in order to acquire or maintain dispositions. Dispositions themselves, for instance. Higher-order dispositions, like reflectiveness about one's values, require lower-order dispositions, like tolerance or attachments to projects. Similarly, the disposition to reaffirm one's commitment to one's values requires some way in which these values may be presented and re-presented to one. I shall suggest later that the experience of art plays an important role here – as well as in cultivating the reflectiveness just mentioned.

In these ways the content of education can be filled out in more and more detail, working from the general towards the particular. This book is not the place to go exhaustively into this task – although I shall be saying a little more about this when I look at the timetabled curriculum below. But the task is obviously of great importance. It is where work on the British Government's National Curriculum should have begun.

Who should decide content?

As argued in Chapter 1, what the content of school education should be cannot rationally be divorced from questions of what kind of society is held to be desirable. Such questions are political questions and call for political decisions. In a democracy, every citizen has ideally equal power to decide political policy. Leaving the content of school education to be determined by the teaching profession, whether as a whole, or school by school, or as individual teachers, is thus anti-democratic: there is no more reason why the teaching section of the population should make political decisions relevant to the well-being of society as a whole than there is for the armed services to decide defence policy.

This is the case for saying that the broad content and aims of school education should be under political control. It is not an argument for *detailed* political control, only for control over the broad framework of education. There are two reasons why teachers at school level should be empowered to make more specific decisions about content. The first, which derives from the nature of democracy and generates a further democratic criterion which we will touch on again, is that if teachers are, like anyone else, self-determining individuals, as much room as possible should be left, in their professional as well as in their personal life, for their autonomous decision-making. The second is that the more specific decisions about educational content become, the more the teacher is in a good position to make judgements: he or she knows the particular circumstances in which learning takes place – pupils' current levels of achievement, for instance, or obstacles to learning arising from local factors. Both reasons taken together point towards democratic decisions about content being taken at whole school level, and being individually interpreted by each teacher when it comes to still more specific planning.

To say that there should be political control of the broad framework is not to say at what *level* this should occur, eg locally, nationally or supra-nationally. As claimed in Chapter 1, in the case of England, the argument against purely local control is that the society of autonomous individuals which a democratic education policy, along with other political policies, is to promote cannot be confined to, say, Norfolk or Liverpool. We think of ourselves as belonging to a national community because our own identity is bound up with a shared language and culture; and it does not make sense to leave smaller communities with full powers to determine the taxation, housing, health, law and order, education and other policies designed to equip every citizen to lead an autonomous life. This is not to rule out either local decision-making within this framework or some coordination with supra-national policies, eg at a European or whole-world level.

If these arguments are sound, they apply to the education of all children, including those in independent as well as maintained schools. In the Education Reform Act statutory requirements concerning the National Curriculum and its assessment were not extended to independent schools. One might think this entirely in order since independent schools are by definition independent of state control. But we need to make some distinctions here. The independence of independent schools is in the first instance financial: they are funded not by local or central government, but by parents and other private bodies. Financial independence does not entail independence of all other sorts; there are, indeed, good reasons why it should not. Health and safety regulations apply to private as much as to state schools; the same should be true of curricular and other matters. Independent schools should not be free to teach just whatever they want to without constraint. Suppose Eton were taken over by parents committed to the ideals of National Socialism who wanted a Nazi curriculum for their children. If we are inclined to say this should not be allowed, on what grounds do we do so? Presumably we take it that in a liberal democracy what goes on in schools should in some way be constrained by the values of that polity. But once we have accepted this, we should also accept the corollary, that in this regard independent schools are no different from maintained. The basic aims of liberal-democratic education, together with the more specific content that these presuppose, should inform what happens in both. If the timetabled curriculum in maintained schools needs to be state-controlled, then so does the timetabled curriculum in independent schools. But constraints on the latter should be even more extensive. I shall argue below that there is a case for state regulation of schools' internal organization and ethos, as well as of their pedagogy. Again, the case applies to *any* school, not just schools in the maintained sector.[2]

The timetabled curriculum

As far as timetabled activities are concerned, I do not intend to provide a fully fledged alternative to the present National Curriculum. Part of my case against it has been that it has been too hastily put together and the impression has been given that making up the broad outlines of a national curriculum is a pretty simple matter: one merely sets out a list of ten subjects, picks out three of them as 'core', and lays down that all ten subjects with the exception of a modern language will be taught throughout the 11 years of compulsory schooling. But a timetabled national curriculum worked out in line with the values outlined in this book is bound to be far more complex than this. It would require a lengthy process of research, collective deliberation, negotiation and compromise, perhaps within a newly established National Educational Council, to do it justice. This would have to take into account not only ethical and epistemological considerations, but also – to give just a few examples – psychological evidence about children's abilities and motivation; sociological points about the attitudes and expectations of sub-cultures; and administrative considerations about the intellectual equipment which teachers currently possess and how long it would take to equip new generations of teachers to teach a different kind of educational content.

Writers about what a school curriculum should be like often end up with a *list* of essential areas to be covered, whether these are called 'forms of understanding', 'areas of experience' or 'selections from the culture'. Those who were responsible for curriculum planning in schools in the days before the National Curriculum when professionals had much more leeway were often grateful for such lists, since they appeared to give them a systematic, research-validated way of carving up curriculum objectives which they could then apply in their more detailed planning. In the same way, many teachers are now grateful for the clear, simple list of subjects enshrined in the National Curriculum. If I could come up with a list or tidy system of my own – which I can't – I would not be doing teachers and other educationists a service in offering it to them. It might make them think framing a curriculum is easier than it is. Part of my task is, on the contrary, to point out over-simplifications. Yet I do also want to be rather more positive, to say something definite about what the timetabled curriculum should include; but this will have to be indicative rather than comprehensive.

There are certain assumptions made in the National Curriculum which need not be made and which may unduly constrain curriculum planning from the start: first, that national curriculum objectives are to be located within *school subjects*; second, that whatever main curricular units are selected are to be studied throughout each year of compulsory schooling.

There are also other assumptions, some of which *may* lie behind the National Curriculum, which are widely current in the educational world and also get in the way of clear thinking in this area. One is that mathematics is of particular importance in education because it trains children in logical thinking and develops their problem-solving abilities. Some such idea may partly lie behind the elevation of mathematics into 'core subject' status. While it is no doubt true that maths can help to develop logical thinking *within maths* and help children to solve *mathematical* problems, it is a further question whether going deeply into mathematics is particularly useful in thinking logically about current affairs, or in solving, say, the kinds of problems that a teacher faces in his or her day-to-day work in a school. The kind of logical thinking found in mathematics is exact and yields conclusions that follow necessarily from their premises. Most of our logical thinking in other spheres is not like this. Planning a new national curriculum would be a good example. Here we are not dealing with exactitudes but with a mass of complex considerations which have to be weighed against each other in order to generate some avowedly imperfect conclusion about what is to be done. There is no room here for anything like a QED. Indeed, if we *do* bring children up to think that their mathematical training will equip them to solve problems in this way in areas beyond the borders of mathematics, we may be crippling them intellectually rather than empowering them: we may be encouraging them to be dissatisfied with the unavoidable imprecision of much of our practical reasoning and to yearn for a more perfect world where rational thought about any problem will yield the certitudes of mathematics.

Much the same is often said about learning a foreign language. This, too, is supposed to be good for 'training the mind'. In the past Latin particularly was labelled in this way; these days one frequently hears the argument applied to foreign languages more generally. I find this puzzling. At least in learning mathematics one is acquiring a mode of reasoning, doubtful though it may be that this is extendable to other spheres, and one is therewith acquiring new concepts, the concepts of mathematics, which extend one's understanding within that domain. But in learning French or German, neither of these things need apply. For the most part one is learning how to express already assimilated ideas in the words of another language: it is new words, rather than new ideas, that one is acquiring. Of course, learning a new language is not a wholly automatic affair: one has to engage in sophisticated judgments in making sense of what is being said and in making oneself understood. But, again, there are no grounds for believing that being good at *that* kind of thinking is going to be particularly helpful when it comes to working out one's holiday plans or managing a department. None of this is to say, of course, that mathematics and foreign languages should not have a place on the timetable. There may well be better reasons for them than these.

If we try to avoid such illegitimate assumptions which may constrain our thinking about a new timetabled curriculum, how, positively, should we proceed? The general direction must be from the top downwards, from the most general aims through further specification of them down to more detailed objectives at school level. I described above (pp 143–4) something of how one might start to do this. We began from the aim of promoting each child's autonomous well-being, took concern for others' well-being within the national community as one facet of this, and then looked at what kinds of knowledge would be required in order to develop this disposition (eg knowledge of its major industries) and what further knowledge this might bring in its train (eg a knowledge of science and technology).

This is only *one* route from the general to the specific; there are innumerable other threads to trace. Going back over the arguments in earlier chapters of the book may help one to tease these out. The first thing to do is to be as aware as possible of the manifold values which I have brought together under the master-aim of promoting each child's autonomous well-being. Even though I have discussed these at some length in this book, I would be the first to admit that the values I have come up with are still very crude and need further refinement and elaboration. There is much philosophical and sociological work to be done here in distinguishing easily confused values from each other and plotting the logical interrelationships between values. The second curriculum planning task is then to see what kinds of personal qualities and kinds of knowledge and understanding children need to have in order to realize these values. About kinds of knowledge I have said something in Chapter 7. Once again, I am very aware that this is little more than an indication of a direction to follow up, and that it is not a comprehensive survey of what pupils need to know.

To give a further example of the kind of thinking required, let us follow a second downward thread. A personal quality necessary to autonomous well-being is courage. In order to flourish one needs to be able to deal appropriately with one's fears, whether this means withstanding them (eg on the battlefield) or allowing them to motivate one to seek safety (eg in coming across an unleashed Rottweiler in the street). Courage can take different forms. The two examples just given are to do with fears for one's physical safety. However, one can also be afraid, for instance, about what others might think of one if one acts differently from the crowd, or afraid of losing one's job if one stands up to an injustice on the part of one's authorities. To regulate these types of non-physical fear one needs what is often called 'moral' courage. If we have got as far as disentangling this virtue from others – and, again, there is much more that could and should be said about what moral courage involves – we can then ask what kinds of understanding and other dispositions one needs in order to possess it. What seems clearly to be required is some measure of reflective awareness of one's conflicting desires: that on the one hand one wants to be approved of by one's group, yet on the other that one wants to do something which goes against their conventions; or that one wants to keep one's job yet wants to stop an injustice. As well as this awareness, one needs to have acquired the disposition to weigh one kind of desire-satisfaction against another in cases of conflict, and the resoluteness to stick to the desire which reflection tells one is the desire which should outweigh the other. As for what more specific qualities and kinds of understanding a pupil needs to acquire, one has to relate the discussion at this point to the broad types of non-physical fear that living in a society like one's own might be expected to engender. Fear of going against the crowd, or of depressing one's prospects of getting a job or promotion are emotions that are likely to affect us all. So is fear of incurring displeasure or anger in more intimate situations: for example, one needs moral courage in being firm with one's children or in not being patronized by one's husband.

Some understanding of the role of public opinion in a mass society, of the psychology of group-conformity, of authority structures in the workplace, of child-psychology and the purposes of upbringing, and of male domination as a traditional strand in our culture, will be necessary background to being able appropriately to cope with fears of the sorts just mentioned.

A more comprehensive study than this would trace threads not only from beneficence and moral courage, but from the whole complex of ethical values. Let us imagine that we have in front of us such a comprehensive picture: how helpful would it be in determining timetabled activities? It would cover too much, since it would be a map of the content of upbringing as a whole and thus include parental education as well as that part of school education which goes beyond the formal curriculum. Ideally one would want to separate out which forms of learning parents can best promote, and which the schools; and within the latter category, which the timetabled curriculum can best cover, and which other things.

This is an interesting conclusion, since it implies that one cannot properly work out the content of a national curriculum without deciding on the content of parental education. As far as I know, no one has systematically addressed this question, but it should not be an impossible task to sketch out in at least a crude way what the personal qualities and kinds of understanding are for which parents should be responsible. We already have some intuitive idea of this – in, for instance, the views of infant teachers on what dispositions, values and common understanding of their world children are expected to have acquired at home (given variations to do with social class, sub-culture or locality).

How far should this vague notion be sharpened up into a more determinate account of parental responsibilities? There is much spoken and written these days about the qualities required in school teachers – about their knowledge of what they have to teach, their ability to relate to children and get them interested in studying, and their readiness to co-operate with colleagues. These days their strengths and weaknesses are the object of evaluation and assessment by themselves, their colleagues and outside bodies. Central government has recently taken a number of initiatives to assure that teachers are up to the mark. Not everyone will agree with all the specifics, but it would be difficult to deny the general claim that the political community has a legitimate interest in ensuring that teachers are suitably equipped and motivated for their tasks.

If teachers, why not parents? In all the clamour in Britain over the last few years for tighter government control over the school curriculum and standards of teaching, why has there not been a similar call for political monitoring of the content of education within the family and of the standards of parenting? Given especially that what children learn in their early years is of vital importance to their later development, there would seem to be a strong case for the community's trying to ensure that parents lay adequate foundations.

There can be no sharp line separating the content of parental education from that of school education. Both are centrally concerned with the formation, extension and hierarchical ordering of desires and there will be considerable overlap between what home and schools do. Virtues, commitments and attachments encouraged in the family should be reinforced at school, and vice-versa. Where parents for whatever reason fail to promote such things, schools must try to make up the deficiency.

A new national curriculum should focus first, therefore, on personal qualities. Knowledge comes second: what knowledge is deemed of most worth is to be determined by reference to ethical values. The central task of the school, like the central task of the parent, is to build into children the dispositions necessary for a life of autonomous well-being. It is in a position to do this in ways that are often not open to parents. Since it is dealing with many children, not just with one or two, it can put much more emphasis on co-operative group activities of many sorts, with all the attendant benefits in the way of shared goods and the consequent blurring of the line between self-concern and altruism mentioned in Chapter 4. It can help children to cope with the value-conflicts which they will increasingly experience as their world of values enlarges, by the distanced reflection on these that is derived from reading literature and from structured class discussion, perhaps under the heading of 'personal and social education'. Finally, schools can enable children to extend desires they already have so as to encompass new objects. This is made possible by the new types of knowledge and understanding to which schools introduce them. The broad desire to help others may crystallize into wanting to become a doctor or a civil servant, where the pupil acquires some realistic awareness of what such jobs involve from studying science, history or social studies. Similarly, affiliative desires connected with face-to-face groups can be extended into an attachment to one's wider national community and to the liberal democratic values which underlie it: again, this is only possible once the child has attained a certain understanding of what this national community is and of what a democratic system of government involves.

I am aware that there is much more to say about the personal qualities which a school can help to foster. Earlier chapters fill this out a little, but at some point there needs to be a more thoroughgoing study of this whole field. Then our curriculum legislators will be in a better position to say what requirements should be laid on schools in this regard. At all events, it should be recognized that the cultivation of desirable personal qualities should be at the heart of the school's work. As Chapter 7 has shown, we would do well to stop thinking of schooling primarily in terms of knowledge-acquisition. The same is true of a national curriculum. The main content of the latter should be the structuring of desire.

But knowledge-content is obviously important, too, as long as its dependence on ethical values is always kept in mind. This means that we must start from the threads that lead downwards from the latter, not from items plucked out of the air like the foundation subjects of the 1988 National Curriculum, or from Hirstian or other taxonomies of knowledge. Looking back to Chapter 7, what kinds of knowledge did we end up with when we traced through what different values require? Although the discussion there was very schematic and we were dealing with isolated examples rather than a comprehensive picture, the resulting idiosyncratic account may even so be instructive. It included knowing about: different types of physical pleasure and how to attain them; types of friendship; other people's desire-structures and how they came about; forming sexual relationships; types of pain and injury, including sickness and poverty; how such things are caused and how they may be prevented; people's legal and moral rights and the roles of the law, the police and democratic institutions in protecting them; the geography of one's locality, country and other countries; the basic needs of autonomous individuals; groups here and overseas whose basic needs most want attention; the ways in which basic needs can be met, including industries and agriculture, health services, transport and financial services; natural and social obstacles to the satisfaction of needs, ranging from drought to racial oppression; the range of activities which may be chosen for their own sake and how to go about engaging in them; and one's own and other's psychic constitution.

I stress again that this is a very sketchy list of kinds of knowledge. It will obviously not do as it stands as the sum-total of knowledge-requirements for a new national curriculum. But it is interesting, nevertheless, in its overwhelming emphasis on types of knowledge about the human world in which we live. In one way this is not surprising: if one begins with ethical values to do with autonomous well-being, it is precisely knowledge about ourselves, other people, and the communities in which we live which we would expect them to require. Science and mathematics, two of the three core subjects in the 1988 National Curriculum, happen not to have been mentioned in this list.

This does not mean that science and mathematics should have no place in an alternative national curriculum, only that they need in some way to be threaded back to ethical values. Mathematics is necessary, among other things, to science; and science is necessary for the proper understanding of the industrial structure of our own and other societies embedded in the desire to help meet people's material needs. Both disciplines, too, can help to enlarge the range of options from which pupils choose their individual version of a flourishing life: they can each be enjoyed for their own sake; and they can open the door to other activities, including vocational activities.

Still, there is no reason why mathematics and science should be elevated, as 'core' subjects, over curriculum activities which help us more directly to understand and orientate ourselves in the human world in which we live. Indeed, it is with those forms of learning which *do* have this more direct connection that the priority ought to lie. We may call these 'the humanities'. They include the arts, especially literature; work often included under the heading of 'personal and social education' to do with the exploration of ethical values, understanding oneself and others, health education, preparation for democratic citizenship; the study of the social structure, economy and institutions of one's national community; less detailed study of similar features of other political communities and of international relations; and the historical and geographical background required by the last two items.

I have not included in this new humanistic 'core' the study of a modern foreign language, despite its traditional place in school curricula that is reflected in its inclusion as a foundation subject in the 1988 National Curriculum. As argued in Chapter 7, it is not, like the other studies mentioned, a derivable prerequisite of central ethical values in either a constitutive or an attached-instrumental way. Opportunities should exist for pupils to take up Russian, Arabic, Spanish or other languages on a voluntary basis if they wish, but I see no good reason, English being the leading world language, why a modern language should be compulsory. It is indeed essential that British children come to learn a lot about other countries, not least about the other countries of Europe, East as well as West, with which our national life is becoming increasingly intertwined. It makes much more sense that they leave school with a sympathetic understanding of an array of foreign cultures and communities, including what they can glean through foreign literature in translation, than that they leave with the smatterings of one other language. The 1988 National Curriculum requires a large slice of the timetable to be given to the latter, far more than can be available for the former – this makes no sense.

Among the new 'core' areas I have included the arts, especially literature. I wish now to say a few words about this area in particular. Of the classical trinity of human ideals – Truth, Beauty and Goodness – while the first and third have been the objects of much of this book, it has so far said nothing about the second, or about the relationships between all three. The following section will, I hope, make up a little for this deficiency, underlining, as it does, the pivotal role that the arts can play in the content of education and the school curriculum.

The arts in the curriculum

First, a clarification. I have been discussing an alternative national curriculum under the headings of 'personal qualities' and 'kinds of knowledge'. Recommendations about the humanities have come up under the second of these headings. Yet there are difficulties, well worked-over in the literature of the philosophy of education, about calling the arts a form of *knowledge*. This is especially so if one has propositional knowledge in mind. While studying history or science straightforwardly involves acquiring well-founded beliefs that such and such is the case, coming to enjoy the Pastoral Symphony is not to be confronted with a proposition or a complex of propositions. Despite this, in some respects involvement in the arts at school *can* enlarge one's knowledge, even though this is not the sole reason for its importance.

We need to look a little more closely at the role the arts can play in cultivating autonomous well-being. An adequate treatment of the topic would fill another book, but here are a few pointers. An obvious rationale for the arts lies in their contribution to the enlargement of options. For many people, the enjoyment of music, painting and literature is of major importance in their hierarchy of personal values: schools should see to it that pupils are not cut off from these as possible sources of intrinsic value for themselves, but sensitively introduced to them. The stress here should be on the whole world of painting, music and literature – that is on pupils' becoming acquainted with a great number of works of art and the artistic traditions from which these have been born. Teaching children to produce paintings, poems and pieces of music themselves may also have some place, but it lacks the priority which should be given to acquaintance with the works of others. This is so even if one imagines someone for whom writing poetry, as distinct from reading it, is to become a major life option: the ability to write poetry depends on having some understanding of what poetry is and the traditions which have informed it; and one does not need to have tried one's hand at poetry at school in order to write poetry in later life.

Enlarging the range of options to be pursued for their own sake is thus one way in which the arts can further autonomous well-being. Another way is in opening doors to further options, including vocational ones. I am thinking here of all the careers and leisure activities which have a foundation in the arts.

It may be said that this justification of the arts in terms of extending options puts them on all fours with other possible curriculum activities which do the same thing. Science and mathematics can do this, as we have seen, and so can any other area of learning you might like to mention – including not only such familiar curriculum items as history or domestic science, but also, for instance, rock-climbing, coin-collecting or bee-keeping, since getting immersed in all these things can open up new option-horizons.

While this is in one way true, one should not forget the extraordinary priority which enjoyment of the arts plays in so many people's lives. This is not surprising when one thinks of the enormous *delight* which art can give us – so immediately and often with so little struggle – as compared with many other intellectual or practical activities. This is not to say that every pupil *must* make the arts a priority, only that we have good grounds for claiming that, if exposed to them, many of them *will* do so. There is reason enough here to lay especial weight on the arts in the curriculum, in so far as we are considering the enlargement of options.

But we need to go beyond the latter consideration. The arts have another rationale too, a rationale which helps to explain this remarkable attachment which so many people have to them.

Values in art are manifold. Some have to do with its sensuous and formal properties: we delight in the perceptual experiences which it reveals to us, in their contrasts and affinities, and in the ways in which they can fit together within a satisfying whole. However, works of art and especially, but not exclusively, literary works, can also have a more intimate connection with personal well-being.

Art unlocks emotions in one – emotions of horror, pity, pride, joy, love. It does so by working on one's imagination: one's horror at the execution scene in Goya's painting *Fusilamientos del 2 de Mayo* is felt from the standpoint of an eyewitness, in whose shoes one finds oneself. Art releases in this way a number of mental powers – the imagination, emotions, perceptual abilities, memories. The greater the work, the more many-sided this release, as more layers of meaning are revealed to us and more associations evoked in us.

Art breaks through the crust of our conventional ways of thinking and behaving, and through our ordinary practical involvement in our affairs. In setting free these other powers it gives us a sense of increased vitality. That in itself might be thought enough to show its value to us.

But this is only half the story. Art liberates, yet it guides at the same time. The releasing of our natural powers takes us closer to the unbounded multifariousness of our experience. We take pleasure in exercising our powers in a spontaneous, unfettered way. In satisfying these desires so deeply implanted in us, art contributes directly to our well-being. But we also have within us an opposite kind of desire – to establish some kind of order among our desires. We are driven from multiplicity in the direction of unity, trying to arrange our desires in priorities of importance. In this task none of us succeeds completely. Conflicts occur at more than one point – from the imperfections of our prioritizings, where a desire we acknowledge to be of higher value to us confronts a recalcitrant desire of lesser value; and from irresolvable tensions between our most important desires themselves. With the first sort of conflict we, or our educators, can do something to minimize it: we can in principle acquire strength of will. But there is nothing we can do, beyond a certain point, in the second realm. It may be impossible for me to be both an artist and a man of affairs; to be fully responsive both to the loyalties which claim me and to my personal projects; to see the world as objectively as possible on the one hand and from my own subjective perspective on the other; to want to be part of the world and to be separate from it – an ephemeral traveller through it. We are beyond the remediation of ethics, but art can still help us. It cannot resolve such conflicts, in the sense of dissipating them – by showing us, perhaps, that one value is to be elevated over another. But it can also cause us to see and feel these conflicts more sharply. In everyday life the tensions affect us in varying degrees, from unease through to despair, but they are rarely the object of our focal attention: their very painfulness to us is likely to prevent them from becoming so. Art enables us to come to grips with them and somehow to cope with them. Once again, it can do this by working on our imagination: we experience the tensions in what we see as the artist's soul, or in those of the characters he or she creates. In this way we approach our own conflicts by contemplating their counterparts in others; and here we do not merely contemplate them, but experience them within the framework of the work itself. The work contains them and enables them to co-exist within a unity, a formal structure. This helps us to reconcile ourselves to the ineluctability – we see our tensions as something we have to live with, something we can hold together within the framework of our own life. A work of art comes to stand proxy in this way for our own life.

These fundamental conflicts, although differing in detailed substance, are common to us all. In seeing them mirrored in works of art we come to experience them not as irredeemably private, but as common. In this way, art binds us to others, sometimes just within our culture, sometimes more broadly. The modern autonomous person, but not the heteronomous member of a traditional society, is riven by the knowledge that choices in one direction close off options in another: via the novel one can make up for this vicariously, by dwelling within characters from very different walks of life. However, being forced to do evil whatever choice one makes creates conflicts for everyone and not only for the autonomous, and in this way the binding power of its expression in art can be more extensive – as in Agamemnon's tragedy, for example.

Because art gives public expression in this way to private feeling, it can help us to cope with one of the conflicts I have mentioned – ie between being part of the world and being separate from it. If I am separate, I am not atomically so: I am at the same time bound within a whole. Yet

I do not lose myself within the whole: I remain, and want to remain, a separate individual. Experience of art can help me to recognize this tension, to accept the inevitability of oscillating between the two poles of my being.

I have mentioned art's power to lead us both towards the rich particularity of our experience and towards psychic unity. Here we have another fundamental tension, perhaps the most fundamental of all. We want life, spontaneity, and wealth of sensory and emotional experience; and we want boundedness, order and framework. We cannot go all the way in one direction: we cannot become purely rational beings, or gods. We need multiplicity of experience, yet it needs to be ordered; and we need substance to our orderliness of soul which only our sensuous, animal nature can provide. A work of art, by embodying this tension within itself, can help us to hold these two opposites together. It shows us how it can be done.

Art is the coping side of the ethical life. Like it, it recognizes the plurality of our values; like it, it seeks reconciliation and harmony where these are possible, but not when they are not. Where art goes beyond the ethical is in creating imagined frameworks in which some kind of aesthetic harmony is found between the most irreconcilable of conflicts. This is the best it, or anything, can do for us. In this way art helps to preserve us from false guides, which would have us believe that a higher perfection than this is possible – that conflict can be eradicated by eliminating value-plurality and setting up one value as supreme. Art preserves us from the false harmonies of religion and of Utopian politics.

It is often said that in our age art has come to take the place of religion. We can see why this should be said. Human beings need a framework within which to fit all their desires: they cannot tolerate fundamental incoherences. In the past, religion has helped them to make sense of this aspect of their lives: it has taught them, for instance, that this life, with all its contradictions, is not the most important life – that the perfect, fully harmonious, life is still to come. Today fewer and fewer of us can accept this kind of story: we see our lives as unique and bounded by our death. Yet we still need a vehicle through which to reconcile ourselves to what we are. We can find this in our experience of art.

I have dwelt on art's role in helping us to cope with fundamental desire-conflicts. In doing so, it makes us more keenly aware of the desires which are opposed. In this way, as has been often remarked, it can both affirm our attachment to these desires and, sometimes, cause us to jettison desires to which we have previously adhered.

It can thus perform another important educational function, since pupils need not only to acquire new desires but also to continue to be committed to them and to reflect, in some cases, on their acceptability.

There needs, therefore, to be some kind of vehicle – or vehicles – to ensure that this takes place. Art is one such vehicle.

In its conservative function, of reinforcing values, art can equip us with confidence in the broad acceptability of our desires. It is all too easy, amid the confusion about moral or ethical values described in earlier chapters, to lose confidence in what we value, to feel that it needs further support or, failing that, that it emanates only from our prejudices. But confidence is what we need. It is a mistake to think that our deepest values *can* be rationally supported; but this does not mean that they are no more than prejudices, and are thus arbitrary and replaceable. If a person will not accept without further reasons that concern for others is a good thing, those reasons cannot be provided for them. Altruism has no rational foundation, but that is no reason to be suspicious of it, to see it as some arbitrary commitment on the part of a person or their culture. We are brought up, rightly, to accept altruism, along with love of sensory pleasures and all the other values I have dwelt on in this book, as the mainspring of our personal and communal life. We need constantly to be recalled to this taken-for-granted world, to hold fast to it. Art helps us to do this in a manner beyond the powers of philosophy or religion.

About how it does this I have said something already. But I need to underline again the publicness of art, the fact that poems, paintings, pieces of music are objects to which we can all gain access and which provide us with common reaffirmations of our values. Not that we all experience the same things from works of art. We each approach them with personal systems of value which differ in detail if not in broad outline, and with different recent backgrounds of degrees of closeness to or distance from our deepest attachments. Works of art are themselves many-layered and many-faceted – great ones most noticeably so – and this gives them the power to engage with us in our differences. Underlying this variation in our experience and response are common values to which we all broadly adhere and which we find expressed in art. Art gives us ethical confidence not only through its reaffirmations, but also through its publicness. It reminds us that our values are not *just* our values, belonging to us as individuals: they are our inheritance from a common culture.

There are analogies between works of art and human beings: we hold both to be, in different ways, intrinsically valuable; both are the locus of a complex plurality of instantiated values and of conflicts and balances between them; both can be the object of an affection that develops with acquaintance. It is because of this affinity between art and our nature that experience of the former has a role in education which goes far beyond its value as an optional activity for those who prefer it to other things. Art is necessary for everyone, because self-knowledge – in its practical aspect

– is necessary for everyone. We saw in Chapter 5 that the autonomous people we have in mind need, for the sake of their own well-being, to be closely in touch with their own structures of desire, including their feelings; and not to be confused or mistaken about their priorities, or in other ways self-deceived. In its power to reveal ourselves to ourselves, and thereby to confirm us in what we take ourselves most deeply to be, and also in our sense that our values are not idiosyncratically our own, but shared with countless others across space and time, art is an unparalleled vehicle of self-understanding, and so of education.

How indispensable is art to our autonomous well-being? If there were no art in the world, could anything else take its place? Could we in principle eliminate experience of art from the content of education and replace it by something that did the same job? Many of us will know people whose existence has no place for it, but who lead thoroughly worthy and fulfilled lives, attached to friends and family, the larger community, their work, and their leisure interests. Their daily contact with others, their conversation and their private reflection, perhaps reinforced by philosophical reading, may be enough to maintain them in the attachment to their values and reflectiveness about them which I mentioned as one role of the arts. But what can they do to match its other role – ie that of providing frameworks within which our most irreconcilable conflicts of value can be contained in some kind of aesthetic unity? If they cannot accept religious forms of reconciliation, what is there left to them?

I have argued that experience of art is a constituent feature of our well-being and not simply one option among others. This is enough to ensure it an important place in education, but this may not be its only place. Viewed only as a pleasurable activity, it is also something which some people would prefer to fill more of their lives than others do. The weaker argument for art, that it should figure in the range of options to which the autonomous person in the making is to be introduced, still stands. There is no need for the liberal's anxiety about the apparent impossibility of developing in pupils a love of art shallow enough to be jettisoned if art is not chosen as an option, and yet not so deep that it unduly sways them in their autonomous choosing. For a love of art is also, for other reasons, to be seen as a desirable – and permanent – disposition to be cultivated in everyone.

Education in the arts is thus not important only because it enlarges options. This still leaves the arts as a dispensable element in the good life. The unparalleled contribution of the arts to self-knowledge gives them an even stronger title to curricular importance. If the arts are irreplaceable as helpmeet in the ethical life, educators are on firm ground in bringing pupils up to see their flourishing as embodying within it a love of the arts. This implies a further shaping which educators should give to the concept of personal well-being in its most abstract form: love of art as well as personal autonomy and care for others should all be built into it as constituents.

The Gulbenkian Report of 1982, *The Arts in Schools*, embraced a curricular egalitarianism about the arts in particular which we have already seen cause to reject more generally. 'The arts are crucial elements in a balanced curriculum: not more, nor less, but certainly as important as other forms of knowledge.'(p 28) Leaving aside problems about whether they are forms of knowledge, the Report is obviously trying to give the arts a solid stake in the curriculum at a time when scientific and technological pressures pose a threat to them: if one could show that the arts were on all fours with science, this would be a valuable achievement. Nevertheless, some of us may still be left wondering how far the Gulbenkian Report is not, even so, *selling the arts short*. Their intimate connection with self-knowledge and personal well-being give them a curricular importance which mathematics, say, or science could not hope to rival.

The timetabled curriculum: conclusion

To be in line with democratic requirements the alternative national curriculum will be built in the ways suggested around personal qualities, various types of knowledge, and experience of the arts. Its core will be humanistic – science, mathematics and technology being less salient than in the 1988 version.

Academic subjects should not be the only foci of classroom activity. As David Hargreaves (1982) has persuasively argued, in proposals echoed in his ILEA Report *Improving Secondary Schools*, practical and collective activities have been undeservedly downgraded *vis-à-vis* 'higher culture'. If such things as co-operation for shared ends, self-confidence, social recognition and imaginativeness in devising means to ends are among the central aims of education, there is every reason why home economics, craft, design and technology, projects in the local community, work experience, drama and sports should be accorded great importance in schools.

Personal and social education (PSE) is also most important. The ideals of many of the enthusiasts for PSE are close, I would suggest, to those put forward in this book. Those who argue for its values to permeate the whole work of the school are on strong ground: there should be no rift between the 'academic' side of the school and the 'personal/social' side, since academic aims should be underpinned by a concern for the pupils' well-being. At the same time there is a place among timetabled activities for work which focuses explicitly on the pupils' lives – on their values, commitments, attachments, ambitions and conflicts. This need not only be the PSE lesson, of course: English teachers in particular have always seen this work as part of their role. So have most primary teachers.

I have not said anything about how much time needs to be devoted to each area. That is a complicated question. An area which is less central may require more of the timetable than something more central: the physical sciences, for instance, as compared with sex education. In addition, the cultivation of personal qualities will often go *pari passu* with the acquisition of knowledge: the aims will not be competing against each other for a slice of the timetable. How much time should be allocated across the years and within particular years can only be determined when the whole complex picture of curricular priorities has been fitted together. Short of this what part, if any, central government should play in this is difficult to say.

As for more detailed objectives, these lie outside the broad scope of this book. I will only refer, once again, to the inadequacies of the 1988 Curriculum. As the different working groups on foundation subjects have produced their reports, there has been predictable disagreement with many of the recommendations, both from government and from educationists. It is difficult to see what criteria these groups can have relied on in reaching their conclusions. How does one work out what specific targets there should be in history, English, mathematics, science or geography without a more adequate set of overall aims than the two or three lines given in the Education Reform Act? Detailed objectives and a fully elaborated account of educational aims go together: it is only when we have the latter that we can sensibly proceed to the former.

Which of the more detailed objectives are to be laid down centrally and which should be left to schools and teachers to decide is a further question. How specific should the nationally prescribed objectives be? It is typical of current government initiatives that they never apparently looked at this, but appear to have assumed that objectives can be as specific as the Secretary of State chooses. We need to shun such arbitrariness and look for sensible criteria. Various initial considerations are these. In some cases specific objectives are logically entailed in more general ones: if some understanding of trigonometry is demanded, pupils have to know what cosines are. In other cases there may be more freedom for schools to decide on specifics: if one of the more general objectives is some understanding of twentieth-century European history, there can be different weights given to sub-objectives beneath this general rubric: one syllabus may include more on Ramsay MacDonald's National Government and less on the *front populaire* in France, and vice versa. In cases like these, I would suggest as one guiding principle that the more specific the objectives become, and thus the more routes become available for realizing the more general aims, the less reason there is for political rather than professional control.

Backing this suggestion are, once again, considerations about auto-nomy. The ideal of 'autonomy for all' applies, among other persons, to teachers. There is also a role-reason, not applicable to other jobs, why teachers should be autonomous agents: we know that children tend to learn by example and if they see that their teachers have plenty of scope in what they do rather than minutely following the instructions of higher authority, their own taste for self-directed activity is likely to be stimulated.

Pedagogy and assessment

State control of the content of school education should go further than laying down the objectives of the timetabled curriculum. Certain forms of pedagogy are at odds with democratic requirements. Schooling based predominantly on rote-learning, on the inculcation of obedience and the discouragement of independent thought is clearly not conducive to fostering personal autonomy. This is not to say that there can never be any place for such procedures, but in a democratic system the onus is against them and a convincing case would have to be made out for adopting them. Teaching should be encouraging, confidence-building, always ready to reward independence of thought and action. If children are to become self-determining adults, they must have some experience of self-determination – eg in the choice of what they are to learn, or when – on the way to this end. This is not at all to say that children must choose their whole curriculum: they are not intellectually equipped to do this while young. But *some* experience of making choices, perhaps increasing with age, there must surely be. One way of encouraging this self-directedness – and this brings us back to the timetabled curriculum – would be by allocating a part of the latter to voluntary rather than compulsory activities, thus giving pupils the chance to pursue personal projects and commitments in some depth. I have long held that one of the attractive features of traditional Soviet education has been the division of the pupil's day into compulsory school activities and voluntary attendance at Young Pioneer's 'circles' where a wide range of academic, practical and aesthetic activities is provided. It is also interesting to see that the reforms embedded in *A Conception of General School Education* allow older children to choose their own subjects for up to a quarter of the timetabled amount of time.

If pupils are to be encouraged to see others' flourishing as inextricably entwined with their own, pedagogy as well as curriculum content can be harnessed to this end. This speaks against treating children always as isolated learners and for engaging them where appropriate in a variety of shared activities and projects. These include many of the practical activities favoured by David Hargreaves and mentioned in the last section; but they go beyond them, since the teaching of even traditional academic subjects like mathematics can be based on shared as well as individual experience.

Assessment of learning must also be in line with democratic objectives. This clearly sanctions formative or diagnostic assessment, since their aim is to facilitate children's learning and bolster their confidence. But there is no place for the kind of publicly recorded summative assessment accompanying the English National Curriculum and taking place at ages 7, 11, 14 and 16. There is no democratic purpose that this serves. There is nothing to suggest that it will promote the well-being of *every* pupil, although *some* may benefit, either by the confidence-boosting knowledge that they have done well in comparison with others or by going to the more favoured schools which will be separated out from others by this device. Correspondingly, other children are likely to be worse off in one or other of these dimensions.

The great weakness of the 1988 national assessment arrangements is that they fail to recognize the ethical tension between diagnostic/formative assessment and summative assessment at 7, 11, 14, and 16 years. Whereas the former is wholly beneficial to learners, the latter may in some cases not do them any good at all. In particular, it may not be good for many slower children to have it borne in on them that they are, say, only at Level 2 when most of their peers are already at Level 5. This tension was obscured from the very inception of a national assessment scheme, even before the Task Group on Assessment and Testing (TGAT) began its work in 1987, for the minister's letter of guidance to this group stressed that he was looking for a single system which met a number of different objectives, both those to do with the improvement of learning through diagnostic/formative assessment and those to do with evaluating the achievements of different schools via summative assessment at different ages. That these purposes might be in tension with each other was never mentioned. It was assumed, rather, that they would *cohere* together rather than conflict: the letter talks of how they 'interrelate with and complement each other' (para 7). In taking on its terms of reference TGAT committed itself to this conflict: the TGAT Report advocated a multiple-purpose single system of assessment which was immediately adopted as government policy.

An alternative system needs to detach these multiple purposes from each other. There is every reason why there should be central regulations about diagnostic and formative assessment: these should be clearly laid down as part of the teacher's contractual role, and steps should be taken to ensure that every teacher is properly trained to carry them out. But there are no good reasons why children should be summatively assessed at 7, 11, 14 and 16 years and therefore, in my opinion, these tests should be scrapped.

But if national summative assessments are ruled out, what will guarantee, a critic may ask, that children progress at a satisfactory rate through the various levels of their learning? What will prevent children in one school or one area from lagging behind comparable pupils elsewhere?

The reply must be that it has not been shown that national testing is the best way of pursuing this goal. There are other ways, ways which avoid the inadequacies of national testing. The most promising is assessment of schools. They can be evaluated on how far they are meeting nationally laid down objectives, including those to do with ethos, organization and pedagogy as well as timetabled curricula. It may be that many of these national standards are not minutely determinate, leaving scope, as I said above, for autonomous teachers to devise their own routes in order to meet them. Schools must have specific objectives, of course, even if these are not centrally prescribed. What could and in my view should be so prescribed is that schools must be able to justify their specifics by reference to defensible wider educational aims, as well as in terms of their suitability to local conditions, including the interests and abilities of their pupils. Like formative assessment of pupils, school evaluation of this kind directly serves educational ends. It does not have to do with sorting institutions out into more popular and less popular, but with helping teachers to see and to articulate the long chain of connections between the minutest of their day-to-day goals and the widest considerations about personal well-being and the good society. All this could go with a central requirement that each school have an adequate system of teacher appraisal.

In so far as another reason for age-related tests is that parents need to be kept in the picture about their children's progress, again there could well be other and humaner ways of meeting this entirely reasonable demand. More resources could be ploughed into ways of increasing contacts between home and school. Cumulative records of achievement, private to pupils and parents, could chart children's progress in all sorts of fields, including intellectual achievements and successes outside the classroom. There is no reason why national regulations should not be extended to make a record of achievement scheme a legal obligation on every school.

In a system like the British, where compulsory education is shared between primary and secondary schools, ways must be found, in the interests of efficiency, of ensuring that the two institutions concerned with the education of any one child coordinate their curricular and other educational objectives. There may be a case for moving away, in time, from the British system of multiple feeder primary schools to the all-age schools that are common in many parts of Eastern and Western Europe.

Until then some less tidy solution must be found. But the problem is not so massive that it needs a system of national testing at 11 to crack it.

The government's critics have rightly emphasized the complexity and cost of the national assessment arrangements. We do not need the complexity, and we need not spend so much money. For once we can turn the Tories' slogans back on themselves. The costly bureaucratic structure which they are creating should be dismantled. Those whom it burdens, both pupils and their teachers, must be liberated.

This is not at all an argument against central political control of the content of education. In many areas we need *new* forms of control. Overall, we need something far lighter and better engineered than our present top-heavy vehicle.

School organization and ethos

We have already touched on the point that democratic principles apply not only at the level of national or local political participation, but also at the level of the workplace. For here, too, decisions have to be made which affect the well-being of all who work there; and in so far as they are autonomous persons the latter should have equal power in making them and seeing them implemented. How far pupils themselves may participate in this depends on their level of maturity as far as autonomy goes, as well as on their competence in particular areas. Pupils apart, the presumption must be that all staff, including non-teaching staff, should be equal members of this democratic community. Many decisions, including some educational decisions – to do, for instance, with the attitudes of adults to children or the non-tolerance of racial abuse – are within the legitimate purview of this larger group. Other decisions – for instance about the organization of the curriculum – must obviously be restricted to the teaching staff as being within their competence alone.

School-level democracy is important not only from the point of view of its participants as self-determining individuals, but also because it may be expected to help pupils to understand and appreciate something of democratic values and procedures, thus fostering their development as democratic citizens.

There are also democratic criteria applicable to the ethos of the school. Its rules and procedures should be framed in accordance with democratic requirements. Thus the demeaning of staff and pupils by racial or sexual discrimination should not be allowed; and neither should forms of organization like streaming in so far as these are known to generate feelings of self-depreciation among least favoured groups.

A national educational council

One last suggestion about democratic constraints. This government has set up a National Curriculum Council, appointed by the Secretary of State, to keep all aspects of the curriculum under review. This needs replacing by a more democratic national education council with a wider remit. The timetabled school curriculum is only one vehicle of education. A more widely focused body would be concerned also with school ethos and pedagogy, and perhaps with parental education and the influence of the media, the legal system and other social institutions. It would not be the tool of a particular government but a quasi-independent public body responsible for recommending aims and overseeing their translation into more specific objectives. It could include representatives drawn from the government of the day, members of the public and professional educators, and be protected from government mishandling by a code of educational principles premised on the constitution of a liberal–democratic state.

Conclusion

These are some ways in which democratic criteria can be applied to the content of school education. No doubt they are not exhaustive; and some may be more controversial than others. There is a strong case for insisting that national curriculum policy, taking this in the wide sense used in this chapter, be built around considerations such as these, so that they become mandatory on all schools. (Again, this applies to fee-paying as well as maintained schools.)

Comparing England with the USSR, it seems that in many ways the latter's current curriculum plans are more in line with democratic requirements than the former's. To many it will seem ironic that the nation which most prides itself on its democratic traditions is now lagging behind a country long associated with autocracy or authoritarianism.

Notes

Introduction

1.   See my 'An unconstitutional National Curriculum' in D Lawton and C Chitty (eds), *The National Curriculum*, Bedford Way Paper 33 (Institute of Education, University of London, 1988).

2.   Throughout the book I mean by 'education' upbringing. In this I follow my practice in White, 1982. On alternative conceptions of education and on the limitations of conceptual analyses of the term, see op.cit. pp 3–6; also Warnock, M, 1977, pp 11ff.

3.   Whereas until the early 1970s ethics operated at an extremely abstract level, concentrating mainly on higher-order, or 'meta-', questions about the logic of the term 'good' or about whether moral judgments can be said to be true or false, Anglo-American ethics – especially American – has for the last 15 years or so turned its attention also to more substantive and practical concerns. Some examples, referred to in this book, are Rawls, 1972; Nagel, 1979; Smart and Williams, 1973; Nozick, 1974; Walzer, 1983; MacIntyre, 1981; Hare, 1981; Dent, 1984; Taylor, 1985; Raz, 1986; Griffin, 1986; Williams, 1972, 1981, 1985. The American journal *Philosophy and Public Affairs* and the British *Journal of Applied Philosophy* are also products of this period.

4.   See the works by Rawls, MacIntyre, Taylor, Raz, Griffin, and Williams (1985) above.

Chapter One: The aims of education in the liberal democratic state

1. See J Raz, 1986, ch 5. I have found Raz's book invaluable for the argument of my first chapter and have drawn on it at several points.

2. I here follow a suggestion in Raz, 1986, p 136.

3. The categories 'moral framework' and 'welfare' are only very rough. They may overlap. Later in the book I abandon this whole way of thinking. Aspects of what is here the 'moral framework' become a *part* of personal well-being, not a frame around it. Other aspects join 'welfare' to form part of our 'basic needs'.

4. As far as I am aware the Thatcher moves towards a national curriculum owe no explicit allegiance to neutralist liberal principles. I leave on one side Conservative onslaughts on peace education. Since security against external attack is one of the deepest foundations on which personal well-being is built, it would be entirely consonant with the welfare aims permitted by neutralism to urge that the government should include work on this topic in its national curriculum proposals.

    I would suggest that present Conservative thinking about education is *not* based on liberal principles at all but has quite another basis. At present there are two strands in Conservative thinking – the 'Scrutonian' strand which emphasizes traditional academic subjects, and the 'Keith Joseph' strand which stresses the needs of the economy. What both views have in common is élitism. The first group would like the country to be run by an intellectual élite, the second by businessmen. Élitism of these sorts or any other sort offends against liberalism in privileging a certain view of the good life over others – ie the conception of the good life favoured by the élite. See also Chapter 8.

5. On the disconnection between autonomy and personal well-being, see Raz, 1986, p 369. He makes it clear that the ideal of personal autonomy belongs to 'a particular conception' of individual well-being.

6. For an example of an ethical theory where liberty is taken as an ultimate moral principle, see R S Peters, 1967.

7. A fuller account of personal well-being will be given in Chapter 2.

Chapter Two: Personal well-being

1. For a fuller account of informed desires, see Griffin, 1986, pp 11ff.

2. In White, J, 1982, pp 39ff, I came down in favour of defining personal well-being in terms of 'post-reflective desire-satisfaction'. I now think that was misguided, as I had not sufficiently separated out personal well-being in general from the personal well-being of an autonomous person. See note 4 below.

3. On higher-order desires, see H Frankfurt 'Freedom of the will and the concept of a person' in Frankfurt, 1988; C Taylor 'What is human agency?' in Taylor, 1985.

4. In White, J, 1973 I did try to derive practical recommendations from a very formal account, being especially concerned about the danger of imposing personal preferences. I was less clear than I am now that I was, however, writing personal autonomy into personal well-being, the latter being seen as a function of what an agent chooses on reflection, having been acquainted with an array of different options. Allowing the agent to choose a non-autonomous way of life (p 23) still left self-determination as an essential element in the concept of well-being. In that book I also began to see (pp 84–7) that my approach made it difficult to cultivate relatively permanent dispositions in pupils to do with their own well-being: at most the argument seemed to justify equipping them only for reflective choice.

   In White, J, 1982 I changed my mind on personal autonomy, writing it into the concept of personal well-being, for reasons given on pp 50–1 (see also pp 40–1). I now think this is too strong, as I explained in Chapter 1: personal autonomy is a feature of well-being in societies like ours, but not others. This does not make it culturally relative in any pernicious sense. It is not something we can jettison as an arbitrary social imposition, once we have seen how it originated: we are part of a culture which is irremediably reflective and whose institutions presuppose self-determination. (See also Williams, 1985, p 163: 'There is no route back from reflectiveness.') Given this, the argument I used in White, J, 1982, p 51 in favour of autonomy still stands, given that it is socially located in this way, and not connected with writing autonomy into well-being.

   Also in that book I suggested that the notion of personal well-being needed to be 'enlarged' so as to include one's moral responsibilities (pp 95ff). This was a further move away from the formal account in the earlier book. I now think this move, although in the right direction, will not do. As I developed it, I made one's own well-being consist in 'leading a life of moral virtue' (p 98). It will become clear from Chapters 3 and 4 below why I no longer think this is true.

Chapter Three: Beyond moral education?

1. See Nagel, 1986, pp 206–7 for discussion of the suggestion that political institutions could 'make it possible for us to lead rich personal lives without denying the impersonal claims that derive from the needs of our billions of fellow inmates'.

2. See Harman, 1977, pp 110–111; Scheffler, 1982, pp 112–3.

3. For classical examples of each of the three theories, see Kant, 1785; Mill, 1861; Rawls, 1972. For introductory discussion of these and other ethical views, see Feldman, 1978. More advanced critiques of all three are found in Williams, 1985. On Kant, see also Aune, 1979; on utilitarianism, Quinton, 1973; Smart and Williams, 1973.

4. On ethical subjectivism and cultural relativism see Williams, 1972, pp 28–51. Feldman, 1978 gives a good introduction to relativism, emotivism and prescriptivism. See also Warnock, 1967 and Hudson, 1983.

5. For critical discussions, see notes 3 and 4 above.

6. For a fuller account of post-Enlightenment ethics see MacIntyre, 1981, chs 1–6.

7. Among recent works which stress the role of the virtues in the ethical life and in upbringing generally are Warnock, 1971, ch 6; MacIntyre, 1981; Dent, 1984; Tobin, 1986. These writers are working within an Aristotelian tradition. See Aristotle, *Nicomachean Ethics*. It is Aristotle who first examined the role of intelligent, flexible response in the acquisition and practice of the virtues. See op. cit., Bks 2, 6.

8. On the rise of views of ethics based on the concepts of law and obligation and replacing Greek emphases on the virtues and on well-being, see Anscombe, 1958; Williams, 1985, ch 10.

9. By attachment to one's national community I do not mean chauvinism. One need not believe that one's nation is *better* in some way than other nations. Neither does this attachment necessarily involve attachment to a particular linguistic/cultural group. It does for the Hungarians and Estonians, but not for the Belgians or Swiss, owing to their multiple languages, or for the British (the inhabitants of Great Britain), partly also because other languages than English are spoken, but more because English is the chief language of a number of other nations. What I *do* have in mind is attachment to the national community in the sense of a *political*

community, ie that community with a 'national' parliament, legal system, etc, which provides a framework in which much of our economic and social life takes place. It is for this latter reason that we can develop an attachment to the whole that makes this life possible for us. As will become clear from later chapters, I do not mean this in any individualistic way. It is not just that it is good for *me* to live within this framework: it is good for *us* who live within it; it is one of the institutions – along with the family, local community, work community etc – which binds us each to each.

In a century desecrated by chauvinism it is not surprising that many of us recoil against the suggestion that national attachments should be strengthened. But we would do well to make the kinds of distinctions just made. We need national sentiment in my sense as a condition of our own individual identity. It could well be a part of our common conception of our nation that it prides itself on *not* feeling superior to other nations, that it is well-disposed towards them and ready to help those of them in need – or to be helped by others if in need itself.

The British people face two particular obstacles, not shared by some other groups, in developing a national sentiment in this benign sense. One is due to the legacy not only of chauvinism (eg 'The British are better than the Germans'), but also of imperialism and racism (eg 'The British are a superior race compared with the Bantu (or the Indians etc)'). The difficulty here is that while the first of these is an attitude towards the national community in my sense, the second goes beyond this since the group to which one feels attached includes British people in other continents, and now in other nations. Although we do sometimes feel warm towards 'Britain' or 'the British people' in a benign sense, localized to our political community, it is hard for us not to be unaffected by these wider, and less benign, associations.

The second obstacle is that, even as a localized political community, we do not know where we begin or end. Is Scotland a separate nation? Even if, as I am inclined to do, we see Britain as the national political community, there is still the question of Northern Ireland or of the Six Counties, depending on the national perspective from which one views it.

All this is of obvious relevance for British education: if preparation for democratic citizenship is a worthy aim, as it surely is, then of what are pupils to become citizens?

Nothing in what I have written here implies that we should not work for, and educate for, supra-national attachments, eg to a European Community. We can have, and we need, attachments at all sorts of levels, from our family to humanity as a whole. Neither does it rule out the possible desirability of the future erosion of national communities within larger units. But at least for the foreseeable future we will continue to live out our lives, for the most part, within the framework of the nation state, and will have to bring up our children with that in mind.

10. I am assuming I can bypass any libertarian objections that this is undesirable because all imposition of 'adult values' on children is wrong. Given my position on liberty in Chapter 1, I would argue that liberty is valuable as a necessary condition of personal autonomy. Since young children are not yet autonomous, I follow Mill (1859) in excluding them from the scope of the principle of liberty. We need to impose 'adult values' on them in order that they *become* autonomous. 'Imposition' here should not be taken as implying coercion, if this is to be associated with a regime of fear or brutality.

11. See note 1.

12. On the diversity of ethical values, see C Taylor 'The diversity of goods' in Taylor, 1985, Vol 2; T Nagel 'The fragmentation of value' in Nagel, 1979; B Williams 'Conflicts of value' in Williams, 1981. Gowans (1987) is a useful collection of well-known papers on conflicts between different values.

Chapter 4: A unified upbringing

1. For a recent defence of the existence of external reasons, see McNaughton, 1988. He attaches the label 'internalism' to the view 'that a moral conviction, coupled with suitable beliefs, is sufficient to supply the agent with reasons to act, and thus to motivate him to act' (p 22). Confusingly for our purposes, 'internalism' brings with it a belief in the possibility of 'external' reasons, as Williams, 1981 uses the term. McNaughton holds that internalism accords better with the phenomenology of our moral experience than its rival, since 'the agent is moved to act by his recognition of moral requirement, a requirement whose nature and existence are not conditional on any desire he may happen to have' (p 49, see also pp 114–5). But it could be that the phenomenology is a misleading guide to what is the case. It certainly *seems* to many people that morality makes demands on them independent of their desires, but their beliefs about this may be mistaken. (See Mackie, 1977,

ch 1.) The 'internalist' still has to show how it is possible for a cognitive state, like recognition, *alone* to provide a reason for action.

Griffin, 1986 argues that 'the distinction between internal and external reasons is unreal' (p 137). He takes the case of a person who has in the past frittered his life away and now comes to value accomplishing something with it (p 29, p 136). In coming to see (understand) what accomplishment is, the person comes to value it. But it is a mistake 'to keep desire out of all understanding. Some understanding – the sort that involves fixing on certain features and seeing them in a favourable light – is also a kind of movement. It requires a will to go for what has those features.' (p29) It is not too clear what Griffin means here. He might mean by 'requires a will' that the person who comes to value accomplishment, for instance, already possesses some desire which he comes to see accomplishment as serving (perhaps in some unobvious way, which it needs deliberation on his part to reveal). If so, the person has an internal reason. If Griffin does not mean this, then he must, it seems, have in mind an external reason. This would *preserve* the distinction between internal and external reasons, rather than showing that the distinction is unreal. It would also leave the nature of the external reason still obscure. It is equally obscure to me how the distinction in question is supposed to be 'unreal'.

2. Joseph Raz, 1986, ch 12, section 6 also deals with the relationship between morality and personal well-being. He too does not want to argue for the unqualified thesis that the latter must always embrace the former, only for a 'rough coincidence' between the two concerns (p 319). He writes:

> Given that the well-being of the agent is in the succesful pursuit of valuable goals, and that value depends on social forms, it is of the essence of value that it contributes to the constitution of the agent's personal well-being just as much as it defines moral objectives. The source of value is one for the individual and the community. It is one and the same from the individual and the moral point of view. (p 318)

The notion of 'social forms' is central to this argument. Raz holds that our major, or, as he calls them 'comprehensive', goals, the satisfaction of which is among the most important elements of our well-being, consist in 'socially defined and determined pursuits and activities' (p 309). Marriage is one example, pursuing a legal career, or being a birdwatcher, are others. Comprehensive goals both depend on social forms for their very possibility, as in these cases; and can also only be acquired by habituation: this, too, is derived from a common culture (pp 310–312). Social forms contribute not only to the agent's own well-being but also to that of others within the community. It is in this way that they are the source of moral as well as prudential value.

There is only a *rough* coincidence between these, however – for two reasons. First, there will be 'occasional conflict in the life of any person between morality and self-interest' (p 319); and, secondly, deviations between the two will occur when the social forms available to one are 'morally wicked, as when a young person grows up in an area where membership in a racist group is the social norm' (pp 319–20). The second qualification leads Raz to talk of 'the essential identity of people's responsiveness to their own well-being and to morality, *provided those social forms are morally sound*' (p 319, his italics).

As with Griffin, Raz's modified claim that personal well-being embraces morality fails to deal adequately with counter-examples like the Thrasymachean despot, the sadistic secret policeman in a totalitarian state, or the member of a criminal gang. Although most people's major goals may have to do with activities shared with others, like marriage or the profession of medicine, others may prefer lonelier satisfactions. The major goals of a Caligula or a Stalin may draw them away from rather than towards shared, cooperative activities. It is true that their well-being *depends on* social forms of all kinds, in which others but not necessarily they themselves participate. If Raz were claiming just that, he could not be faulted. But 'depends on' for him must carry the different implication of actual participation.

The sadistic policeman and the member of a criminal gang do participate in shared activities. Are they covered by the second of Raz's categories of exception, in that the social forms in which they take part are morally unsound? In describing this category, Raz seems to confine it to cases where one *cannot help* engaging in morally unsound practices, as when one grows up in a racist community. If so, this leaves out cases where other options are open to one but one deliberately prefers the immoral path. Some people opt for crime in preference to drudgery or unemployment, or for reasons of personal enrichment, fame, or adventure.

In so far as sadists and criminals *are* covered by Raz's second category, the damaging criticism still remains that this part of his argument is in any case vacuous, since it runs in effect: personal well-being embraces morality except where it includes elements which are morally unsound.

3. In discussing Griffin and Raz I did not go into what each of these writers meant by 'morality'. We cannot assume, therefore, that in arguing for morality's inclusion within well-being they are both advocating the same thing. Griffin's argument

> is not an argument for morality in the narrow sense. A person might be able to live a life of value and substance by single-mindedly painting his pictures, ignoring all his family responsibilities. But it is a life of value and substance only if his paintings are also of substantial value and, in the end, valuable to the rest of us. (op. cit., p 157)

Morality in the wider sense seems here to have to do with actions whose consequences are of general benefit. Raz rejects the idea of 'morality in the narrow sense' as the limiting of the pursuit of one's well-being in the interest of others (p 318): this would imply that personal well-being is inherently in conflict with others' interests, a position which as we have seen, he rejects. Morality in the wider sense is necessarily linked with personal well-being via the notion of collective goods, which 'provide the source both of personal goals and of obligations to others' (p 216). It seems by implication that the concept of obligation is central to morality in Raz's wider sense as it is to it in the narrow sense. What relationships there are between Raz's wider sense and Griffin's are not clear.

4. Since altruism is often considered to be an essential element in morality, some arguments for the inclusion of morality within personal well-being, if sound, might also have been enough to show that well-being involves altruism. Raz's argument, for instance, may generate that conclusion, via the connection which it makes between well-being and participation in shared activities. (Griffin's argument may not do so. If the person who single-mindedly paints his pictures generates moral value only because his work *happens* to prove of general benefit and not because of any altruistic motivation on his part, then the conclusion may not follow. I say 'may not' because it may still be argued that painting is itself a shared activity. See the quotation from Alasdair MacIntyre on page 59.)

   At all events, if the arguments to do with morality are unsound, we cannot derive sound conclusions about the necessity of altruism for well-being. We need to turn to more direct arguments to this conclusion.

5. MacIntyre's account has affinities with Raz's position. See note 2.

6. This is influenced by MacIntyre's account of a 'practice'. See the section on altruism and well-being above.

7. I am indebted to Peter Walwyn for bringing home to me the importance of recognition in education in his PhD thesis 'Some implications for philosophy of education from the works of Hegel' (University of London, 1986, unpublished). See also Glover, 1988, chs 16, 19.

8. Marx and Dewey were both brought up as Hegelians. Hegel himself worked within an Aristotelian framework which began not from people considered as atomic individuals, but from people as members of communities (eg the family, the political community). In the history of British educational thought and practice, as in other aspects of British life, individualistic assumptions have been dominant on the whole. Communitarian ideas, again inspired directly by Hegel, were, however, influential between the mid-nineteenth century and the First World War. Rugby School and especially Balliol College, Oxford played a large part in this. T H Green, the Balliol philosopher, was a pivotal figure. The communitarian ethos of the British public school, the extension of educational opportunities for ordinary people, the concept of the Welfare State, the adult education movement in Britain, Toynbee Hall, the new civic universities, the harnessing of academic studies, not least in philosophy, to social reform – all these owe much to the British Hegelians. Among those brought up in this tradition were Haldane, Tawney, Beveridge and Attlee. For a fuller account of the ideas and achievements of this movement of thought, see Gordon and White, 1979.

    It will be interesting to see how far people turn back to this tradition of civic life in reacting against the individualism now dominant in British politics. I note that Matthew Arnold's *Culture and Anarchy* is now often used as a stick with which to beat contemporary 'philistinism'. Arnold, son of Thomas Arnold, and product of Rugby and Balliol, shared much of the thinking of the British Hegelians. See also A Vincent and R Plant, *Philosophy, Politics and Citizenship: The Life and Thought of the British Idealists* (Oxford: Blackwell, 1984).

    On the other hand, it would be wrong to see contemporary Conservatism as wholly opposed to these communitarian ideas. Roger Scruton's work in philosophy and political and educational thought is thoroughly Hegelian, although in my view his proper emphasis on our shared life within the political community needs to be detached from his élitism and excessive reverence for tradition. More broadly, it remains to be seen whether such things as current

Conservative appeals for the revitalization of family life, moves within some parts of industry towards more participatory ways of working (Lawn, 1987), the introduction of common objectives in education via the National Curriculum will help us to see our personal well-being as involving a common life with others. I suspect that the more individualistic and authoritarian strands in today's Conservatism will prove more powerful, but the future is always unpredictable. In the education service, anti-individualist currents, *not* in this case emanating from the right, began to gather force in the later 1970s and throughout the 1980s. One sees this in the welcome given to Hargreaves' book, already mentioned, in moves towards whole-school policy-making, closer co-operation between teachers and parents, and the rise of personal and social education. Again, it remains to be seen how far contrary ideas, not least some enshrined in the Education Reform Act 1988, will win the day.

9. See also the first section of Chapter 7.

10. On the charge that any such balances will be arbitrary, see the final section of Chapter 3.

Chapter Five: Education for personal autonomy

1. I am assuming educators who are working on the lines suggested in this book. Other educators perhaps *should* be troubled. Those religious parents, for instance, who bring their children up dogmatically to believe in the tenets of their faith. In a society premissed on universal personal autonomy these fail to respect their children's future autonomy in steering them towards a determinate set of beliefs and values.

   But not all religious parents are so dogmatic. These more liberal parents want their children to grow up to lead a self-determined life, but at the same time are often bound by a precept of their religion that children must be brought up within the faith. How far is it possible for them to strike a compromise between religious and liberal demands? A logical stumbling-block is that if their upbringing is successful their children will, it seems, grow up believing both that they must lead such and such a religious way of life, and that they should be self-determined. A reply might be that this obstacle can be avoided by bringing children up in their early years wholly in the religious belief and only later introducing them to the liberal one. But a difficulty here is that early beliefs may well become entrenched and hard to overturn later. If liberal parents try to prevent this by softening the early learning in a liberal direction, perhaps by indicating the tentative nature of the beliefs, pointing out that other people have quite different beliefs etc etc, the children are likely to grow up confused and not knowing where they stand. (This is over and above the confusion which might emanate from trying to hold the religious beliefs themselves, if those critics of religion are right who see it as basically incoherent.) Given the belief accepted both on the religious and the liberal side that early education should be founded on dispositions which are firmly and securely acquired, this way of striking a compromise fails to satisfy both sets of demands. It seems to sacrifice the child's well-being to the parent's attempt to square the upbringing circle.

In my view liberal religious people bound by the requirement that if they have children the latter must be brought up as believers should think twice before they decide to have children at all. In some religions this might mean thinking twice about getting married at all.

Religious people who do not accept liberal notions of autonomy avoid the problems mentioned, although in an autonomy-supporting society they do face others. See the section in Chapter 6 on children from minorities who do not value autonomy.

I am grateful to Terry McLaughlin for many discussions on these and related issues. There has been a long-running debate in the *Journal of Philosophy of Education* on this topic. See articles by McLaughlin, Vol 18, no 1, 1984; Callan, Vol 19, no 1, 1985; McLaughlin, Vol 19, no 1, 1985; Gardner, Vol 22, no 1, 1988.

2. I have in mind here Wittgenstein's 'private language argument' in Wittgenstein, 1953, Part I, Sections 242ff. See also Hamlyn, 1978, chs 6, 7.

3. More has been built into the concept of personal autonomy which I am using than is often the case. This is especially true of altruistic dispositions. As should be clear, in this book I am not 'analysing' *the* concept of autonomy, but constructing a concept useful to my purposes. In its root idea of self-determination, however, it has many affinities with others' concepts. In this it comes close to David Cooper's concept of 'authenticity' (see Cooper, 1983). I agree with his criticism of Dearden, 1972 for its 'exaggerated stress on rational criticism' (p 21). I am also indebted to Lindley, 1986, although I have problems with his account which I spell out in Chapter 6, note 1.

    Finally, I should also point out that 'personal autonomy' is to be distinguished from 'moral autonomy', where this term is used to describe those who follow only those moral rules which have satisfied certain rational criteria, eg Kant's categorical imperative. See Raz, 1986, p 370, note 2.

4. Williams (1981) criticizes the life-planning model as 'of one's life as a rectangle, so to speak, presented all at once and to be optimally filled in' (p 33). His objection to it is that 'it implicitly ignores the obvious fact that what one does and what sort of life one leads condition one's later desires and judgments' (p 34).

5. Griffin (1986) identifies desire-structures with plans of life. He writes (p 34) 'This talk of plans of life does not mean that valuable lives must be highly planned. One could have a life plan to take each day as it comes. Or one could have a minimal plan to live for short-term pleasures that, in aggregate, reach the greatest total. But for us to evaluate any approach to life, even these, we have to see them in the fairly long term: as ways of living, which exclude other ways of living.'

    Griffin does not explain why well-being *must* involve life-planning. Apart from points I raise in the main text, issues to do with life-planning surely only arise with autonomous ways of life: heteronomous members of traditional societies may lead fulfilled lives but allow themselves to be directed by custom. For anyone, heteronomous or autonomous, their 'way of living' need not be a planned way of living. Autonomous people may find themselves *drawn* into certain activities and modes of behaviour which can together be said to constitute a 'way of life'.

6. Slote (1983) argues that it is undesirable for young children to have 'any sort of life plan at all' (p 46), although he leaves it open whether this applies to adolescents. He writes that 'once one has reached a certain point of maturity, life-planfulness is a virtue of practical rationality; but the disposition to have and follow a life plan is the opposite of a virtue, an anti-virtue, in (relation to) childhood.' This raises the question, as he indicates in a note referring to Williams (1981), 'whether life-planfulness is a virtue even in adulthood' (p 47).

7. On the importance of our emotions for self-understanding, see C Taylor, 1985, Vol 1, paper 2 'Self-interpreting animals'.

8. For discussion of this 'genealogical' tracing of the origin of our values, especially in relation to Nietzsche, see Cooper, 1983, pp 23–5 and ch 6.

9. See, for instance, Bernard Barker 'Production and progress' in C Chitty (ed), *Redefining the Comprehensive Experience*, 1987, Bedford Way Paper 32, Institute of Education, University of London.

10. Some of these strands as well as others are well brought out in Charles Taylor's critique of contemporary capitalist society in his 'Legitimation crisis?' in Taylor, 1985, Vol 2.

Chapter Six: Justifying personal autonomy as an educational aim

1. One finds a similar conflation of autonomy and autarchy in Richard Lindley (1986). He writes

   > A is conatively heteronomous with respect to a particular action or set of actions if either A acts through domination by lower order desires, or A acts through weakness of will. (p 70)

   On this view a sufficient condition of acting autonomously is that one lives by the desires one desires to rule one, not by lower-order desires or desires one would rather be without. But, once again, this would make a well-brought up, virtuous member of a tradition-directed community an autonomous person – even though he or she never questioned the conventions in which he or she had been brought up.

2. One or two further points about Callan's rejected arguments for autonomy. The first argument was that autonomy is instrumental to happiness. Is Callan right to deny this? If we take happiness as personal well-being, then Callan may be right if he is making a universal claim about all human beings. But it still may be true *for us* – ie in our kind of society – that autonomy is broadly necessary for well-being. (Agreed, this would not make it instrumental, necessarily.) Part of Callan's objection to the first argument is that a return to a tradition-directed society is a feasible option for us. But in the light of Williams's remark about reflectiveness, is this so?

   In the course of his objection to the second argument – from the alleged absence of ethical experts – Callan says that it would be arbitrary for educators to lead children towards autonomy. But would it be? If their flourishing demands this, is this not reason enough?

3. A version of this chapter is to be found in Spieckev, B, and Straughan, R, *Freedom and Indoctrination in Education*, London: Cassell, forthcoming.

Chapter Seven: The place of knowledge in education

1. See Peters, 1967; Hirst, 1974; Lawton, 1983; Cox *et al.*, 1986; Harris, 1979, ch 6; Anderson, 1980.

2. Mackie in 'Anderson's theory of education' in Anderson, 1980, p 16 writes 'A university is, more than any other, the social institution which might have education as its special concern, the place where the intellectual way of life might flourish and perpetuate itself, and also the centre from which education might spread out into the rest of society, or at least the base from which it could carry on the struggle against uncritical and philistine tendencies.'

3. For a variety of political perspectives see Cooper, 1980 on the right, Bailey, 1984 and Wringe, 1988 on the social democratic left.

4. For further expressions of similar views, see Scruton, 1980; O'Hear, 1981.

5. It would be wrong to see these three theories as limiting themselves to autonomy aims. True, these are at the heart of each of them; but somewhat more peripherally, or so it would seem, they all acknowledge the importance of 'moral' aims or 'moral education'. See Dearden, 1968, ch 8; O'Hear, 1981, ch 5; White, J, 1973, pp 53–4. The separate provision which moral aims receive in these texts underlines the ethical dualism which runs through them.

6. See McNaughton, 1988 for a defence of 'moral realism', the view 'that there is a moral reality which is independent of our moral beliefs and which determines whether they are true or false' (p 7). Having abandoned talk of 'morality' in Chapter 4, I am concerned at this point in the main text with whether or not there is an 'ethical reality'. My disbelief in it stems from my disbelief in the possibility of 'external' reasons for action (see Chapter 4, note 1): ethical values do not constitute a reality independent of our desires. As for ethical naturalism, I do not understand how ethical claims can be grouded in non-ethical statements; neither do I see why all ethical claims need to be grounded at all.

Chapter Eight: The 1988 National Curriculum

1. For problems surrounding attempts to ground ethics in religion, see B Williams, 1972, pp 77–86.

2. *Education Reform Act 1988*, Section 7.1. See Cox and Cairns, 1989, ch 10.

3. See White, 1975; Lawn, 1987.

4. For clear examples of intellectual élitism, see Cooper, 1980; Letwin, 1988. Roger Scruton, who is often branded an 'élitist', has a more complicated position. Unlike Cooper and Letwin, he does not

advocate one sort of education for the few and another for the many. In Cox *et al.*, 1986 he supports, along with his Hillgate Group co-authors, a national curriculum similar to that enshrined in the 1988 Education Reform Act, based on traditional subjects. On the other hand he clearly believes in the desirability of a society stratified by class (Scruton, 1980, ch 8); connects the middle class, but not the working class, with an interest in education (op. cit., p 181); and sees the content of education in terms of academic disciplines pursued for their own sake (op. cit., pp 148ff). What would make all his 1980 and 1986 views consistent would be the proposition that all children should be introduced to academic subjects to be pursued for their own sake, but only some – perhaps those with a middle-class background together with intellectually inclined children from the working classes – may be expected to take to this regime. 'Even when all men are forced through the mill of education, some emerge formed, and others emerge formless' (1980, p 159). Parents who favour education, as thus defined, will be accommodated by the opting out arrangements and City Technology Colleges urged in Cox *et al.*, 1986.

The upshot of this seems to be that Scruton, too, is rightly seen as an intellectual (as well as a social class) élitist. He would like to privilege those people who possess a certain – ie intellectualist – view of the good life. The same may also be said, I think, of Anthony O'Hear, 1987. How Scruton can justify a regime that may be expected to leave large numbers of young people 'formless' is hard to see.

5. See Wiener, 1981 for the view that since 1850 British people have never really accepted the Industrial Revolution and have preferred to be guided by more bucolic ideals.

6. On utilitarian élitism see Williams, 1972, pp 111–2; Williams, 1985, pp 108–110.

7. It is sometimes argued, by writers opposed to making education instrumental to the economy, that education should be seen as an 'intrinsic' good. (See, for example, R S Peters, 1967, ch 1.) There is a danger of confusion at this point. While education should certainly treat pupils as ends in themselves, it does not follow that the only legitimate content of education should be 'intrinsically valuable activities' – that is activities which among other things are pursued only for their own sake. It should be clear from early chapters of the book that I am advocating an education which both makes the promotion of the pupil's well-being for its own sake the central objective, and also, as part of that promotion, encourages him or her to engage in various activities intended to

serve others' well-being. These may include activities which help the economy to prosper – to do with numeracy, for instance, science, or computing.

Chapter Nine: Towards an alternative National Curriculum

1. 'Kontsepsia obshchevo srednevo obrazovaniya', a report by the 'Shkola' research group of the USSR State Committee on Education, Moscow 1988.
2. For arguments criticizing the claim that parents have the right to determine the content of their children's education see White, J, 1982, pp 166-7; White, P, 1983, ch 5; Gutmann, 1987, pp 28–33. For a view more sympathetic to independent parents' rights, see Crittenden, 1988.

Bibliography

Abbreviations

JPE *Journal of Philosophy of Education*
PPES *Proceedings of the Philosophy of Education Society of Great Britain*

Official publications

Curriculum 11–16 (HMI Red Book One), 1977, London: HMSO.
Improving Secondary Schools, 1982, London: ILEA.
Better Schools, 1985, London: HMSO, Cmnd. 9469.
The National Curriculum 5–16: A Consultation Document, 1987, London: DES.
Education Reform Act, 1988
Interim Report of the National Curriculum History Working Group, 1989, London: DES.
National Curriculum: From Policy to Practice, 1989, London: DES.

Anderson, J., 1980, *Education and Enquiry*, Oxford: Basil Blackwell.
Anscombe, E., 1958, 'Modern moral philosophy' *Philosophy*, Vol **33**.
Aristotle, *Nicomachean Ethics*.
Arnold, M., 1869, *Culture and Anarchy*.
Aune, B., 1979, *Kant's Theory of Morals*, Princeton: Princeton University Press.
Bailey, C., 1984, *Beyond the Present and the Particular*, London: Routledge and Kegan Paul.
Barrow, R., 1984, *Giving Teaching Back to Teachers: A Critical Introduction to Curriculum Theory*, Brighton: Wheatsheaf.
Bond, E.J., 1983, *Reason and Value*, Cambridge: Cambridge University Press.

Callan, E., 1985, 'McLaughlin on parental rights', *JPE*, Vol **19**, No 1.

——, 1988, *Autonomy and Schooling*, Kingston and Montreal: McGill-Queen's University Press.

Calouste Gulbenkian Foundation, 1982, *The Arts in Schools*.

Chitty, C. (ed), 1987, *Redefining the Comprehensive Experience*, Bedford Way Paper 32, London: Institute of Education, University of London.

Cooper, D.E., 1980, *Illusions of Equality*, London: Routledge and Kegan Paul.

——, 1983, *Authenticity and Learning*, London: Routledge and Kegan Paul.

——, (ed), 1986, *Education, Values and Mind*, London: Routledge and Kegan Paul.

Cox, C. *et al.*, 1986, *Whose Schools?*, London: The Hillgate Group.

Cox, E. and Cairns J., 1989, *Reforming Religious Education*, London: Kogan Page.

Crittenden, B., 1988, *Parents, the State and the Right to Educate*, Melbourne: Melbourne University Press.

Dearden, R.F., 1968, *The Philosophy of Primary Education*, London: Routledge and Kegan Paul.

——, 1972, 'Autonomy and education' in R.F. Dearden *et al Education and the Development of Reason*, London: Routledge and Kegan Paul.

——, 1975, 'Autonomy as an educational ideal' in S.C. Brown (ed) *Philosophers Discuss Education*, London: Macmillan.

——,1984, 'Education and politics', in his *Theory and Practice in Education*, London: Routledge and Kegan Paul.

Dent, N., 1984, *The Moral Psychology of the Virtues*, Cambridge: Cambridge University Press.

Downie R., Loudfoot E. and Telfer E., 1974, *Education and Personal Relationships*, London: Methuen.

Dworkin, R., 1978, 'Liberalism', in S. Hampshire (ed.), *Public and Private Morality*, Cambridge: Cambridge University Press.

Eaglesham, E., 1967, *The Foundations of 20th Century Education in England*, London: Routledge and Kegan Paul.

Feldman, F., 1978, *Introductory Ethics*, Englewood Cliffs: Prentice Hall.

Flew, A., 1988, 'Meeting needs: charity or justice?' *Applied Philosophy* Vol **5**, No 2.

Frankena, W.K., 1973, *Ethics*, Englewood Cliffs: Prentice Hall.

Frankfurt, H., 1988, *The Importance of What We Care About*, Cambridge: Cambridge University Press.

Gardner, P., 1984, 'The compulsory curriculum and beyond: a consideration of some aspects of the educational philosophy of J.P. White', *JPE*, Vol **18**, No 2.

——, 1988, 'Religious upbringing and the liberal ideal of religious autonomy', *JPE*, Vol **22**, No 1.

Glover, J., 1988, *I: The Philosophy and Psychology of Personal Identity*, London: Allen Lane.

Godfrey, R., 1984, 'John White and the imposition of autonomy', *JPE*, Vol **18**, No 1.

Gordon P. and White J., 1979, *Philosophers as Educational Reformers: The Influence of Idealism on British Educational Thought and Pratice*, London: Routledge and Kegan Paul.

Gowans, C.W., (ed) 1987, *Moral Dilemmas*, Oxford: Oxford University Press.

Gray, J., 1983, *Mill on Liberty: A Defence*, London: Routledge and Kegan Paul.

Griffin, J., 1986, *Well-being*, Oxford: Clarendon Press.

Gutmann, A., 1987, *Democratic Education*, Princeton: Princeton University Press.

Hamlyn, D., 1975, 'The concept of development', *PPES*, Vol **9**.

——, 1978, *Experience and the Growth of Understanding*, London: Routledge and Kegan Paul.

Hare, R.M., 1981, *Moral Thinking*, Oxford: Clarendon Press.

Hargreaves, D., 1982, *The Challenge for the Comprehensive School*, London: Routledge and Kegan Paul.

Harman, G., 1977, *The Nature of Morality*, New York: Oxford University Press.

Harris, K., 1979, *Education and Knowledge*, London: Routledge and Kegan Paul.

Hirst, P.H., 1974, *Knowledge and the Curriculum*, London: Routledge and Kegan Paul.

——, and Peters, R.S., 1970, *The Logic of Education*, London: Routledge and Kegan Paul.

Holmes, E., 1911, *What Is and What Might Be*, London: Constable.

Hudson, W.D., 1983, *Modern Moral Philosophy* (2nd ed.), London: Macmillan.

Kant, I., 1785, *Foundations of the Metaphysics of Morals*.

Lafollette, H., 1980, 'Licensing parents', *Philosophy and Public Affairs*, Vol **9**, No 2.

Lawn, M., 1987, 'The spur and the bridle: changing the mode of curriculum control', *Journal of Curriculum Studies*, Vol **19**.

Lawton, D., 1983, *Curriculum Studies and Educational Planning*, London: Hodder and Stoughton.

——, and Chitty, C., (eds), 1988, *The National Curriculum*, Bedford Way Paper 32, London: Institute of Education, University of London.

Letwin, O., 1988, *Aims of Schooling*, London: Centre for Policy Studies.

Lindley, R., 1986, *Autonomy*, London: Macmillan.

Lukes, S., 1985, *Marxism and Morality*, Oxford: Oxford University Press.

MacIntyre, A., 1981, *After Virtue*, London: Duckworth.

——, 1988, *Whose Justice? Whose Rationality?* London: Duckworth.

Mackie, J., 1977, *Ethics: Inventing Right and Wrong*, Harmondsworth: Penguin.

McLaughlin, T., 1984, 'Parental rights and the religious upbringing of children', *JPE*, Vol **18**, No 1.

——, 1985, 'Religion, upbringing and liberal values: a rejoinder to Eamonn Callan', *JPE*, Vol **19**, No 1.

McNaughton, D., 1988, *Moral Vision*, Oxford: Blackwell.

Mill, J.S., 1859, *On Liberty*.

——, 1861, *Utilitarianism*.

Moore, G.E., 1903, *Principia Ethica*, Cambridge: Cambridge University Press.

Nagel, T., 1979, *Mortal Questions*, Cambridge: Cambridge University Press.

——, 1986, *The View from Nowhere*, Oxford: Oxford University Press.

Norman, R., 1983, *The Moral Philosophers*, Oxford: Clarendon Press.

Nozick, R., 1974, *Anarchy, State and Utopia*, Oxford: Blackwell.

Nussbaum, M., 1986, *The Fragility of Goodness*, Cambridge: Cambridge University Press.

O'Hear, A., , 1981, *Education, Society and Human Nature*, London: Routledge and Kegan Paul.

——, 1987, 'Taking Liberties', *Times Educational Supplement*, 16.1.87

Palma, A.B., 1988, 'On wanting to be somebody', *Philosophy*, Vol **63**, No 245.

Parfit, D., 1984, *Reasons and Persons*, Oxford: Clarendon Press.

Peters, R.S., 1967, *Ethics and Education*, London: Allen and Unwin.

——, 1981, *Moral Development and Moral Education*, London: Allen and Unwin.

Plato, *The Republic*.

Quinton, A., 1973, *Utilitarian Ethics*, London: Macmillan.

Rawls, J., 1971, *A Theory of Justice*, Oxford: Clarendon Press.

Raz, J., 1986, *The Morality of Freedom*, Oxford: Clarendon Press.

Ross, W.D., 1930, *The Right and the Good*, Oxford: Clarendon Press.

Sandel, M., 1982, *Liberalism and the Limits of Justice*, Cambridge: Cambridge University Press.

Scheffler, S., 1982, *The Rejection of Consequentialism*, Oxford: Clarendon Press.

Scruton, R., 1980, *The Meaning of Conservatism*, London: Penguin Books.

——, 1987, 'Expressive education', *Oxford Review of Education*, Vol 13, No 1.

Slote, M., 1983, *Goods and Virtues*, Oxford: Clarendon Press.

Smart, J. and Williams, B., 1973, *Utilitarianism: For and Against*, Cambridge: Cambridge University Press.

Tawney, R.H., 1926, *Religion and the Rise of Capitalism*, London: Penguin Books.

Taylor, C., 1985, *Philosophical Papers Vols I and II*, Cambridge: Cambridge University Press.

Tobin, B., 1986, 'Development in virtues', *JPE*, Vol **20**, No 2.

Walzer, M., 1983 *Spheres of Justice*, Oxford: Martin Robertson.

Warnock, G., 1967, *Contemporary Moral Philosophy*, London: Macmillan.

——, 1971, *The Object of Morality*, London: Methuen.

Warnock, M., 1977, *Schools of Thought*, London: Faber and Faber.

White, J., 1973, *Towards a Compulsory Curriculum*, London: Routledge and Kegan Paul.

——, 1975, 'The end of the compulsory curriculum' in *The Curriculum: the Doris Lee Lectures*, Studies in Education 2, London: Institute of Education, University of London.

——, 1982, *The Aims of Education Restated*, London: Routledge and Kegan Paul.

White, P., 1983, *Beyond Domination*, London: Routledge and Kegan Paul.

Wiener, M., 1981, *English Culture and the Decline of the Industrial Spirit, 1850–1980*, Cambridge: Cambridge University Press.

Williams, B., 1972, *Morality: An Introduction to Ethics*, Harmondsworth: Penguin Books.

——, 1981, *Moral Luck*, Cambridge: Cambridge University Press.

——, 1985, *Ethics and the Limits of Philosophy*, London: Fontana.

Wittgenstein, L., 1953, *Philosophical Investigations*, Oxford: Blackwell.

Wringe, C., 1988, *Understanding Educational Aims*, London: Unwin Hyman.

Index